CliffsNotes®

Guitar Songs

by Chad Johnson

ISBN 978-1-4584-2127-2

HAL•LEONARD®
CORPORATION
7777 W. BLUEMOUND RD. P.O. BOX 13819 MILWAUKEE, WI 53213

Visit Hal Leonard Online at
www.halleonard.com

Table of Contents

Introduction

Welcome to *Guitar Songs.* In this book, you'll learn the cornerstone riffs to 150 classic songs, but that's not all. You'll also learn key biographical information about the artist, details about the song, tips on the gear used (which will help you in recreating the sound), and the ins and outs of the riff, including theoretical analysis and performance tips. I get straight to the meat of the songs here — discussing the first riff that pops into your head when you first hear the song mentioned. In other words, you learn what other people want to hear you play!

A broad range of styles is covered here, so there's something for everyone — acoustic, electric, hard rock, old time rock 'n' roll, punk, folk, and so on. In fact, you can't help but become a more well-rounded player by working through this book, as you'll no doubt be exposed to new styles and techniques; Not to mention the fact that you'll have a whole lot of fun in the process. So grab your guitar and get ready to fill your minds with facts and your fingers with notes — CliffsNotes, that is! Enjoy!

Ain't Talkin' 'Bout Love

Performed by Van Halen

From *Van Halen* (1978)

It's easy nowadays to overlook the impact that Van Halen's debut album had on the music world. Bands like the Beatles, Jimi Hendrix, and Led Zeppelin consistently get more recognition for altering the musical terrain that followed them. This is no doubt helped by the fact that, whereas the music of the 1960s and 1970s has since come fully back into fashion, much of the world still hasn't forgiven the many excesses (musical and otherwise) of hair metal. However, 1978's *Van Halen* undeniably reshaped the musical world as we know it, and Eddie shot out of the gates like a steam-blowing rodeo bull, sending *everyone* back to the woodshed.

Along with the other colossal rock standards that populate this album, "Ain't Talkin' 'Bout Love" has clearly stood the test of time. Though the song didn't chart, it's become a favorite of many fans due to its slightly punk bent and its restrained (for Eddie), melodic guitar solo.

The song begins with the main riff, which Eddie plays on his homemade "Frankenstrat" through his trusty 100 watt Marshall Plexi Super Lead. He famously used the Variac (a voltage limiter similar to a light dimmer) to lower the voltage on his amp, allowing for a more distorted tone at lower volumes. (Do not try this at home!) Also in the signal path is an MXR Flanger pedal and an Echoplex (tape delay).

The song is in the key of A minor, and Eddie arpeggiates (plays the chords one note at a time) through the chord progression of Am–F–G5 while palm muting — which means laying the palm lightly on the strings near the bridge to produce a muffled tone. It's a bit uncommon to mute the higher strings as Eddie does here, and it'll take a little practice to get a feel for it. The string pattern here is also deceptively tricky, so play it slowly until you don't need to watch your picking hand at all. He finishes off the riff with another trademark move: the pinch harmonic. Allow the tip of your thumb to brush the fifth string while you pick to generate this squeal, and follow it by hammering from B to C to wrap it up. Be sure to tune down a half step if you want to play along with the original recording!

Ain't Talkin' 'Bout Love

Words and Music by Edward Van Halen, Alex Van Halen, Michael Anthony and David Lee Roth

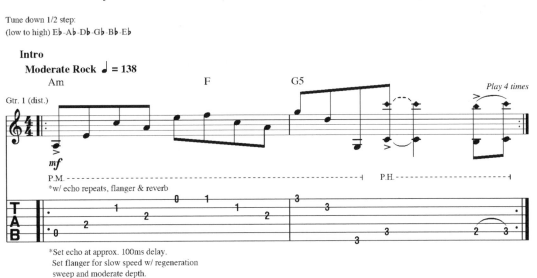

All Day and All of the Night

Performed by the Kinks
Released as a Single (1964)

Although they didn't make quite the splash that the Beatles or the Rolling Stones did, the Kinks were still a powerfully influential part of the British invasion that took place in the early 1960s. Leaning more toward the punk sound than other bands of the time, their sound was a bit rawer and sometimes sounded as if their sanity may be in question, although their songwriting maintained clear pop-driven sensibilities. The song was first released as a single in both England and the U.S. (1964) and in England only as part of an EP known as *Kinksize Hits* (1965).

The band enjoyed a long string of success throughout the 1960s, highlighted by such influential albums as *Face to Face* (1966), *Something Else by the Kinks* (1967), and *The Village Green Preservation Society* (1968). These albums helped to demonstrate the band's versatility, both in writing and production, because they ran the gamut from sensitive acoustic ballads to all-out rock anthems. Although the Kinks are fully appreciated now and their widespread influence is acknowledged by many, the band never really received its due when held up against the towering accomplishments of the other British giants (the Beatles, the Rolling Stones, and the Who).

"All Day and All of the Night" rocks hard with a nervous energy and a tightly unified sense of direction and is similar in more than one way to their first single, "You Really Got Me,". Making use of a similar distorted guitar tone, "All Day…" begins as "You Really Got Me" does — with a high-energy power-chord riff in the key of G. Guitarist Dave Davies achieved this revolutionary (for the time) tone with an unusual approach. After slicing the speaker cone of his low wattage Elpico combo amp, he plugged in his 1962 Harmony Meteor and cranked it all the way up. He plugged the speaker leads into his Vox AC30, essentially using the Elpico as a preamp to drive the Vox. The result was a dirty, raspy, distorted sound that, when paired with sliding power chords, perfectly complimented the band's aesthetic.

To perform the riff, simply grab a power chord, slide it around, and hang on. Note that the two-note F5 at the beginning and end can be performed by barring the first finger on the third fret in preparation for the following G5. The first finger then remains on fret 3, and fingers 3 and 4 cover the fifth fret on strings 5 and 4, respectively. Be sure to notice how this same riff is transposed to several different pitch levels throughout the song!

All Day and All of the Night

Words and Music by Ray Davies

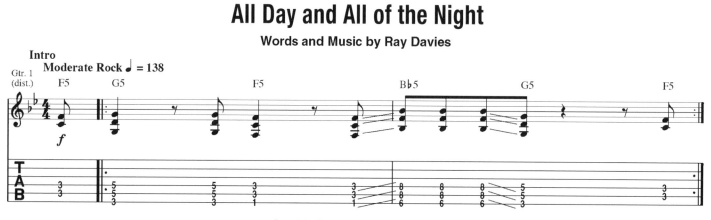

All Right Now

Performed by Free
From *Fire and Water* (1970)

With two of the most powerful players in British rock — vocalist Paul Rodgers and guitarist Paul Kossoff — Free were certainly a force to be reckoned with. And if they weren't given their due in terms worldwide adoration, they have certainly been credited, and rightly so, with their influence in helping to shape the sound of British hard rock. They were there from the beginning and helped lay the foundation for the arena rock of subsequent bands like Foreigner, Humble Pie, and Bad Company — the latter of which featured Paul Rodgers on vocals.

Though their 1968 debut, *Tons of Sobs,* and the eponymous follow-up a year later failed to make much of a dent in the charts, that all changed with 1970's *Fire and Water.* On the strength of the #4 single "All Right Now," the album hit #17 on the charts, and the band was invited to headline the illustrious Isle of Wight festival, where they performed in front of 600,000 people. Though the stage seemed set for their rise to the top, alas, it was not to be. When 1971's *Highway* failed to meet expectations, the band began to implode and broke up shortly after the release of *Free "Live"* later that year. Though they tried to reconcile with the release of *Free at Last* in 1972, the tension quickly returned and grew even worse. They called it quits for good and each moved on to other projects. (Kossoff's career was cut tragically short in 1976 when he succumbed to a drug overdose.)

In one of the most recognizable intros in all of classic rock, "All Right Now" begins with drums only supporting Paul Kossoff's legendary guitar riff, which he played on his Les Paul through either a Marshall Super Lead/Bass or a Selmer T&B 50. If you listen closely, you'll discover that the sound is not actually all that distorted, but it's made to sound bigger because Kossoff doubled the riff, and the two performances are panned left and right in the mix for a massive sound.

The song is the key of A, and the riff, for the most part, alternates between five-string A5 voicings and D/A voicings. But a careful listen to measure 3 reveals that Kossoff allows the open G and E strings to ring against the F♯ and D notes, creating a dense Dadd4/9 sound. This is an often-missed ingredient of the riff; many players play the same D/A voicing in both measures, but the Dadd4/9 adds a layer of depth, so don't neglect it!

All Right Now
Words and Music by Andy Fraser and Paul Rodgers

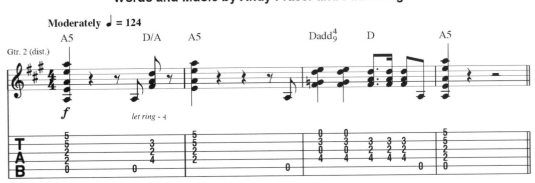

American Woman

Performed by The Guess Who
From *American Woman* (1970)

Initially led by singer/guitarist Chad Allen, The Guess Who released their early material under the name of Chad Allen & The Expressions. However, in an attempt to build mystique, their record label released their 1965 single "Shakin' All Over" under the name of Guess Who? Eventually the band's true identity was revealed, but by that time, so many DJs had introduced the song on the radio as being by The Guess Who that the band was forced to rename itself. In 1966, Burton Cummings joined the band on keys and vocals, and Chad Allen left soon after. Cummings and guitarist Randy Bachman began to take the reigns as composers, and the band's sound began to transform.

It's almost hard to believe the same band that produced the sweet, acoustic-tinged "These Eyes" in 1968 (from *Wheatfield Soul*) would produce this rock staple. In 1969, they released *Canned Wheat,* which included the first version of the folky "No Time," but they revamped the song to be included on *American Woman* a year later. By that time, the rest of the world had fully taken notice, and on the strength of "No Time," "No Sugar Tonight," and "American Woman," the band became worldwide superstars. Bachman soon left the band to form Brave Belt, which would eventually become Bachman-Turner Overdrive. The Guess Who continued to enjoy a few more hits over the next few years, but they eventually disbanded in 1975.

"American Woman" actually began its life as an impromptu onstage jam in Ontario. In an attempt to liven up the crowd, The Guess Who began jamming on the main rhythmic riff while Burton Cummings improvised lyrics. That riff is built exclusively on A-form barre chords played on strings 5–2. In the key of E major, it has a few interesting things happening. First of all, it contains both B (V) and D chords (♭VII) repeatedly in close proximity. This is a bit unusual, because the prominent use of one or the other is more common in classic rock. The other interesting fact is that the riff is consistently misquoted. Most players mistakenly repeat the same move from D to E in measure 2 that happens in measure 1.

Randy Bachman achieved the classic rhythm tone of the intro riff by plugging his '59 Fender Strat (with a Telecaster bridge pickup) into a Fender Concert amp. The volume was raised enough so that just a hint of break-up appears, and the tremolo was set to a moderate speed and depth.

American Woman
Written by Burton Cummings, Randy Bachman, Gary Peterson and Jim Kale

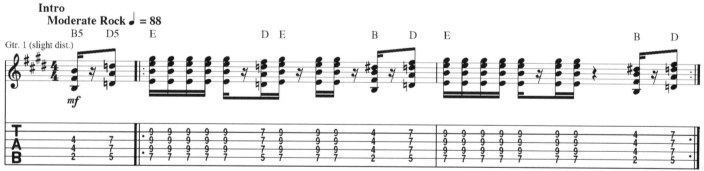

Aqualung

Performed by Jethro Tull
From *Aqualung* (1971)

Jethro Tull, with their concoction of folk-meets-classical-meets-blues-meets-hard rock-meets-lyrical surrealism, were quite a rare breed. Although many bands of the 1970s, such as Led Zeppelin, fused several genres to create hard-to-categorize stylistic offshoots, few did it as boldly as Tull and with such unique results. They had no trouble selling records and remained atop the charts for the better part of the 1970s, though they were rarely taken seriously by the critics. The band's personnel rotated often, with only the founder Ian Anderson (vocals/guitar/flute) and Martin Barre (guitar) remaining through almost the entire life of the band. With the change in members came changes in sound, and the largest shift in sound occurred with the onset of the 1980s, which is when the band began to lose favor with the public.

The *Aqualung* album (1971) was quite a bold statement in a time that saw a rise in Christian-based rock — particularly evidenced by the huge success of the rock opera *Jesus Christ Superstar* only a year earlier. Filled with disdainful messages pertaining to organized religion, *Aqualung* still managed to resonate with the public, shooting to #7 on the *Billboard* chart. Interestingly, the most well-known song on the album — the title track — was never released as a single. The tale of a dirty homeless man and his often impure thoughts, the song was originally inspired by a photo taken by Anderson's wife. The original version has a running time of 6:34 and marries two disparate sections: an angular hard rock assault with winding, nomadic harmonies, and a more delicate, acoustic-driven tale (which is split into several different tempos and feels itself).

Martin Barre performed this classic tune with his 1958 Les Paul Junior, which he purchased after seeing Mountain's Leslie West play one. He ran that through his Hornsby Skewes Treble Booster and into a Hiwatt. Martin has remarked that the Hornsby Skewes was so horribly designed (using bare, uninsulated wires) that it was constantly picking up radio signals when they played live. The intro begins with the song's signature riff: a wicked-sounding six-note phrase derived from the G blues scale (G–B♭–C–D♭–D–F). Because it fits neatly into the blues box position, it can be easily handled in third position and actually makes a nice fingering exercise, with each finger being used.

Aqualung
Words and Music by Ian Anderson and Jennie Anderson

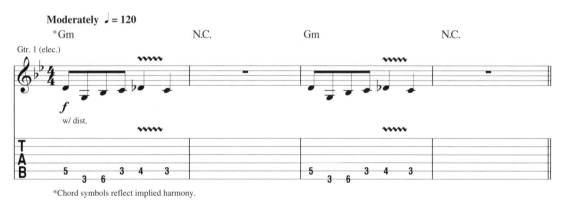

*Chord symbols reflect implied harmony.

Are You Gonna Go My Way

Performed by Lenny Kravitz

From *Are You Gonna Go My Way* (1993)

With a 1970s obsession worn on his sleeve, Lenny Kravitz burst onto the scene in 1989 with *Let Love Rule* — riding the crest of the soon-to-be retro craze that was eventually epitomized later by bands such as Jet, Wolfmother, and the Black Keys, among countless others. Kravitz was essentially a one-man band in the beginning, performing most of the instruments on his first several albums as well as producing them. Although he continues to produce most of his work, he did eventually start to bring more players into the studio in the hopes of broadening his sound.

The moderate success of *Let Love Rule* (#61) helped introduce the world to his still-evolving brand of hippie rock. But it was the follow-up, 1991's *Mama Said* (#39), on which Lenny hit his artistic stride. Although the album only contained one *huge* hit in the soulful R&B number "It Ain't Over Til It's Over" (#2), several of the album's other tracks became huge fan favorites. However, it was 1993's *Are You Gonna Go My Way* that made Kravitz a star. With the title track, he had fully tapped into the retro-rock pulse of America, and the song went on to become one of the anthems of the 1990s. One of his most successful period pieces of rock and roll, there's absolutely nothing about the production of the song (or the accompanying video, for that matter) that suggests the date is any later than 1973.

An avid collector of vintage amps and guitars, Kravitz has quite the gear arsenal available to him come guitar-tracking time. He likely ran either a Les Paul or his Flying V through a fuzz — most likely his Dallas Arbiter — and then into a Marshall plexi. The tone is bone dry and in your face, with some mids scooped out (most likely enhanced by the fuzz). As for the riff itself, the song is in E minor, and Lenny remains in the open-position E minor pentatonic (E–G–A–B–D) box for the entire intro. It works the classic bend and pull-off on the G string and resolves it to the E on string 4, interrupting a second accented E note with a jab at the open low E string — a classic Hendrix move. In the answer to measure 1's question phrase, he ends measure 2 with a biting G/D dyad on strings 1 and 2, respectively.

Are You Gonna Go My Way

Words by Lenny Kravitz
Music by Lenny Kravitz and Craig Ross

The Attitude Song

Performed by Steve Vai

From *Flex-able* (1984)

For many fans of Steve Vai's work with David Lee Roth and Whitesnake (and his 1990 groundbreaking *Passion and Warfare* album), the music on his first, self-produced solo album, *Flex-able* (1984), is usually quite a shock. After learning a bit of background info on Vai — the fact that he had worked in Frank Zappa's band for three or four years before recording the album — it makes a bit more sense. *Flex-able* is rife with Zappa-like humor, unpredictability, and just plain weirdness. You're hearing an incredibly creative guitarist and musician producing music without a single thought to the commerciality of it. Indeed, it's safe to say that, if Vai's career hadn't taken off the way it did — with a short stint in Alcatraz giving way to the massive exposure he received during the David Lee Roth gig — most guitar players probably wouldn't be aware of the album at all.

Of course, this isn't to say that the album is completely devoid of the scary guitar work for which Vai would be worshipped in the years to come. In fact, it contains one of his scariest tracks of all: a little piece of guitar insanity called "The Attitude Song." Although his tone is completely different than his post-Roth years, Vai's fingerprint (one of the most unique in guitar history) is all over the song. Although the *Flex-able* album didn't crack the charts, the lessons he learned in the process helped with his future projects, including the monumental *Passion and Warfare* six years later, which hit #18 — an impressive feat for an instrumental rock album.

For nearly all of *Flex-able*, Vai used a 1970s Fender Strat (equipped with a Floyd Rose tremolo) and a Carvin X100B amp; "The Attitude Song" is no exception. The sound isn't nearly as distorted here as on his later work. The riff is quite a piece of work. Working with only three chromatic notes (A, G#, and G) and open low E string, he creates a descending, syncopated phrase that keeps you off balance the whole time. Consisting of three eighth notes and one sixteenth note, each repetition begins on a different sixteenth-note subdivision of the beat, which means it takes seven beats to right itself again — hence, the 7/4 time signature. Also notice that Vai changes the articulation with each repetition of the phrase, alternating between pinch harmonics and palm muting. To make matters worse, the drums play a straight 4/4 drum beat, which means you really have to concentrate to keep your place!

The Attitude Song

Babe, I'm Gonna Leave You

Performed by Led Zeppelin

From *Led Zeppelin* (1969)

With their debut album in 1969, Led Zeppelin emerged with a near fully-developed style combining distorted blues with acoustic textures and catchy choruses with mythology-based lyrics. Even though they refused to release singles in the U.K., instead focusing on the AOR (album-oriented-rock) format, *Led Zeppelin* became a huge success, reaching #10 on the charts and immediately finding favor on both sides of the Atlantic — despite the many negative reviews by the critics. (Critics nowadays, with their 20/20 hindsight, seem to consider the material much more acceptable.)

The rest, as they say, is history; Zeppelin continued on and all but ruled the 1970s. Beginning with *Led Zeppelin II* (1969), they enjoyed a nearly unprecedented string of success, with every single album reaching the #2 or #1 spot, save for the final *Coda* (#6, 1982), which was assembled from leftovers after drummer John Bonham's untimely death in 1980. Although Page had far-reaching musical ambition, it was truly the combination of the four that fueled their sonic creativity. This is no doubt a huge part of why the band didn't continue after the loss of Bonham; it simply wasn't Led Zeppelin without all four of them.

It was through Joan Baez's 1962 recording of "Babe, I'm Gonna Leave You," that Page and Plant became aware of the song. Because Baez had no songwriting credit listed on her album, Page and crew assumed it was an old traditional song, crediting it as "Trad. arr. Page" on the *Led Zeppelin* album. In fact, the song was written by Anne Bredon in the late 1950s, who received a healthy sum of back royalties after becoming aware of the Zeppelin version in the late 1980s. Jimmy performed this song in the studio on a borrowed Gibson J-200. In the key of A minor, the Zeppelin arrangement makes use of a common arpeggiated progression that uses a descending bass line, slowing moving from the tonic i chord (Am) down to the V chord (E). What really sets this riff apart is Page's subtlety, as he alters the top note of each four-note pattern (with additional variation on the repeat in measures 5–8) to create a sort of melody within the accompaniment part.

Babe, I'm Gonna Leave You

Words and Music by Anne Bredon, Jimmy Page and Robert Plant

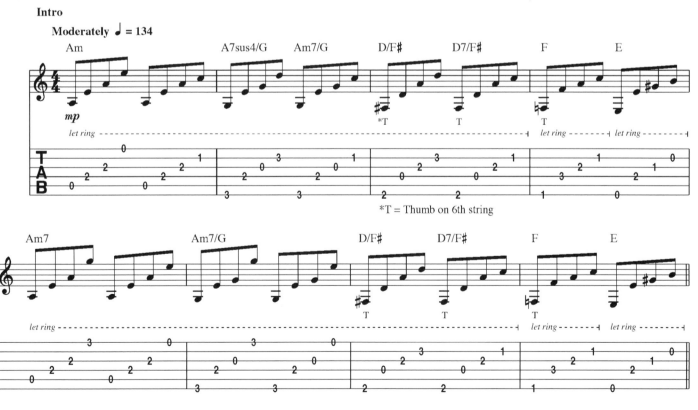

Back in Black

Performed by AC/DC
From *Back in Black* (1980)

Since their debut *High Voltage* in 1975, brothers Malcom and Angus Young have been fueling the stripped down, no-nonsense rock of AC/DC with some of the best riffs rock guitar has to offer. The Australian band's long and lustrous career can basically be divided into two broad categories: before singer Bon Scott's death (1974–1979) and after (1980–present). Though Scott's tragic death (from alcohol poisoning) nearly resulted in the end of the band, they decided to press on, hiring Englishman Brian Johnson — one of the few that could accurately simulate Scott's strained howl. The result of the new lineup's first trip into the studio was *Back in Black,* the second AC/DC album produced by Mutt Lange. That album quickly made it clear that the band would be able to continue without Scott. Although it peaked at #4, its staying power has been nearly without peer. With over 49 million copies sold to date, it ranks second only to Michael Jackson's *Thriller* (which leaves all else in the dust with 110 million copies sold!) in best-selling albums of all time.

Written by Malcom Young, the "Back in Black" riff almost never made it to the record. Malcom was just about ready to erase his cassette demo of the riff when brother Angus claimed it for his own. According to an interview in *Guitar Player* magazine, Angus plugged his Gibson SG into a Marshall 100W Super Lead to create the holy grail of rock tones. The riff is in the key of E and uses the most ubiquitous of all classic rock chords: the I (E5), ♭VII (D5), and IV (A5). Note that the rests are every bit as important as the notes here, and it wouldn't rock half as hard without them. The famous descending sixteenth-note lick comes straight out of the open-position E minor pentatonic scale, and the ultra syncopated bass-note lick at the end alternates chromatically rising lower notes (G♯–A–A♯–B) on string 6 against a repeated B note on string 5. It's nothing terribly fancy; it's just perfect!

Back in Black

Words and Music by Angus Young, Malcolm Young and Brian Johnson

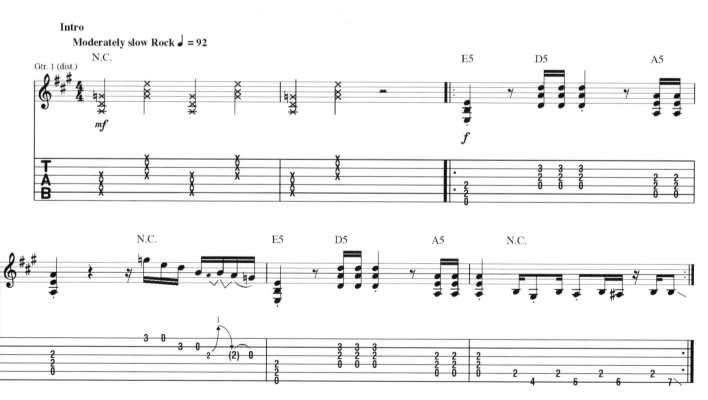

Bad to the Bone

Performed by George Thorogood & The Destroyers

From *Bad to the Bone* (1982)

Although he rarely received much love from blues purists, George Thorogood took his bar-band brand of blues stylings to the people in the 1980s, scoring two platinum and six gold albums along the way. Originally hailing from Delaware, Thorogood gave up his dreams of playing professional baseball for a music career in the early 1970s and relocated to Boston with his newly formed band, the Destroyers. After cutting their teeth on the bar scene, they secured a deal with Rounder Records and released their eponymous debut in 1977. It was the band's second album that put them on the map, with the cover of Hank Williams' "Move It on Over" becoming an FM radio staple and broadening their audience substantially. The album hit #33.

The final album Thorogood did with Rounder, 1980's *I'm Wanted,* helped keep him in the public eye long enough for his breakout smash to arrive. *Bad to the Bone* (1982), his first major label album (EMI Records), made him a household name, thanks to the title track's heavy rotation on radio and MTV. It's since been featured in countless movies, TV shows, and commercials, including *Terminator 2: Judgment Day,* Stephen King's *Christine, Major Payne, Joe Dirt, Married… with Children, Renegade,* and *Miami Vice,* among many others. If you need to introduce a villain in a film or poke fun at a character's inflated sense of machismo, "Bad to the Bone" never disappoints.

Borrowing heavily from and/or paying tribute to Chicago blues classics such as Muddy Waters' "Hoochie Coochie Man" or "Mannish Boy" and Bo Diddley's "I'm a Man," George kicks off "Bad to the Bone" with his Gibson ES-125 plugged straight into most likely a blackfaced Fender Bassman with a 2x12 cabinet. With his P90 pickups and a brass slide, he distills the essence of those Chicago blues classics into six notes: duh-duh-DUH-duh-DUH-DUH. In open G tuning (D–G–D–G–B–D, low to high), this means alternating chords on the open fourth, third, and second strings (G) with those on the fifth (C) and third (Bb) frets. It's simple and effective, but it rocks hard and loose. Note that, although the slide is used to play both chords — on frets 5 and 3 — only the third fret is treated to a quick gliss up the fretboard before it's released. This helps to affirm the fact that, just because you're playing with a slide doesn't mean you need to slide into or out of every note.

Bad to the Bone

Words and Music by George Thorogood

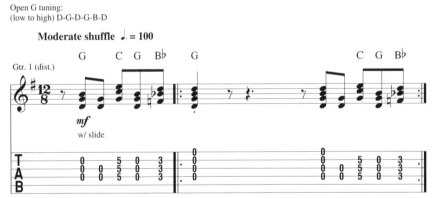

Barracuda

Performed by Heart

From *Little Queen* (1977)

In a time when most women were folk-rock, singer-songwriters, the Wilson sisters helped to liberate their sex in the rock world, paving the way for future femme-rockers like Pat Benetar. In fact, they had earned the nickname Female Zeppelin after their first album — a fitting nickname considering Zeppelin's influence on Ann Wilson, in particular. After reaching #7 with their debut *Dreamboat Annie* in 1976, which contained the hard-rocking hits "Magic Man" (#9) and "Crazy on You" (#35), they continued trailblazing with the follow-up, *Little Queen* in 1977, which shot to #9 on the strength of "Barracuda" (#11). Though their popularity (and their relationship with Epic) slowly began to wane in the 1980s, they experienced a huge commercial revival in 1985 with *Heart*, resulting in four Top Ten singles and their first #1 album.

"Barracuda" is in the hard rock- and metal-approved key of E minor and makes use of the most typical of devices for riffs in those genres: palm muting and power chords. With palms firmly planted on the strings near the bridge, Howard Leese and Roger Fisher chug along an open E5 chord in the galloping metal rhythm — an eighth note and two sixteenth notes — before breaking the monotony with a brief F#5 leading to a sustained G5 chord. Measures 3 and 4 are decorated with twelfth- and fifth-fret harmonics treated to whammy bar dips — another hard rock staple. The repeat closely mimics the first four measures, but the G5 at the end of measure 6 is expanded in measure 7 to a six-string G6 voicing, which is created by allowing the top three strings to ring open against a G5 chord on strings 6–4.

The notes aren't the only appeal of this riff. The thick tones on the song were created by Roger Fisher's Strat plugged into a hybrid (solid state preamp, tube power amp) Music Man head and cabinet and Howard Leese's 1966 Tele (with humbucker) running through a cranked 4x10 1956 Fender Bassman. The famous flanger effect was achieved with a rackmounted flanger kit from Phoenix Systems (Massachusetts). Fisher (Gtr. 1) ran the flanger through the Music Man's effects loop with the speed set as slow as he could.

Barracuda

Words and Music by Nancy Wilson, Ann Wilson, Michael Derosier and Roger Fisher

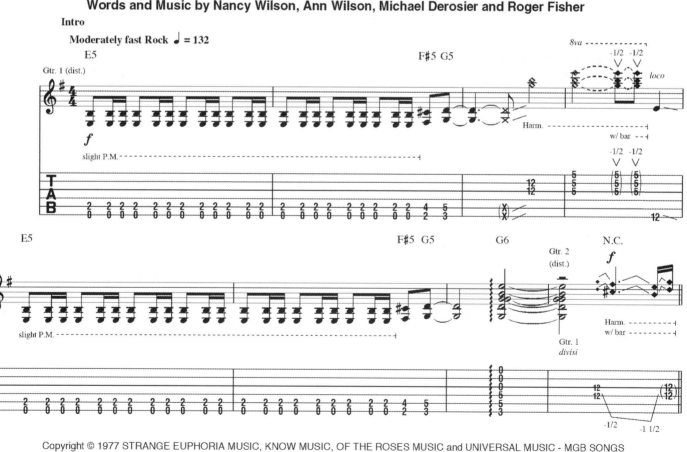

Beast and the Harlot

Performed by Avenged Sevenfold

From *City of Evil* (2005)

Although they were still in high school when they formed the band, Avenged Sevenfold quickly carved out a niche for themselves and their brand of death/glam/punk-meets-British metal. Building a steady following with their first two albums on the Hopeless label — 2001's *Sounding of the Seventh Trumpet* and 2003's *Waking the Fallen* — the band moved to Warner Bros. for their third album. Released in 2005, *City of Evil* reached #30 on the charts on the strength of "Bat Country" and "Beast and the Harlot." Their releases since then have only fared better, with *Avenged Sevenfold* (2007) reaching #4 and *Nightmare* (2010) climbing to #1.

To create the wall-of-sound distortion tones heard on "Beast and the Harlot," Synyster plugged his custom Schecter into a Bogner Uberschall and 4x12 Celestion-loaded cabinet. Similarly, Zacky played his Schecter S-1 through either a Bogner Uberschall head and 4x12 Bogner Uberkab cabinet or a Mesa Boogie Dual Rectifier head and Mesa Triple Recto Cab. Moving by at the brisk tempo of 154 beats per minute (bpm), the guitar team fuels the appetite of the beast with a classic metal rhythmic device: one eighth note alternated with four sixteenth notes. You can hear this same type of thing in dozens of metal songs, including Ozzy Osbourne's "Crazy Train" (verses), Yngwie Malmsteen's "I'll See the Light Tonight" (intro), and Iron Maiden's "Wasted Years" (intro), to name but three. This creates an on-the-beat, off-the-beat feel syncopation with enormous forward momentum; paired with a speedy tempo such as this one, it takes the listener on quite a wild ride.

Taking full advantage of the one-fingered power chord afforded by drop D tuning (D–A–D–G–B–E, low to high), Zacky and Synyster alternate an open, palm-muted low D string in sixteenth notes with F5, G5, and A♭5 chords on strings 6–4. In the key of D minor, this translates to the ♭III, iv, and ♭V chords, respectively — the A♭ lying a particularly wicked tritone away from the tonic. Notice that, in measures 3–4, the riff is altered, and the same abbreviated phrase is played twice to maintain interest and unpredictability — a nice touch for sure.

Beast and the Harlot

Words and Music by Matthew Sanders, James Sullivan, Brian Haner, Jr. and Zachary Baker

Beat It

Performed by Michael Jackson
From *Thriller* (1982)

After singing his way into the hearts of Americans everywhere as the youngest member of the Jackson 5, Michael Jackson began his solo career (though still part of the Jackson 5) with the release of the successful *Got to Be There* and *Ben* in 1972. However, as the Jackson 5 craze began to die down, so did Michael's built-in publicity machine, and his next two releases — *Music & Me* (1973) and *Forever, Michael* (1975) — didn't fare nearly as well. Career fatigue had also clearly caught up with Michael, and he'd grown tired of Motown's heavy hand.

Jackson signed to Epic Records for his fifth album. With producer Quincy Jones at the helm, Michael released *Off the Wall* in 1979. A startlingly fresh album, blending elements of disco, rock, and funk, it became his breakthrough album, legitimizing him as a true talent in the music world and reaching #3 on the Billboard charts. However, all of this was merely a prelude to what lay ahead. With the release of *Thriller* in 1982, nothing was left to question. Michael was undisputedly the biggest star in pop music, and the album broke nearly every record it could. Racking up eight Grammy awards in 1984, the album sold over 40 million copies in its original run, with seven tracks reaching the Top Ten, and oh yeah — it became the best-selling album of all time.

For the disco-rock track "Beat It," Michael and Quincy recruited Eddie Van Halen to play the solo — an occurrence that's become the stuff of studio legend. Some claim Eddie was only paid $75 for his services, while others claimed he was cheated out of millions in royalties. The truth is that Eddie knowingly did it as a favor for free (and it's not as though he was hurting for cash at the time). The song's main riff, however, was performed by legendary studio guitarist Steve Lukather, also a member of Toto.

Wielding his 1959 Gibson Les Paul, "Luke" ran through a cranked Fender Princeton and doubled his part to achieve the warm overdriven tone heard on the track. The song is in the key of E minor, and the main riff ascends from the open low E string up a broken Em arpeggio to outline an Em harmony and then descends stepwise F#–E–D to outline the D chord. Notice the subtle difference in measure 4, in which the D note is not repeated, book-ending the phrase nicely. Also pay close attention to the subtleties, including the grace-note hammer on from E to F# and the deliberately placed rests in the D measures. With the use of the pinky, the entire riff can be comfortably played in second position.

Beat It
Words and Music by Michael Jackson

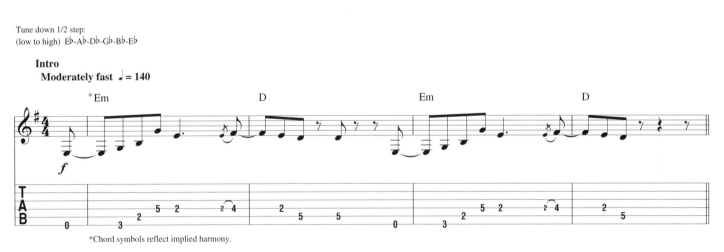

*Chord symbols reflect implied harmony.

Behind Blue Eyes

Performed by the Who
From *Who's Next* (1971)

The Who is perhaps the most famous archetype of the standard rock quartet: drums, bass, guitar, and vocals. This model would be adopted by dozens of great bands to follow through the 1970s — most notably of course being Led Zeppelin. Though largely guided by the creative genius of guitarist/songwriter/vocalist Pete Townshend, the Who were anything but a one-man show. Each member's unique take on his instrument was critical in determining the sound of the band. What would they have been without Keith Moon's bombastic approach to the drums or John Entwistle's furious bass lines? Certainly, they'd still be noteworthy, but they wouldn't be the Who.

After bashing it out on the British club scene for a few years, the Who captured England's attention with one of Townshend's first compositions, "I Can't Explain," which was released in January 1965 and cracked the British Top Ten. Later that year, the band followed up with the mod-anthem "My Generation," which could be considered their signature song. Reaching #2 in England and #74 in the U.S., the song catapulted them to British stardom and firmly established them among the highest ranks of the British Invasion bands. It wouldn't take long for them to dominate the world, scaling the charts with *A Quick One (Happy Jack)* (1966) and *The Who Sell Out* (1967). With the release of the bona fide rock opera *Tommy* (1969), the band settled into a long series of Top Ten albums that they managed to sustain for several years after Keith Moon's untimely death in 1978.

Working with his trusty Gisbon J-200 jumbo and an Esus4 chord, Pete crafts one of the most instantly recognizable intros in all of classic rock for "Behind Blue Eyes" — the #34 hit from 1971's *Who's Next.* He had an obvious penchant for sus4 chords in those days, as evidenced by his other ode to the sus4, "Pinball Wizard." As if traversing through a series of hills and valleys, Pete arpeggiates the chord in straight sixteenth notes, gently rolling up and down through the strings. Although he mostly works with adjacent strings, there are several leaps thrown in to provide a nice contrast. Even though Pete played this riff with a pick, it makes a nice fingerstyle exercise as well, because you'll be forced to shift string groups a few times throughout. Note that by simply beginning measure 2 on the 5th, B, a dominant harmony of B7sus4 (B–E–F♯–A) is suggested — even though the F♯ is not heard — which provides a stronger sense of resolution for the Em chord that follows at the beginning of the verse (not shown).

Behind Blue Eyes
Words and Music by Peter Townshend

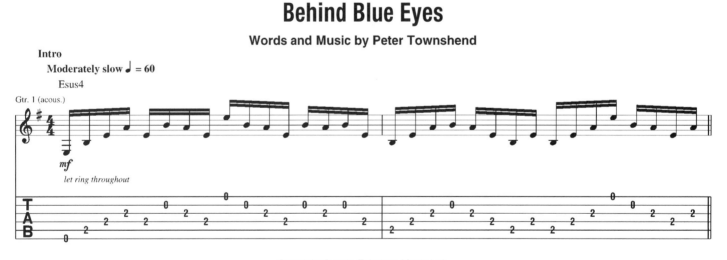

Blitzkreig Bop

Performed by the Ramones
From *Ramones* (1976)

Often cited as the first punk rock band, the Ramones fall into the same category as Velvet Underground — not stylistically, of course, but in terms of influence and commercial success (or lack thereof). Much like Velvet Underground, the Ramones barely cracked the charts throughout their career, but their influence has been immense

With their self-titled debut in 1976, the Ramones made clear their focus: fast, catchy songs played with bottomless wells of energy. There are 14 songs on the album, and none breach the 2:30 mark. (Unbelievably, these songs don't sound all that fast when you compare them with bands that fell under the Ramones' influence.) Although the album only reached #111 on the Billboard charts, it's been ranked #33 on *Rolling Stone's* list of the 500 Greatest Albums of All Time. Working with a miniscule budget of less than $7,000, the album took only seven days to record from top to bottom. In keeping with their adoration of the Beatles, the band used similar recording and mixing techniques, mixing the instruments on extreme ends of the stereo spectrum and doubling the vocals.

"Blitzkreig Bop" epitomizes three-chord punk rock. Play barre chords, play 'em fast, and dig in with all downstrokes. Johnny Ramone ran his Mosrite Ventures II guitar through a Marshall, turned it up, and let loose. Notice that he switches between E-form barre chords (for the A) and A-form barre chords (for the D and E), which is not always the case with punk rockers, who often use the movable E-form. The only thing you have to watch out for is the syncopated E chord, which arrives on the "and" of beat 2, whereas everything else is straight on the beat. This syncopation, although brief, is quite affecting and is hugely responsible for the song's relentless drive forward.

Blitzkreig Bop

Words and Music by Jeffrey Hyman, John Cummings, Douglas Colvin and Thomas Erdelyi

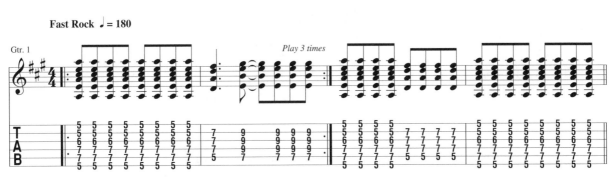

Boom Boom

Performed by John Lee Hooker
From *Burnin'* (1962)

The undisputed king of the boogie, John Lee Hooker left behind him a blues legacy like few others. With a recording career spanning over half a century, he influenced countless blues giants and defined the minimalist approach to blues. Hooker rarely played anything flashy, but what he played was always on the money. Originally recorded in Chicago in 1961, "Boom Boom" featured John Lee out in front of a stellar Motown band, including James Jamerson on bass, Benny Benjamin on drums, Larry Veeder on guitar, and Hank Crosby and Mike Terry on horns. The song became a hit for Hooker, reaching #16 on the R&B charts and even climbing to #60 on the *Billboard* Hot 100.

The song's popularity was spurred along by a few other sources as well. The English band the Animals included a cover on their debut U.K. album from 1964, *The Animals*, which hit #43 on the *Billboard* Hot 100, and the Yardbirds released their version as a single in 1966, which appears on the 2001 compilation, *Ultimate!* (Rhino Records). It was also prominently featured in a 1992 commercial for Lee Jeans and in the 1980 film *The Blues Brothers*, although it wasn't included on the film's soundtrack. The song was inducted into the Rock and Roll Hall of Fame's list of "The Songs That Shaped Rock and Roll" in 1995.

Manhandling his favorite 1959 Epiphone Zephyr plugged into a Fender Twin, John Lee distills the blues down to six or seven golden notes with the intro to "Boom Boom." He works out of the open E blues scale, making use of several slides to lend a vocal-like quality to his lines. Starting on the second finger for each measure will put you in good position to finger the rest of the phrase. Notice that you'll need to tune up a half step in order to play along with Hook's original recording. Alternatively, you could place a capo on fret 1 and achieve the same effect. This song uses a stop-time feel, meaning that every other measure, the band stops on the downbeat to let the vocal take over for a measure. This is in turn answered each time with a lick supported by the band. Although "Boom Boom" begins with a 12-bar form, Hooker rarely stuck to a set number of measures. Instead, he required "big-eared sidemen" to pay close attention so they could follow him as he went where the music took him.

Boom Boom
Words and Music by John Lee Hooker

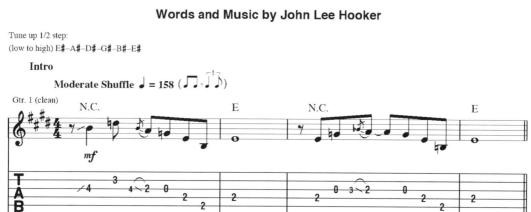

Born to Be Wild

Performed by Steppenwolf
From *Steppenwolf* (1968)

Steppenwolf burned brightly in the late 1960s, scoring a #6 album with their self-titled debut in 1968 and a #3 album with *Steppenwolf the Second* that same year. Although they scored six Top 40 hits in those early days, including "Magic Carpet Ride" and "Rock Me," "Born to Be Wild" has to be their most shining accomplishment. Featured on their debut, the song reached #2 on the charts, but that was hardly the beginning. The band managed to hold things together until 1974, when internal strain tore apart the core lineup and effectively brought an end to the Steppenwolf everyone knew.

After being featured in the 1969 film *Easy Rider* starring Dennis Hopper, the song became a bona fide biker anthem and the go-to song for biker scenes in any movie or TV show. The song is also famous for its first documented use of the term "heavy metal." Although some feel that this merits crediting the band with the invention of the genre, most disagree and simply acknowledge their naming of the genre, reserving the credit of invention for Black Sabbath's eponymous debut in 1970.

Michael Monarch used an all-Fender chain to generate his mammoth, heavy metal thunder tone. He plugged a 1950s Esquire into an early 1960s brownface Fender Concert and cranked it. Although he was repeatedly asked to turn it down, he recounts that he would temporarily oblige but would always sneak over and turn it back up before they hit "record." The riff is a lesson in simplicity and letting the tone do the work for you. Combining the low open E string with an A-form E barre chord in seventh position, Monarch generates a huge crunch with minimal effort. After a few syncopated strums on the E chord, he finishes the two-measure phrase with the biggest hook of all: E6 and E7 dyads atop the low E string that logically lead the ear back to the full E chord. Borrowed from the boogie woogie patterns popularized by Chuck Berry and used by everyone and their mother, the dyads will require a slight stretch in the fret hand, but the fact that you're in seventh position helps out quite a bit in this regard.

Born to Be Wild
Words and Music by Mars Bonfire

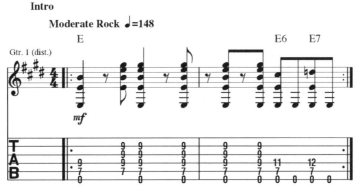

Born Under a Bad Sign

Performed by Albert King

From *Born Under a Bad Sign* (1967)

Albert King had experienced minor celebrity in the blues circles up to 1966 when he moved to Stax Records. But his recordings made at that studio, which featured the house band, Booker T. & The MG's, made him a star in both the blues and rock worlds. With endorsements from both Eric Clapton and Jimi Hendrix in the form of cover versions and obvious tips of the hat, Albert soon became a household name and a huge concert draw everywhere. Although the title track from 1967's *Born Under a Bad Sign* only reached #49 on the R&B charts, the album's impact as a whole was far greater, and its influence on modern blues and rock players is truly incalculable. Over the years, the song has been covered by Cream (*Wheels of Fire,* 1968), Peter Green (*Little Dreamer,* 1980), Robben Ford (*Talk to Your Daughter,* 1986), and Jimi Hendrix (released on *Blues,* 1994), among many others.

Although it's clear that Albert King preferred solid state amps, mostly Acoustics and Rolands, from the early 1970s on, he experimented with many different amps. However, the riff shown here wasn't played by Albert; it was Steve Cropper as part of the house band backing Albert — Booker T. & The MG's. Steve's weapons of choice in those days were a Fender Esquire (early Tele) and the 10w Fender Harvard combo amp.

Working out of C# minor pentatonic, Cropper doubles the bass line for this song. Notice how he uses a slide to move from the low F# to G#. If you begin with your third finger on F#, you'll be in perfect position to finish it off. There are subtle quarter-step bends on the higher E notes and some smooth vibrato on the sustained C# tonic notes. Both of these details provide depth to the riff, so don't neglect them. Perhaps the coolest thing about this riff is the variation that occurs every other time. Instead of just repeating the first phrase over and over (which you will hear some players doing), Steve and the gang insert a low, fat, open E string to break up the monotony and add serious weight to the riff. Oh yeah!

Born Under a Bad Sign

Words and Music by Booker T. Jones and William Bell

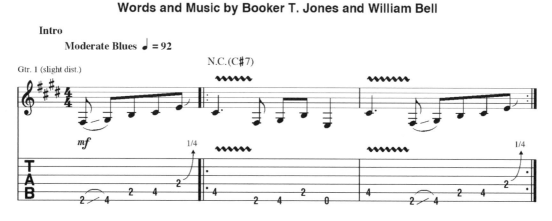

Brain Stew
(The Godzilla Remix)

Performed by Green Day
From the Motion Picture Soundtrack *Godzilla* (1998)

Green Day represents all that's ironic about punk rock. The message is almost always one of defiance and rebellion against authority and anything else that stands in the way of originality and expression. The people that listen to and relate to this type of music don't usually want its purveyors to sell a lot of records, because it diminishes and dilutes this message; it makes them a functioning part of the system they so openly protest. Whereas Nirvana (and especially Kurt Cobain) never learned how to shoulder the adoration, Green Day seemed to adapt fairly easily.

After earning their share of punk fans with their first two releases on the independent Lookout label, the band struck commercial gold (platinum, actually) with 1994's *Dookie*. On the strength of the incredibly catchy "Basket Case" and "When I Come Around," the album shot to #2, and the sell out accusations started flying in. Of course, these accusations were all but drowned out by the sound of cash registers across the country, as the album quickly reached multiplatinum status. With the release of 1995's *Insomniac,* the band fared almost equally well, reaching #2 on the charts on the backs of singles "Brain Stew" and "Geek Stink Breath." From that point on, Green Day wore its pop crown loudly and proudly.

To craft the wall-of-sound distortion heard on "Brain Stew," Billie Joe doubled his guitars throughout. He has an extensive collection of guitars but most likely played either a Gibson Les Paul or Les Paul Jr. for "Brain Stew." As for amplification, he combined the sound of two different Marshall stacks to form a composite tone. The riff is power chord rock 101, but the rests are just as important. Clamp the palm down on the strings after strumming each chord to keep them quiet in between each note. (Note that if you want to play with the original recording, you'll need to tune down a half step.) Billie Joe works through a I (A5)–♭VII (G5)–VI (F♯5)–♭VI (F5)–V (E5) progression in A, voiced all as power chords. Although the first three chords could be seen as coming from A Mixolydian (A–B–C♯–D–E–F♯–G), the F5 is borrowed from the parallel A minor mode, which gives the riff its darker, twisted sound.

Brain Stew
(The Godzilla Remix)
from the TriStar Motion Picture GODZILLA
Words by Billie Joe
Music by Green Day

Breaking the Chains

Performed by Dokken
From *Breaking the Chains* (1983)

Dokken first arrived on the scene in 1983 with their debut album, *Breaking the Chains*. After failing to crack the Top 100 on the *Billboard* charts, the Elektra label was ready to drop them. However, the smooth-talking management team of Dokken was able to get them one more shot. Although it didn't top the charts, the 1984 follow-up, *Tooth and Nail*, did manage to claw its way to #49, mostly on the strength of the power ballad classic, "Alone Again." This bought them enough clout with Elektra to continue on with 1985's *Under Lock and Key*. The album slightly outperformed its predecessor, reaching #32 and producing the hit single "In My Dreams."

Back for the Attack (1987) became their biggest selling record and reached #13, largely on the strength of "Dream Warriors," which first appeared on the soundtrack to *A Nightmare on Elm Street 3: Dream Warriors.* After the ensuing tour, which resulted in the 1988 live album *Beast from the East* (#33), Don Dokken and George Lynch called it quits on the basis of creative differences.

On "Breaking the Chains," Lynch (a.k.a. "Mr. Scary") played his custom-made Tiger M1 guitar. This was a Superstrat-style guitar with a solid maple body, Floyd Rose bridge, maple neck, and ebony fretboard. He ran through a Dallas Rangemaster treble booster and a tube Echoplex before hitting his 71 Marshall Super Lead and 4x12 cabinet. The intro (and verse) riff is basically a lesson in 1980s metal rhythm playing. You have the three elements: power chords, palm muting, and the i, ♭VII, and ♭VI chords. As is done in probably 50 percent of all metal songs from the day, Lynch alternates power chords on strings 5–3 with a palm-muted open E string, which serves as a pedal throughout the riff. Be sure to tightly clamp down the palm mute each time the open E comes around, because this adds to drama of the riff: the stark contrast between the wide open chords and the tightly muted bass string. The tempo is not an issue here, so using all downstrokes is the way to go.

Breaking the Chains
Words and Music by Don Dokken, George Lynch and Mick Brown

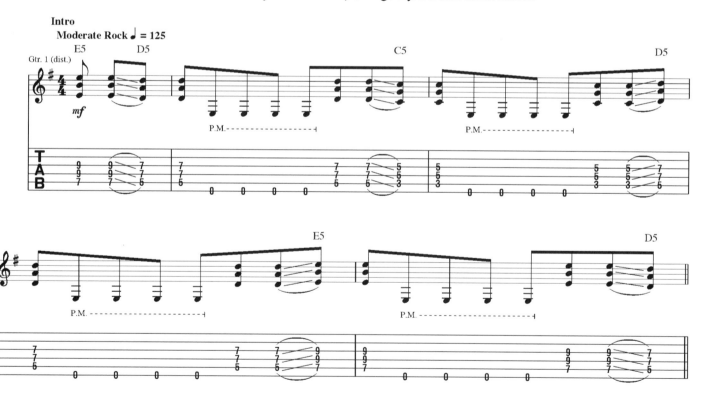

Breaking the Law

Performed by Judas Priest

From *British Steel* (1980)

Judas Priest is one of the forefathers of British Metal, arriving on the scene only a few years behind Black Sabbath. Decked in leather and chains and sporting a twin guitar attack, they helped solidify the formula to which so many future bands would adhere. After spending their formative years redefining the genre with increased emphasis placed on speed and precision, the band took a turn back to simplification for the landmark *British Steel* album in 1980. This album helped usher in a whole new era of mainstream metal. For the first time in their careers, Priest began headlining stadiums and arenas, which helped break down barriers for other metal bands as well. Although *British Steel* topped out at #34, it brought into focus the band's strengths, which they continued to mine on future albums — most notably on *Screaming for Vengeance* (1982), which contained one of the band's signature songs, "You've Got Another Thing Comin'."

"Breaking the Law" contains one of the all-time great metal riffs and teaches a great lesson in simplicity. There's nothing difficult about it, but it rocks hard and is seriously catchy. Though the notes are important, the rhythm is just as big of a hook. The syncopation at the end of measures 1 and 3 spurs the phrase along with a great sense of anticipation. The tune is in the key of A minor, and this riff is built upon notes from the A minor scale (A–B–C–D–E–F–G). Notice how each chord change (A5, F5, and G5) is acknowledged in the riff with a root note sounding at each respective chord. But perhaps the coolest element of this riff is the question-and-answer aspect of it. Take a look at the last two notes in measures 2 and 4. In measure 2, the "question" phrase, we have B and C, which sends the riff charging forward. In measure 4, this is "answered" by C and B, which logically leads us back to the beginning of the riff for the repeat. Both Glenn Tipton and K.K. Downing used the metal-approved rig of Gibsons into Marshalls to drive this riff into the metal history books.

Breaking the Law

Words and Music by Glenn Tipton, Rob Halford and K.K. Downing

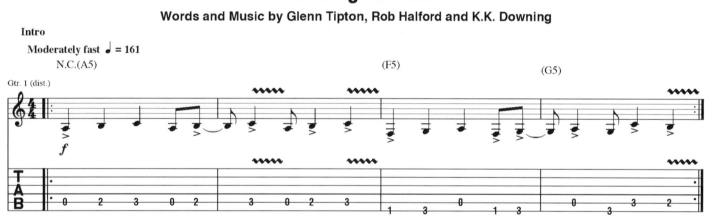

Bring It on Home

Performed by Led Zeppelin

From *Led Zeppelin II* (1969)

After the out-of-the-gates success of their first album, Led Zeppelin hit the road on its first North America tour. When they had the time between shows, they holed up in the studio to record what would become *Led Zeppelin II*. Due to the limited time available, the album consisted of many blues standards that they had reworked in typical Zeppelin fashion. On the strength of such immortal classics as "Whole Lotta Love," "Heartbreaker," "Ramble On," and "Moby Dick,", the album had no problem reaching #1, beginning a long string of chart-toppers for the band. Page had shed the famed Tele and Supro amp combination for *Led Zeppelin II,* replacing it with more standard fare in the world of rock guitar. The result is a more direct sound that has more in common with the rest of the band's repertoire.

After a down-home, shuffled blues intro lures you into a peaceful state that brings to mind an afternoon spent rocking on the porch with a tall glass of lemonade, things change rather abruptly. With a musical punch in the nose, the band cranks up to full volume and embarks on a high-wattage blues rock romp. Page straps on his '58 Les Paul Standard, dimes his 100W Marshall, and creates a diamond of blues-rock riffery. The tone is raunchy and wide open, with plenty of bite and grit.

Working from the open E position, he plays out of the E Mixolydian mode (E–F♯–G♯–A–B–C♯–D), mixing open strings with whole-step bends and pull-offs. The major 3rd here (G♯ on fret 1, string 3) is a bit of a surprise, because the open G string is probably more often used with a lick like this. Whereas measure 1 resolves nicely to the root note, measure 2 comes to rest on beat 4 with an A note, suggesting an A major harmony. This is an interesting take on question-and-answer phrasing in the sense that it feels more like an answer first (with the tonic E note resolution) and a question second (with the suspension on the A note). Realize that the sound of the riff is augmented with two Page overdubs as well — one doubling the riff exactly and one on octave higher (not shown) — which creates the huge sonic footprint you hear on the recording.

Bring It on Home

Written by Willie Dixon

Brown Eyed Girl

Performed by Van Morrison
From *Blowin' Your Mind* (1967)

After making a name for himself with Them in the mid-1960s, Van Morrison set out on his own. In his haste to get started, he quickly signed a deal with Bert Berns' Bang Records in New York. On that label, he released his first solo album, *Blowin' Your Mind*, in 1967. Although it only peaked at #182, it put him on the map with "Brown Eyed Girl," which is far and away his signature song. Bert Berns died that same year from heart failure, and Warner Bros. bought out Van's recording contract. His first record for Warner Bros., *Astral Weeks* (1968), is considered by many to be his masterpiece. Although it failed to make a dent in the charts, its influence has been far-reaching. The follow-up, 1970's *Moondance,* reached #29 and began a successful string of Top 40 albums that stretched through to the mid-1970s.

The music that comprised the *Blowin' Your Mind* album was recorded quickly in March of 1967 with a group of session musicians backing up Van. In fact, he didn't even realize the album was going to be released; he was under the impression that four singles would be chosen from the sessions. He was also upset about the album artwork, because he was not a drug user and didn't appreciate its suggestive nature. Due to a hastily signed record contract, however, he had surrendered nearly all creative control over his material.

Three guitarists are listed for the *Blowin' Your Mind* sessions: Eric Gale, Hugh McCracken, and Al Giorgioni. One of them played the famous signature riff, but which one is not clear. The riff is a veritable lesson in harmonizing 3rds. Over the G chord, a G–A–B–A–G melody is harmonized a 3rd above to form dyads of G/B, A/C, and B/D. This same exact riff is transposed up a 4th for the C chord, resulting in the dyads C/E, D/F, and E/G. Notice that the F note is not diatonic to the key of G, which has F♯ in its key signature. Therefore, the riff takes on a G Mixolydian quality over that chord, which adds a bit of tartness that serves the lick well. Over the D chord, a 5th of D/A sounds at first, followed by a climb up from the 3rd of D (F♯) to the 5th (A), leading you logically back to the G dyad.

Brown Eyed Girl
Words and Music by Van Morrison

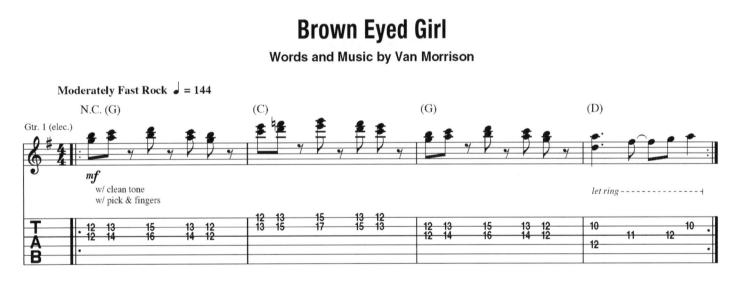

Can't Stop

Performed by Red Hot Chili Peppers
From *By the Way* (2002)

Although the Red Hot Chili Peppers originally made their name with their freaked-out brand of funk rock, they changed quite a bit throughout the years, eventually incorporating melodic pop rock into the fold. This shift occurred most noticeably on their #3 smash *Blood Sugar Sex Magik,* which not only contained the Grammy-winning funk rap of "Give It Away," but also the soulful #2 ballad, "Under the Bridge." The success of the latter in particular was liberating for the band, freeing them to veer even further away from the hyper-energetic sound with which they had so long been associated. Though they stumbled briefly with 1995's *One Hot Minute,* which featured Dave Navarro on guitar, the Chili Peppers resurfaced stronger than ever with the massively successful *Californication* (#3) in 1999.

Although they continued to explore the pop side of songwriting with *Californication* and subsequent releases, they occasionally reach back to their funkier past and filter it through their new, more focused sound. Such is the case on "Can't Stop," which appears on 2002's *By the Way* (#2). Although the track begins similar to a vintage Chili Peppers track, it never opens up with full abandon. And by the time the layered vocal harmonies and guitar parts show up, it's clear that the band is forging new ground.

With his trusty Strat and Marshall, John Frusciante seriously lays it down as the band lays out. Supporting an ostinato of D–E, he supplies the implied harmony of Em–Dsus2–Bm(add11)–Cadd9 all by himself, alternating between bass notes played on strings 4–6 and the melody D and E notes played on string 3. The tone is dry and in your face, with Frusciante using the bridge pickup to really cut through. Notice the abundance of dead notes, particularly in measures 3 and 4, when the bass notes move to string 6. By laying his fret-hand's first finger lightly across the strings, he's able to strum freely but only sound the notes on strings 6 and 3. This kind of fret-hand muting is absolutely necessity in funkier styles like this, besides the fact that it's part of the sound. Those muted notes add considerable weight and would be sorely missed if they weren't there.

Can't Stop

Words and Music by Anthony Kiedis, Flea, John Frusciante and Chad Smith

Carry On Wayward Son

Performed by Kansas
From *Leftoverture* (1976)

Perhaps because they were American, and their most famous song, "Dust in the Wind," was a fairly straightforward acoustic affair, people tend to downplay Kansas's progressiveness. But make no mistake; they were just as art rock as Genesis or Yes. Although they trolled along the depths of the charts with their first few albums, they hit it big with their 1976 classic, *Leftoverture.* No less progressive than its predecessors, this album is set apart by the inclusion of the band's #11 hit, "Carry On Wayward Son," which helped the album scale all the way up to #5. No doubt tuned in to the reception of "Carry On…," they laced the follow-up, 1977's *Point of Know Return* (#4), with two more pop-tinged tracks: the title track, which hit #28, and their signature-song, "Dust in the Wind," which blew its way up to #6. This would prove to be their career climax, however, as other musical ambitions began to splinter the band's focus.

After the famous a cappella intro, guitarists Kerry Livgren and Rich Williams kick off the tune in style with the famous, muscular single-note riff. Kerry works his Gibson 335, while Rich most likely plays a Gibson Les Paul, both of them running straight into Marshall 100W amps. Almost entirely comprised of notes from the A minor pentatonic scale (A–C–D–E–G), the riff also contains one F# at the very end, which stems from the A Dorian mode (A–B–C–D–E–F#–G). This is a common rock scale that fits a major IV chord in a minor key song. In this case, you have a D major harmony in the key of A minor.

One of the most salient features in this riff is found in its rhythm. Notice how the rhythm of the first four-note phrase, A–G–A–C, is mimicked starting on beat 4 with A–G–A–D. This is known as playing across the barline and interjects the riff with an air of sophistication that's typical of the band's brand of progressive rock. This is contrasted nicely in measure 3 with two nonsyncopated melodic dyads of D–G and D–F#. What's also interesting here, and par for the course with Kansas, is that the phrase is three measures long as opposed to the much more common two or four measures.

Carry On Wayward Son
Words and Music by Kerry Livgren

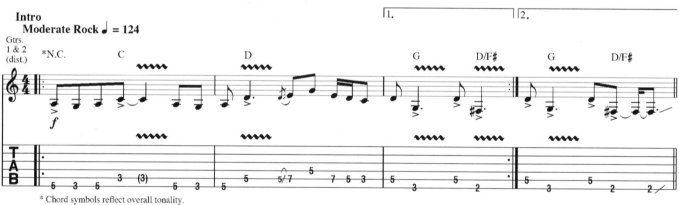

* Chord symbols reflect overall tonality.

Cheap Sunglasses

Performed by ZZ Top

From *Degüello* (1979)

ZZ Top got its start in 1969 when guitarist Billy Gibbons and drummer Dan Mitchell, both formerly in the Moving Sidewalks, joined bassist Lanier Greig. After a few lineup shuffles, their final incarnation, including bassist Dusty Hill and (beardless) Frank Beard, established itself later that year. After developing a following in Texas based on their live show, they signed a deal with London records and released their *ZZ Top's First Album,* in January of 1971. This album established their somewhat crude sense of humor and gritty approach to blues rock. After gaining a bit of ground with their follow-up, 1972's *Rio Grande Mud,* which included the minor hit "Francine," the Top enjoyed their first real commercial breakthough in 1973 with *Tres Hombres.* On the strength of the #41 hit "La Grange," the album reached #8 on the charts — "La Grange," went on to reach legendary status.

After a bit more success with *Fandango* (#10, 1975) and a bit less with *Tejas* (#17, 1976), it seemed as though ZZ Top was running out of steam. The band decided to take a hiatus to get refreshed and it paid off. Although 1979's *Degüello* only reached #24, it contained two charting singles with "I Thank You" (#34) and "Cheap Sunglasses" (#89), both of which are Top classics. After treading a bit of water with *El Loco* (#17, 1981), the boys from Houston, Texas, struck gold with *Eliminator,* the worldwide smash that made them indisputable superstars and earned them diamond platinum sales status (over 10 million copies sold in the U.S. alone).

To achieve the gritty, half dirty tone on "Cheap Sunglasses," the Reverend Billy Gibbons plugged his 1959 Les Paul (known as "Pearly Gates") into a Marshall Major — basically a 200W variation of the classic 100W Marshall. The song is in the key of G minor and is on the funkier side for ZZ Top. Gibbons breaks his part into two different segments — a chordal accent on top, and a syncopated, funky riff on the bottom — resulting in what sounds like two separate guitars. The chord appears on the downbeats, where Gibbons slides into a Bb triad from a half step below. In this context, the Bb triad functions like a rootless Gm7 chord. Gibbons then answers this with several syncopated 5ths and 6ths played on strings 6–4 that require a few serious stretches. Note that, for all its complexity, the basic progression happening is Gm7 (beats 1–3)–Bb6 (beat 4)–C5 (beat 4.5).

Cheap Sunglasses

Words and Music by Billy F Gibbons, Dusty Hill and Frank Lee Beard

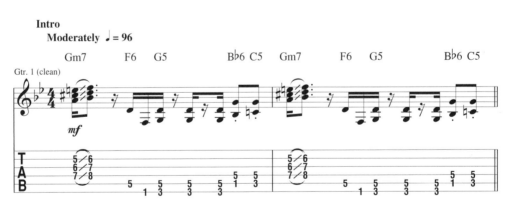

Cochise

Performed by Audioslave
From *Audioslave* (2002)

Audioslave is one of the few supergroups to emerge thus far in the new millennium. Like many supergroups before, their star shone brightly but burned itself out quickly. After Zack de la Rocha left Rage Against the Machine, the remaining members started searching for a replacement. On the suggestion of legendary producer Rick Rubin, they contacted Chris Cornell, who was working on his second solo album at the time. The chemistry between the Rage guys and Cornell was evident almost immediately, and they formed a new band, Audioslave, reportedly writing 21 songs in 19 days of rehearsals. Released in 2002, the eponymous debut album delivered in a big way, reaching #7 and spawning several charting singles. Two songs also enjoyed prominent film placement; "Shadow of the Sun" was featured in *Collateral* (starring Tom Cruise), and "Cochise" was featured in *Talladega Nights: The Ballad of Ricky Bobby* (starring Will Ferrell) as well as the game *Guitar Hero* for Playstation 2. According to Morello, "Cochise" tells the story of the last American Indian chief to die free and unconquered.

To create the mighty, thunderous riff of "Cochise," Morello worked with fairly standard tools: a Strat and a Marshall amp. The guitar is a Fender Aerodyne Strat (nicknamed "Soul Power") that features an Ibanez Edge Floyd Rose tremolo, Fender Noiseless single coils in the neck and middle positions, and a Seymour Duncan Hotrails (stacked humbucker) in the bridge position. It also has a toggle switch wired, and the body is routed out behind the tremolo so that the bar can be pushed down or pulled up. As for the Marshall, it's Morello's trusty JCM 800 2205, which he used while in Rage Against the Machine.

"Cochise" is in the key of E minor — although, in typical Cornell fashion, he mixes in the parallel major mode at times by singing G# notes — and the riff is pretty much Heavy Rock 101. Sounding like something straight off a Zeppelin record, it's composed entirely from notes of the E minor pentatonic scale (E–G–A–B–D) and features one somewhat tricky position shift from fifth position down to third. The tempo is fairly slow, however, so it's certainly manageable. Like many hard rock riffs in the key of E, the basic contour leads from a higher E note down an octave to a lower E note. The syncopation on beat 3 is largely responsible for the riff's swagger, so make sure you're getting the rhythm right!

Cochise

Lyrics by Chris Cornell
Music written and arranged by Audioslave

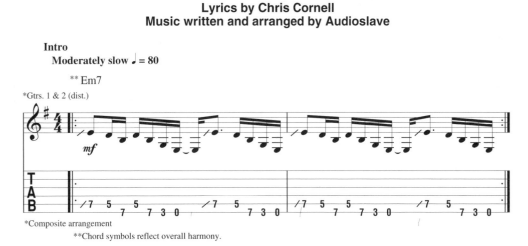

*Composite arrangement
**Chord symbols reflect overall harmony.

Cold Gin

Performed by Kiss

From *Kiss* (1974)

After being together as a band only a little over a year, Kiss released their eponymous debut album in 1974 on Casablanca Records. This was made easier by the fact that much of the album's material had been written by Paul Stanley and Gene Simmons while they were members of a previous band known as Wicked Lester. Although no singles were issued from the album, it managed to sell 75,000 copies on its initial release and reached gold status three years later. With their comic book-themed stage wardrobe and party-til-you-drop song themes, Kiss quickly scaled the charts with each album. It was the 1975 release of *Alive* (#9) the live album that catapulted them to mega-stardom, however, largely based on the immortal version of "Rock and Roll All Nite," which gave them their first Top 20 single and still enjoys heavy radio rotation nearly forty years later. The rest is history, as the band went on to rule the charts for the remainder of the decade and amass a fortune on merchandising.

The classic intro riff from "Cold Gin," the fourth cut from their debut album, comes at you full blast in the right speaker. To achieve the thick, fuzzy tone, Ace Frehley plugged his Gibson Les Paul Standard, which had a rewound hot pickup, into either a Marshall Stack or tweed Fender Bassman. Because James Marshall basically copied the Bassman schematic when he built his first amp, the sounds are very similar — the only differences being the speaker/cabinet configuration and the transformers used. Granted, those elements do make a big impact on the sound, but Fender and Marshall amps never sounded as similar in any other incarnation.

"Cold Gin" is in the key of A, and Ace crafts a catchy, syncopated riff using a clever device: a pedal tone. Using the open A string beneath dyads played on strings 4 and 3, he achieves a thick, sophisticated timbre and full-range sound in the process. Working with three dyads on strings 4 and 3 — A/E, G/D, and F#/D — the harmonies of A5, G5/A, and D/A are created, and Ace uses specifically placed rests to add drama and anticipation to the riff. Be sure to tune down a half step if you want to play along with the original recording.

Cold Gin

Words and Music by Ace Frehley

Come as You Are

Performed by Nirvana

From *Nevermind* (1991)

Rarely has the term "overnight success" been so fitting as with Nirvana. They might tell you otherwise, because they had spent years scraping by prior to their explosive popularity. But to the majority of music fans, they seemed to spring up overnight — instantly becoming the biggest band in the world. Diehard fans knew of their Sup Pop debut in 1989, *Bleach,* which featured former drummer Chad Channing. But for many, "Smells Like Teen Spirit" was their introduction to the band. And rock music would never be the same again.

"Come as You Are" opens with a mesmerizing riff that's clever on more than one level. Its efficiency is quite brilliant, because it can be played entirely in first position with minimal movement. Two dyads make up the core of the riff, both of which are played on strings 6 and 5 (as is the entire riff, for that matter): F#/A, which implies F#m, and E/B, or E5. With the song being in the key of F#m, this results in a i–bVII progression. Besides the obvious symmetry created on the guitar fretboard with these shapes (the 2 and 0 on tab strings 6 and 5, respectively, being flipped to 0 and 2), Kurt adds a chromatic passing tone, F♮, to link each chord, both when ascending and descending. The result is a somewhat cyclical sound that, like an M.C. Escher work, seems to never have a beginning or an end.

It's unclear as to which guitar Kurt actually played on this track, but a safe bet would be his late-1960s Fender Mustang, which he picked up at a pawn shop. At that point, those guitars had been unfashionable for quite a while and could be had for next to nothing. He played through a Vox AC30, which was owned by the studio of producer Butch Vig. To obtain the watery, warbling effect, Kurt used an Electro-Harmonix Small Clone chorus pedal. Set the rate on the slower side with the depth switch set to the maximum position. Remember to keep the fingers arched so that all the notes are allowed to ring throughout.

Come as You Are

Words and Music by Kurt Cobain

Come Out and Play

Performed by the Offspring

From *Smash* (1994)

With the massive success of the young punk-rock band Green Day in early 1994, the stage was set for the Offspring, who had barely made a dent in the charts with their first two releases on the independent Epitaph label. When they released their third album in April of 1994, *Smash,* little did they know it would go on to hold a record of its own. With the slowed-down punk catchiness of "Come Out and Play" and "Self Esteem," the indie album reached #4 on the charts and has gone on to sell over 12 million copies to date, making it the best-selling independent album of all time.

Dexter Holland (lead vocals) and Noodles Wasserman keep it simple in regard to their tones on "Come Out and Play" — Ibanez guitars and Mesa Boogie amps. Specifically, the guitars are customized Ibanez RG models with Dimarzio Super Distortion pickups, and the amps are Mesa Boogie Mark IV heads with Boogie 4x12 cabinets. On the record (and when playing live), Dexter handles the clean melody, and Noodles chunks along with the power chords.

The song is in the key of B minor, and while the arrangement is simple for the most part, the notes, in Dexter's part at least, are a bit unorthodox. Over a B5–F#5–A5 (i–V–♭VII) progression provided by Noodles, Dexter plays a melody derived from the B Spanish scale: B–C–D#–E–F#–G–A. This unusual scale could be also be described as the fifth mode of the E harmonic minor scale. In other words, if you start this scale on the note E, you have the E harmonic minor scale: E–F#–G–A–B–C–D#. Dexter only plays up and down the first five notes of the scale, so the only note that strays from a B major scale is the b2, but what a difference one note can make! Dexter uses a grace slide from E to F#, heightening the exotic nature of the riff. With regard to the power chords of Gtr. 2 (Noodles), be sure to keep the palm mute locked down tightly throughout.

Come Out and Play

Words and Music by Dexter Holland

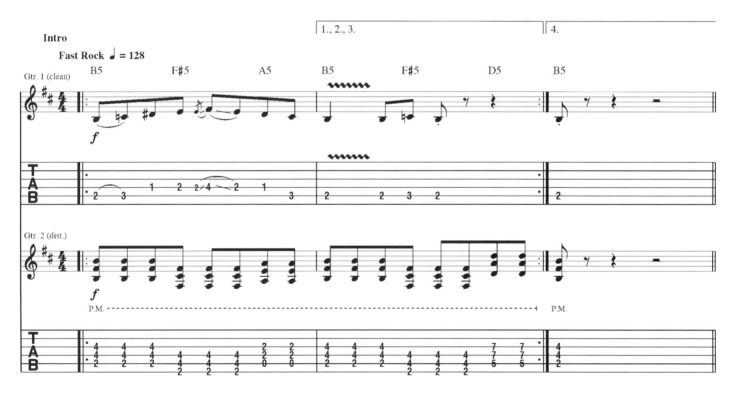

Couldn't Stand the Weather

Performed by Stevie Ray Vaughan and Double Trouble
From *Couldn't Stand the Weather* (1984)

Stevie Ray Vaughan was a force of nature. Rarely, if ever, has a guitarist so aptly combined chops, feel, and tone. As if this weren't enough, throw into the pot that he was also a charismatic showman and a talented songwriter, and you have the makings of the legend. Jackson Browne offered him free studio time to record a demo. Stevie and Double Trouble got their big break in 1982 when, after hearing the demo, legendary producer John Hammond got them signed to Epic Records. The demo tapes were released as *Texas Flood* in 1983, which shuffled up the charts to #38, and a star was born. The follow-up, 1984's *Couldn't Stand the Weather* (#31), confirmed that he was indeed the real deal — not to mention instrumental in launching a full-fledged blues revival.

You simply can not think of Stevie Ray without his indelible sonic signature coming to mind. Thick, meaty, yet still defined, it's been the goal of thousands of tone-seekers for decades now. On "Couldn't Stand the Weather," Vaughan made use of Charley, a custom Strat built by Charley Wirz — owner of the famous Dallas guitar shop, Charley's. This guitar featured Danelectro lipstick pickups, one volume and one tone knob, a white headstock (to match the body), an ebony fretboard, and a hardtail bridge. It's hard to be as certain about the amp, because Stevie made a habit of carrying a staggering number of amps into the studio and combining several to create the final composite tone on any one song. However, a blackfaced Fender Vibroverb or Super Reverb would get you in the ballpark.

As for the famous intro riff, it's sparse, but it grooves with a vengeance. In the key of D, its backbone is the D–C–D phrase that kicks off measures 1 and 3. The first time, it's answered by a long, syncopated climb up the D blues scale starting from the low F note. Although a long pause on G suggests the IV chord, it's never confirmed, because the bass is doubling Vaughan exactly. The second time, after an exaggerated pause, which creates great anticipation, you can hear a syncopated, chromatic climb beginning on the *major* 3rd, F♯ — the mixing of major and minor 3rds being a common move in funkier styles. Remember to tune down a half step to play along, and be sure to dig in!

Couldn't Stand the Weather
Words and Music by Stevie Ray Vaughan

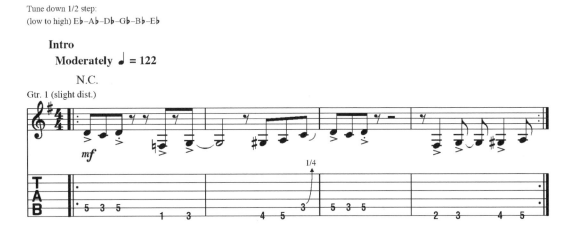

Crazy Train

Performed by Ozzy Osbourne
From *Blizzard of Ozz* (1980)

After leaving Black Sabbath in 1979, the Ozzman was on the hunt for a guitar player to suit his new project. Just before his final gig with Quiet Riot, Randy Rhoads was called for an audition on the recommendation of a magazine editor who was interviewing Ozzy at the time. After Rhoads showed up with his Les Paul and a practice amp and played a few riffs, Ozzy almost immediately offered him the gig. Rhoads was shocked but ecstatic all the same. After recommending a replacement for himself in Quiet Riot, he was winging it to the U.K. to begin work on what was to become *Blizzard of Ozz.*

Blending his love for heavy metal with his classical background, Rhoads became a huge force in Ozzy's sound at the time, and both Ozzy and then-bassist Bob Daisley encouraged him to play what he wanted. His explosive playing ignited the album and turned the guitar world on its ear, launching him to the top of several magazine polls. The album hit #21 and eventually went on to sell 6 million copies without the benefit of a Top 40 single, making it quite unique among the list of 100 best-selling albums in the 1980s.

A good candidate for the most famous metal guitar riff of all time, "Crazy Train" is on top of the "must-know" list for aspiring young metal players of any generation. Although it's not a difficult riff, it does make a great frethand exercise, because it works the pinky a good deal. The iconic intro riff in F♯ minor is performed in second position and makes famous use of a pedal tone: one tone repeated in alteration against changing tones above (or below). In this case, the low F♯ acts as the pedal tone in measure 1, while C♯ (the 5th) and D (the ♭6th) tones are heard above. Measure 2 answers with two scalar runs — B–A–G♯–A and B–A–G♯–E — which lead elegantly back to F♯ for the riff's repeat.

To create the creamy yet aggressive tone on the record, Randy Rhoads used his classic cream-colored Gibson Les Paul-and-Marshall stack combination, which served as his main live rig at the time as well. To achieve more gain, he ran through an MXR Distortion+ pedal, which also helped with his trademark pinch harmonics. As with almost all of his tracks, Rhoads doubled the part throughout.

Crazy Train

Words and Music by Ozzy Osbourne, Randy Rhoads and Bob Daisley

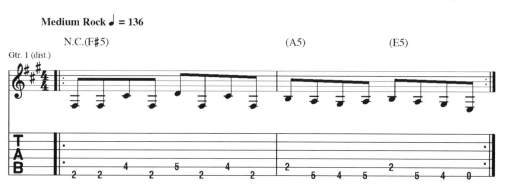

Cross Road Blues
(Crossroads)

Performed by Cream
From *Wheels of Fire* (1968)

Cream was the ultimate supergroup; there's no denying that. And Clapton's mythical stature at the time added to the mystique. After establishing the first power trio with *Fresh Cream* in 1966 (#39), the band teamed up with producer Felix Pappalardi for *Disraeli Gears* in 1967, the psychedelic-tinged masterpiece that hit #4, largely on the strength of the #5 über classic, "Sunshine of Your Love." By the time the #1 *Wheels of Fire* was released in 1968, containing the mammoth "White Room" and "Cross Road Blues," the end was in sight, as personalities began to clash and Clapton began to suffer hearing loss due to ridiculous stage volumes. With the appropriately titled *Goodbye* (#2), the band called it quits in 1969.

There's a great debate regarding Clapton's instrument of choice on the famous live recording from the *Wheels of Fire* album. Although Clapton himself has reportedly referred to his famed cherry red Gibson 335 as the guitar used on this song, many feel adamantly that it was, in fact, his famous, psychedelic Gibson SG (painted by The Fool) on the iconic recording. It's clear that Clapton did play the 335 on the farewell tour in 1968, and this could possibly be what Clapton was referencing, but the version featured on the *WOF* album was recorded in 1967 with no video documentation. He was definitely running through his 100W Marshall head and 4x12 cabinet to achieve his sonic nirvana.

Clapton is credited for the arrangement of "Cross Road Blues," and he did quite an impressive job making it his own. Though the original Robert Johnson version lumbers along at a lazy 95 bpm, the Cream version sounds like hyper blues at 124 bpm with a hint of a double-time feel. The laid back swing of Johnson's version was also replaced with a relentlessly charging straight eighths feel. Working from an open A chord's framework, Eric crafts a super-catchy A–G–A motive on string 3 that immediately follows the A5 chord struck on the downbeat. The legato move that follows effectively reverses this with G–A–G before Clapton skips down to string 5 for the final C note, which is bent a bluesy half step and leads back to the open A5 for the repeat.

Cross Road Blues
(Crossroads)
Words and Music by Robert Johnson

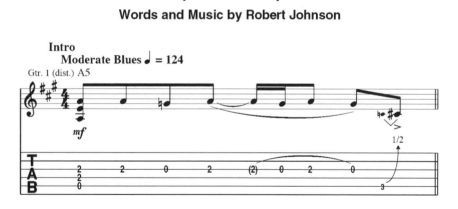

Cult of Personality

Performed by Living Colour
From *Vivid* (1988)

Vernon Reid founded Living Colour in the mid-1980s, and the group was discovered by Mick Jagger in 1987, which helped secure them a deal with Epic Records. The result of their first effort was *Vivid,* the #6 album that contained two Top 40 singles: the Grammy-winning "Cult of Personality" (#13) and "Glamour Boys" (#31). The album also helped to demonstrate that they had more than a gimmick going for them — being an all-black heavy metal band. However, the magic didn't last long, and with their next two albums, *Time's Up* (1990, #13) and *Stain* (1993, #26) failing to produce a substantial hit, the band parted ways.The band did reunite in 2003 but have failed to garner much commercial success.

Vernon Reid, heavy metal's left-brained guitarist, was never one to rely heavily on clichés. This is aptly demonstrated on his angular riff to "Cult of Personality," which has no doubt remained Living Colour's signature song. To create the razor-like distorted tone heard on the track, Vernon played his custom ESP guitar (with active EMG pickups) through Mesa Boogies. Although the song is in the key of G minor, the riff makes heavy use of the note E. This results in a G Dorian tonality (G–A–B♭–C–D–E–F), which is a jazzier take on minor keys than the usual natural minor scale or the classical-sounding harmonic minor scale — a favorite of Yngwie Malmsteen and other neoclassical shredders.

Taking place entirely on the fourth and sixth strings, the riff is all over the place in terms of intervals — the smallest interval being a minor 3rd. The core of the riff is the root G on string 6, which serves as the anchor against the target F and E notes above. The open D string is pulled off to after each F note as well. In addition to the striking effect of the notes, the rhythm is a major hook as well. Notice that the first set of five notes (G–F–D–G–E), which occupies three eighth notes, is repeated verbatim beginning on the "and" of beat 2, creating a wicked syncopation. And don't miss the added E note at the end of measure 2, which provides just enough variation to keep things interesting (not that the riff was in danger of being dull).

Cult of Personality

Words and Music by William Calhoun, Corey Glover, Muzz Skillings and Vernon Reid

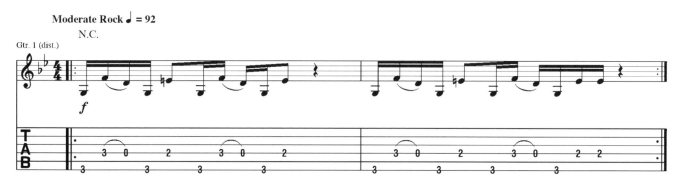

Day Tripper

Performed by the Beatles
Released as a Single (1965)

During the recording sessions for the monumental *Rubber Soul* album (although, which Beatles album wasn't monumental, really?), the band was under pressure to release a single for the approaching Christmas season. Lennon's response was "Day Tripper," which he completed, save for a few verse lyrics from Paul, on his own. (Paul contributed the flip side of the "double A-side" single with "We Can Work It Out.") A #1 smash, "Day Tripper" contains typical Lennon wordplay, telling the story of someone who's only a "weekend hippie." Interestingly, the song contains one of the most obvious of all studio mistakes to appear on a Beatles song. At 1:50, the lead guitar and tambourine drop out (disappear) — the result of rerecording over the same tape repeatedly. This glitch was corrected, however, for the *1* (2002) and *Past Masters* (1988) compilations.

Although the famous intro riff was penned by Lennon, George got to kick off the song on the recording. Picking on either a Gibson ES-345 or a Fender Strat (there's plenty of debate on this), he played through a Vox AC15 to generate the classic, half-dirty tone. The riff is doubled by another guitar (which is evidenced by the slightly out-of-tune D strings that you can hear on the recording), and McCartney joins in an octave lower on the bass for the repeat.

The song is in the key of E, and it begins with a typical move: the root note (E) followed by a minor-to-major 3rd move — in this case, G to G♯. This is a classic device in rock and roll found heavily in the work of Chuck Berry and just about everyone who followed him. The riff continues up an E major arpeggio with B on string 5 and E on string 4 before landing on the ♭7th by way of the open D string, resulting in an E7 tonality. Just when you think you've figured it out, though, Harrison (by way of Lennon's riff) throws another wrench into things with B followed by F♯, which is the 9th, before finishing up with a classic 5–♭7–1 move (B–D–E) at the end of measure 2. Taken altogether, the riff suggests an E9 tonality. Certainly not a common occurrence in rock, it proves once again how daring the Fab Four were in their sonic explorations.

Day Tripper

Words and Music by John Lennon and Paul McCartney

Dr. Feel Good

Performed by Mötley Crüe

From *Dr. Feel Good* (1989)

After years and years of extremely decadent lifestyles, the Crüe boys decided to get sober after Nikki Sixx's near death (in fact, he was pronounced dead) experience from a heroin overdose in 1987. Ironically, their first album recorded after this experiment in sobriety was 1989's *Dr. Feel Good,* which was produced by Bob Rock. Although the album hit #1 (a first for the band) and spawned four Top 40 singles (another first), it would be singer Vince Neil's last with the band until their reunion in 1997. Two of the hit singles from the album were directly related to drug abuse: ""Dr. Feel Good" and "Kick Start My Heart," which was influenced by Sixx's 1987 revival, during which a medic injected two shots of adrenaline into his heart.

To create the heavy-handed tone for "Dr. Feel Good," Mars worked with his custom Kramer and a combination of Marshall and Soldano amps. After a good fourteen measures or so of rumbling and noise-making to set the vibe, he settles into the signature riff of the song. In the key of E, he starts off with the root on the open sixth string and stutters his way chromatically from F♯ to A before leaping to strings 3 and 2 for the syncopated chord stabs of D5 and A in measures 1 and 3 and G5 (implying the E7♯9 harmony) in measures 2 and 4. Of course, the rhythm is half of this riff's appeal, as the syncopated low E note, which enters on the last sixteenth note of each measure, drives forward the momentum relentlessly.

Although Mick Mars makes it sound easy, the chromatic climb from F♯ to A is deceptively difficult. Be sure that your hands are perfectly synchronized at a slow tempo, especially on the notes that are doubled up, before you increase it to match the original recording. This is the kind of thing where most players think, "If I can play this many notes as sixteenth notes, I can surely double each note with no problem." But double-picking notes is a unique skill that takes work if you've never done it before.

Dr. Feel Good

Words by Nikki Sixx
Music by Mick Mars and Nikki Sixx

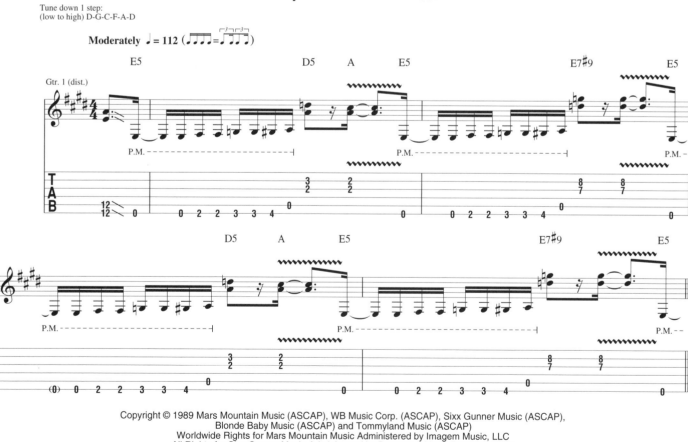

Don't Fear the Reaper

Performed by Blue Öyster Cult
From *Agents of Fortune* (1976)

Blue Öyster Cult, the band consisting of two New York rock critics, spent the first half of the 1970s slowly climbing the charts. It wasn't until 1976 with *Agents of Fortune* that their fortunes would be made. Largely on the strength of the anthemic "Don't Fear the Reaper," which climbed to #12 and remains the band's biggest single, the album hit #29 and has enjoyed tremendous staying power, regularly appearing on "Top 500" lists. The song itself has fared even better, with over 930,000 digital copies sold in the U.S. alone as of 2010. Although the band continued to release albums well into the 1980s and beyond, the only one that came close to matching the success of *Agents of Fortune* was 1981's *Fire of Unknown Origin,* which burned its way up to #24 on the strength of the hit "Burnin' for You."

Donald "Buck Dharma" Roeser has claimed that he was thinking of his own mortality when he composed "Don't Fear the Reaper." The famous riff, which he recorded on a Gibson ES-175 through a Music Man 4x10 combo amp, came to him "out of the ether" as did the first two lines of lyrics. The song has aged well, sounding nearly as fresh today as it did in 1976. And yes, the cowbell is clearly audible.

The song is in A minor and makes use of one of the most famous minor chord progressions of all: i–♭VII–♭VI–♭VII. Arpeggiating throughout the progression, Roeser's masterpiece employs a power musical device called a common tone; note how the last note in each chord is the open G string. This lends a great sense of continuity to the proceedings and creates a very smooth transition from chord to chord as well. But Roeser also makes use of another common tone, by way of the open D string, to bridge the G and F chords, resulting in the F6/9 (no 3rd) chord. Taken altogether, the chords cascade effortlessly into each other and create a lush bed of harmony over which the vocals glide. Be sure to keep your fingers arched so that all the notes can ring out as long as possible.

Don't Fear the Reaper

Words and Music by Donald Roeser

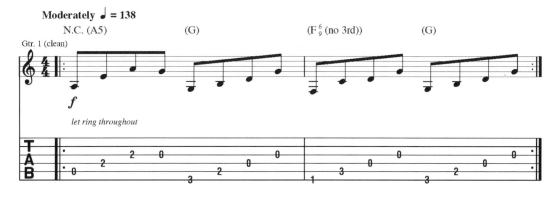

Drive

Performed by Incubus
From *Make Yourself* (2000)

Formed by friends Brandon Boyd (lead vocals), Jose Pasillas (drums), Alex Katunich (bass), and Mike Einziger (guitar) while in the tenth grade, Incubus released their first major label EP, *Enjoy Incubus,* in 1997. *S.C.I.E.N.C.E.* followed shortly thereafter, and with the help of constant touring in support of bands such as Korn and 311, they moved over 100,000 copies of it without any radio or TV exposure. The band returned to the studio in 1999 to record *Make Yourself.* The first single, "Pardon Me," failed to make much of an impact until Boyd and Einziger performed the song acoustically at a few interested radio stations. With renewed interest in the song, the band filmed a video, and it eventually climbed to #3 on the Modern Rock Tracks chart. It was the acoustic-driven "Drive," however, that made the band a household name, eventually helping the album reach double platinum status.

Mike Einziger gets the ball rolling on "Drive" with his Guild D40, crafting a memorable riff over the i–♭VI–iv progression. In E minor, this translates to Em–C–Am. However, thanks to Einziger's creative and colorful voicings, the harmonies produced are actually Em–Em9–Cmaj7–A7(no 3rd). Mike mixes muted strums with incidental open strings — open strings that are sounded during a move from one chord to the next — throughout, resulting in a loose but solid groove. It should be noted that, although the transcription here shows specific strings being struck throughout, the most important thing is to have the chord voicings fretted properly, because Mike would probably never strum it *exactly* this way again.

Mike begins in seventh position by only fretting strings 5, 4, and 2 of an Em barre chord, allowing the open G and E strings (both high and low) to ring out. For beat 4 only, he switches to fifth position for the sophisticated Em9 voicing, which is a standard in jazz but not nearly as common in rock. He makes use of a fairly standard voicing for Cmaj7, which is derived from an A-form barre chord, and resorts to only the root (A) and ♭7th for the A7(no 3rd). On the repeat, he keeps most things the same, but he turns the final A chord into an A9(no 3rd) by adding unison B notes on top — fret 4 of string 3 and the open second string.

Drive

Words and Music by Brandon Boyd, Michael Einziger, Alex Katunich, Jose Pasillas II and Chris Kilmore

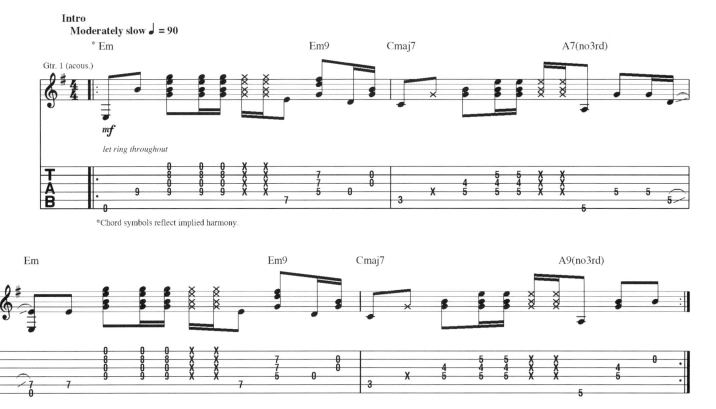

Dust in the Wind

Performed by Kansas
From *Point of Know Return* (1977)

"Dust in the Wind," written by guitarist Kerry Livgren, captured the ear of a nation, hit #6, and continues to serenade campfires and FM radio in the new millenium. Although 1976's *Leftoverture* was their first commercial triumph, it was 1977's *Point of Know Return* (#4) and the most un-Kansas of all the band's songs for which they became famous. Apparently, the acoustic guitar was so uncharacteristic for Kerry Livgren that he had to borrow a Martin D-28 from fellow guitarist Rich Williams to record "Dust in the Wind" because he didn't own a high-quality instrument of his own. Thankfully, Rich obliged, and the world received one of its all-time enduring fingerstyle classics. On the original recording, the guitar is at least double-tracked (if not more), which results in the full, wide tone.

This intro riff is pretty much the Travis picking proving ground for a would-be fingerstyle guitarist. If you can make it through this, you're on your way in the world of fingerstyle. Making use of one singular pattern throughout, Livgren creates a real gem by altering the top note (on string 2) every two beats, maintaining a C–B–D–C–B–D pattern throughout. The magic stems from the fact that, although the chords change every two measures (moving between C and Am), the "melody" on top, which contains only three notes, repeats every measure and a half. So each time the chords come around, they arrive with a different melody note on top. This results in the colorful harmonies of Cmaj7, Cadd9, Asus2, and Asus4.

Dust in the Wind
Words and Music by Kerry Livgren

18 and Life

Performed by Skid Row

From *Skid Row* (1989)

Formed in 1986 by bassist Rachel Bolan and former Bon Jovi guitarist Dave "The Snake" Sabo, Skid Row spent most of 1987 playing east coast clubs and making a name for themselves. Snake, who had remained in touch with Jon Bon Jovi, contacted the superstar and convinced him to help the band land a deal with Atlantic Records. The resulting eponymous debut album (#6), released in 1989, enjoyed multiplatinum success on the strength of the hit singles "18 and Life" (#4) and "I Remember You" (#6). The success was short-lived, however, because they suffered severe backlash from vocalist Sebastian Bach's reckless, offensive behavior. They eventually fell off the radar with the grunge takeover in 1991 that overthrew the rest of the metal crew.

Like many metal players in the late 1980s, Sabo plugged his custom Spector into a then-all-the-rage ADA MP-1 preamp for "18 and Life." He ran that into an H&H power amp driving Marshall cabinets that were miked up for the recording. The song is in C♯ minor, and the intro/verse riff uses the most ubiquitous chords in all of metal: the i, ♭VII, and ♭VI; in this case, that's C♯m, B, and A, respectively. (You can play just about 90 percent of Iron Maiden songs with those three chords!)

In a creative display of efficiency, Snake arpeggiates through C♯m using the fourth-position barre chord form and remains there for the B chord, simply removing his second, third, and fourth fingers to reveal a B triad barred by his first finger on strings 4–2. The arpeggio pattern he chooses for the B chord begins at the top (D♯) and moves down, so the low, sustained C♯ on string 5 doesn't muddy things up. In fact, he even takes advantage of it with the little hammered ornament at the end of measure 1 as he transitions back to C♯m. Measure 2 repeats exactly with the exception of the last eighth note, where Sabo uses the pinky to nab the low B note on fret 7 of string 6. Measure 3 is similar to measure 1, without the hammered ornament at the end, and gives way to the "turnaround," as it were, where Asus2 and Bsus4 are arpeggiated. Notice that both the chords are created by clever use of the open B and E strings atop A5 and B5 fingerings, respectively, on strings 5–3.

18 and Life

Words and Music by Rachael Bolan Southworth and David Michael Sabo

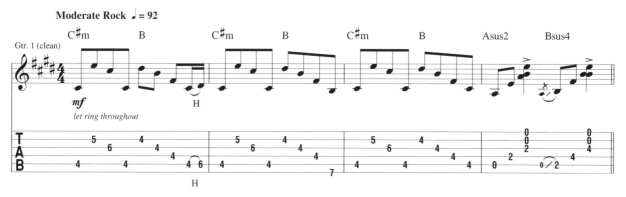

Even Flow

Performed by Pearl Jam
From *Ten* (1991)

The somewhat delayed success of Pearl Jam's *Ten* is well-documented, as is the formation of the band by ex-members of Mother Love Bone Jeff Ament (bass) and Stone Gossard (rhythm guitar). With the addition of Mike McCready (lead guitar), Dave Krusen (drums), and Eddie Vedder (vocals), the band clicked into place in a big way; and the rest is history. According to McCready, the band "played 'Even Flow' over and over until we hated each other." The extra effort was apparently worth it, because the track was instrumental, along with "Alive" and "Jeremy," in helping the album eventually reach #2 and sell over 10 million copies in the U.S. alone.

"Even Flow" is, for the most part, in D major — or D Mixolydian to be more precise — although it does use some borrowed chords from the parallel D minor in the chorus. The implied harmony for the intro, however, is basically just C and D, or ♭VII and I. Here we're looking at Mike McCready's guitar part, which is most likely the part you'd play in a one-guitar band, because the bass would be playing something similar to Stone Gossard's low-resister riffing (not shown). McCready plugged his 88 Les Paul Deluxe into a tweed Fender Bassman, engaging a Boss DS-2 Turbo Distortion pedal for solos. Although the Bassman was cranked and therefore overdriven (especially with the use of the Les Paul), the sound isn't fully distorted. With super distortion comes super compression, and that's not what's happening here; this tone breathes a bit more than that.

McCready stabs at C and D triads in fifth and seventh position (though the C is actually a dyad), respectively, in a syncopated rhythm that's sounded by the whole ensemble. On beat 4, he runs straight down the D blues scale in sixteenth notes on string 4, starting from the ♭5th, to set up the repeat. After three times through, the entire band joins in (with Stone Gossard doubling him an octave lower, not shown) for a measure of 2/4 that features a two-beat, sixteenth note riff from the D blues scale, resolving conclusively to the tonic D, which is held for a full two measures (back in 4/4 time) while the band (and audience) catches their breath for the coming verse.

Even Flow

Music by Stone Gossard
Lyric by Eddie Vedder

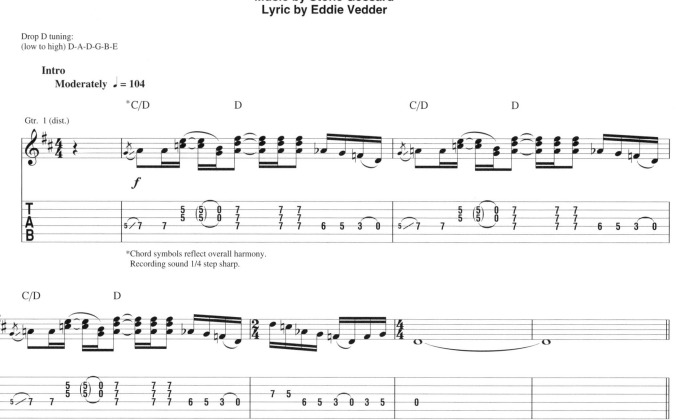

Every Breath You Take

Performed by the Police

From *Synchronicity* (1983)

Synchronicity (1983) was to be the Police's final studio album, and they certainly went out with a bang. With three Grammy Awards and two Top Ten singles — "Every Breath You Take" (#1) and "Wrapped Around Your Finger" (#8) — the album dethroned Michael Jackson's *Thriller* to top the charts. According to Sting, "Every Breath You Take," though considered by many to be the band's signature song, is one of the most misunderstood of all his songs; its lyrics tell the story of an obsessed, jealous stalker — not a pretty love story. After Sting gave Andy Summers a demo of the song with only bass, drums, and lead vocal and told him to "make it your own," Andy set out to do just that.

Finding inspiration in a classical piece by Béla Bartók that made extensive use of 5ths, Andy crafted the famous riff heard on the recording, which features two stacked 5ths on top of each root note. This results in the lush harmonies of Aadd9, F#m(add9), Dsus2, and Esus2 — the first two being quite difficult on the fret hand! To save yourself much pain and suffering, take a cue from the man himself. When Andy performs this song live, you'll see that he's not fretting all of the notes at once. On the Aadd9, for example, he frets the A, E, and B notes on strings 6, 5, and 4, respectively, with fingers 1, 2, and 4. On beat 3, he moves his first finger up to grab the C# on string 3 while leaving fingers 2 and 4 where they are. Because he's palm muting the entire time, the abandoned low A note is not missed! The same economical solution is applied to the F#m(add9) as well.

To create the thick, crisp tone heard on the recording, Andy relied on his trademark heavily modified 1961 Fender Telecaster. He ran through an MXR analog delay for the short, slapback echo effect, and an Electro-Harmonix Electric Mistress flanger pedal created the thickness — not a chorus pedal. Two 100W Marshall half stacks, run with the volume about half up to obtain a fairly clean tone, supplied the amplification.

Every Breath You Take

Music and Lyrics by Sting

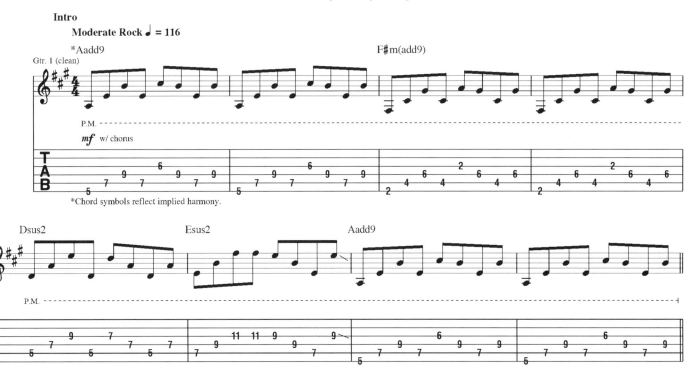

Eye of the Tiger

Performed by Survivor
From *Eye of the Tiger* (1982)

Chicago-based Survivor spent two albums paying their dues before they became soundtrack juggernauts with 1982's *Eye of the Tiger.* After being contacted by Sylvester Stallone to compose a theme song for the upcoming *Rocky III* film (Sly was unable to get the rights to Queen's "Another One Bites the Dust," which was his first choice), the band responded with "Eye of the Tiger" — a song so perfectly suited that its mark on the movie is indelible. You simply can't think of one without thinking of the other. After barely breaking into the double digits with their second album, Survivor suddenly found themselves with a #2 album and a #1 single.

After a brief stumble with 1983's *Caught in the Game,* the band looked in sad shape, when vocalist Dave Bickler was forced to quit due to voice problems. The band soldered on, replacing him with Jami Jamison (formerly of Cobra) and tackled another movie project; "The Moment of Truth," which appeared prominently in *The Karate Kid,* gave them a minor hit at #63. Things looked up, as 1984's *Vital Signs* reached #16 on the strength of three Top 20 singles: "High on You" (#8), "I Can't Hold Back" (#13), and "The Search Is Over" (#4). Reuniting with Sly once more, the band added "Burning Heart" to the *Rocky IV* soundtrack, which scored them a #2 hit. Unfortunately, the well dried up after that, and the band failed to outlive the decade, calling it quits after two more unsuccessful albums.

"Eye of the Tiger delivers one of the most recognizable hard rock riffs of all time. Frankie Sullivan simply plugs a Les Paul into a Marshall and cranks out some power chords. Over the constant, sixteenth-note drone of another guitar pedaling the low tonic C note (not shown), Sullivan jumps into the ring dynamically with a series of staccato, syncopated C5 (i) and B♭5 (♭VII) power chord jabs before allowing the energy to rebuild with a G5 (V) and sustained A♭5 (♭VI). Dramatically heightening the effect is the fact that entire band joins in for the accented chords and then quiets itself just as quickly, allowing the single, low tonic note (not shown) to jog along, determined and alone, in between the hits. Also dig that, on the original recording, the band flipped the tape over to achieve a backwards swell into the first hit, which makes it really pop.

Eye of the Tiger

Theme from ROCKY III

Words and Music by Frank Sullivan and Jim Peterik

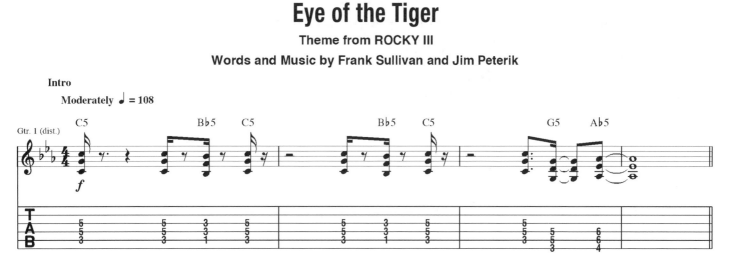

Foolin'

Performed by Def Leppard
From *Pyromania* (1983)

After establishing their brand of carefully crafted British metal on their first two albums, Def Leppard was hungry to capitalize on their growing success — thanks in part to the rotation of "Bringing on the Heartbreak" on MTV, which gave them a minor hit at #61. They continued working with Mutt Lange at the helm, who had produced their second album, and the legendary knob-tweaking perfectionist took his obsessions to new heights for *Pyromania* — a super glossy production/performance package that helped set the standard for melodic hard rock. The results speak for themselves: *Pyromania* burned all the way up to #2 on the charts and spawned three Top 40 singles in "Rock of Ages," "Photograph," and "Foolin'."

Details on the recording of *Pyromania* are sketchy at best and subject to years of folklore embellishment, so it's tough to know exactly which acoustic guitar was played on "Foolin'" or who played it. My money is on Pete Willis, as he performed most of the rhythm tracks before he was given the boot. This haunting intro is in the key of A minor, although the rest of the song strays from that key, as is the case with many Def Leppard songs. Consisting of arpeggios throughout, the basic chord progression of Asus2–F(♭5)–Fmaj7♯11 is articulated cleverly and economically.

Instead of using the open B string to create Asus2, as is commonplace in acoustic playing, the fourth fret on string 3 is used to access the B (2nd) note. Not only does this begin to move the hand into a better position to handle the following chords, it also allows the note to come to life by way of a subtle vibrato. At the beginning of measure 2, that fourth fret note rings in unison against the open B string as the first finger moves from E to F on string 4 for F(♭5). On the "and" of beat 2, the fourth fret B note is slid up to fret 5, while the open E and B strings are arpeggiated, transforming the chord into the lush but dense Fmaj7♯11. Note that the only difference in measures 3–4 occurs at the very end, when the order of the last three notes changes from E–C–B to E–B–C.

Foolin'

Words and Music by Joseph Elliott, Steve Clark, Peter Willis, Richard Savage, Richard Allen and R.J. Lange

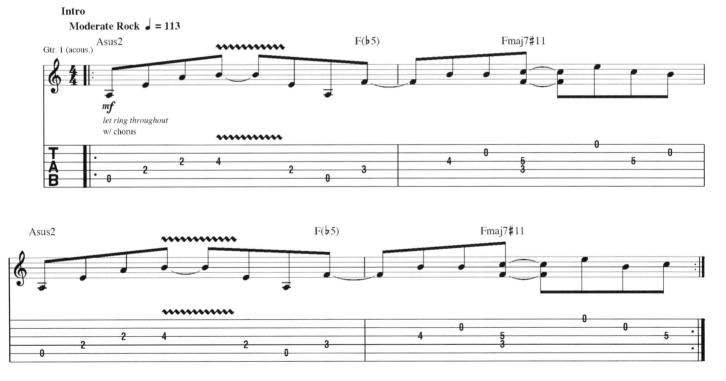

Frankenstein

Performed by the Edgar Winter Group

From *They Only Come Out at Night* (1972)

Edgar Winter enjoyed success shortly after his critically acclaimed debut, *Entrance* (1970), with two albums backed by his White Trash band. *Edgar Winter's White Trash* (1971), although it failed to chart very high, became a huge fan favorite, but *Roadwork* (1972) became a bona fide hit at #23. When he decided to bring together Ronnie Montrose (guitar), Dan Hartman (bass, vocals), and Chuck Ruff (drums) to form the Edgar Winter Group, little could he have known what was in store. The band's first release, 1972's *They Only Come Out at Night*, shot to #3 on the strength of the classic "Free Ride" (#14) and the surprise #1 hit, the instrumental "Frankenstein." Though the follow-up, *Shock Treatment* (1974), made a respectful showing at #13, The *Edgar Winter Group with Rick Derringer* (1975) failed to make much of a dent, and Edgar returned to his solo project soon thereafter.

Ronnie Montrose strapped on a Les Paul, plugged into a Marshall, and laid it down with the boys on "Frankenstein," ending up with over ten minutes of tape in the process. (Producer Rick Derringer is also credited with playing guitar on the track.) As they went about the painstaking task of editing it down to the album length, which is just under five minutes, they ended up with a patched up tape that looked like something out of a monster movie. When drummer, Chuck Ruff, exclaimed, "Wow, man, it's like Frankenstein," Edgar Winter knew he had the song's title. Winter has stated that the title fits the lumbering, heavy-handed beat of the song as well, which is certainly true.

In the vein of other dyad-driven riffs, such as the king of them all, "Smoke on the Water," the main riff to "Frankenstein" makes its home on strings 5 and 4 with a D/G 4th dyad. With the G tonality provided by the bass, the dyad is actually masquerading as an inverted 5th and therefore sounds like G5. Sputtering the dyad out in a syncopated fashion, conjuring up images of electronic sparks flashing on and off, Derringer quickly adds a lower neighbor F5 before two nonsyncopated G5 dyads set up the accented B♭ chord on beat 4. Measure 2 answers with an abbreviated sequence, giving way to silence on beats 3 and 4. What really makes this riff groove is the articulation, so don't neglect the subtleties, such as the staccato and accent marks.

Frankenstein

By Edgar Winter

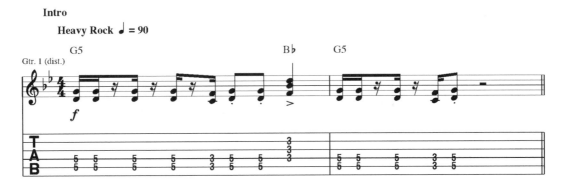

Free Ride

Performed by the Edgar Winter Group

From *They Only Come Out at Night* (1972)

Though Edgar Winter had experienced a good degree of success with his debut album, *Entrance* (1970), and his two follow-ups with his White Trash band, he assembled quite a team when he formed the Edgar Winter Group in 1972. In bassist/guitarist/vocalist Dan Hartman, he found a true collaborator indeed, and Hartman contributed to almost half of the material that appeared on 1972's *They Only Come Out at Night,* including the classic rock staple "Free Ride." Reaching #14 on the charts, the song helped to propel the album — along with the #1 instrumental "Frankenstein," of course — to #3 and to eventual double platinum sales.

One of the all-time classic Strat riffs, songwriter Dan Hartman opens "Free Ride" with his Fender probably running through a Fender Twin Reverb. The sound is clean with just a tiny hint of tube breakup, and the riff is doubled, with the two guitars panned left and right for a huge sound. The tone is a bit on the darker side of Strat territory, so he's most likely using either the neck pickup or neck/middle combination. "Free Ride" is in the key of A, and Hartman gives quite a lesson in chord inversions with his brief, incredibly catchy gem. In the pickup on beat 4, he articulates a broken D chord in first inversion (3rd, F♯, on bottom) on strings 5–3. He then kicks off beat 1 with another first-inversion triad, the tonic A major, but on strings 4–2 this time, sliding into it from below. He follows this with a quick nab of the first-inversion G triad (♭VII chord in the key of A with B on bottom) a whole step below en route to the second-inversion D triad (IV chord in the key of A), which contains the 5th (A) on the bottom. The first part of the riff complete — the "question" is this question-and-answer form — he fills up beat 3 with percussive dead strums for a purely rhythmic effect before using the same D chord pickup phrase to lead into measure 2. In measure 2, he "answers" his A–G–D chord riff with a G–D–A riff, making use of the same voicings for G and D and sliding the latter down to second position to form the familiar open A chord, to create a solid conclusion.

Free Ride

Words and Music by Dan Hartman

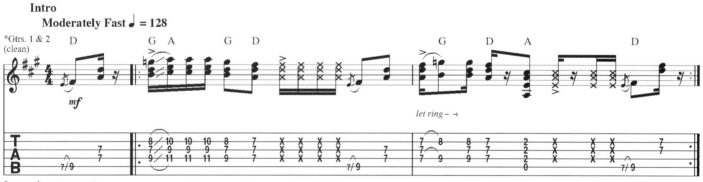

Funk #49

Performed by James Gang

From *Rides Again* (1970)

James Gang followed the trend of the power trio established early on by the likes of Cream and Hendrix but tinged their sound with a bit of country and southern flair. Though *Yer' Album* (#1969) barely broke into the Top 100, they fared better on their sophomore release, 1970's *Rides Again,* which rode all the way up to #20 largely on the back of the infectious "Funk #49." Although their highest charting single, "Walk Away" (from *Thirds,* 1971), would only reach #51, the band became more recognized over time as Joe Walsh made a name for himself as a solo artist and with the Eagles.

Long known for his love of burst Les Pauls, Joe's given the Tele plenty of love at times as well; such is the case for the intro to "Funk #49." Running through a cranked Fender tweed amp (most likely a Champ), the distortion is all power tubes, and how sweet it is! "Funk #49" begins unaccompanied with Walsh pecking out a stuttering, falling bend on string 3, making use of the chicken picking technique to create the clucking effect heard on the recording. Pick the first note of measure 2 normally, and then touch the string with your pick hand's second finger. Pick the deadened string to produce the "click" sound. Then immediately use your second finger to pluck the gradually released bent note. Repeat this process for each descending pitch. The end of the measure, though scary looking, is actually a fairly natural move; don't spend hours trying to replicate it exactly. Joe played it loosey-goosey, so you can too!

At measure 3, Joe settles into the main riff that supports the verse. Allowing the gorgeous tone to shine, he mixes triads, open strings (the A string), bluesy hammer-ons, and a healthy dose of the scratch rhythm technique (strumming deadened strings to produce a scratchy effect) to craft a hooky riff that not only grooves like nothing else, but also fills up enough space to work in a trio format. Check out how the E-form A7 chords are alternated with an A-form D chord ("and" of beat 2, measures 3 and 5), and the A-form D chords are alternated with C-form G chords ("and" of beat 4, measures 3 and 5). Brilliant!

Funk #49

Words and Music by Joe Walsh, Dale Peters and James Fox

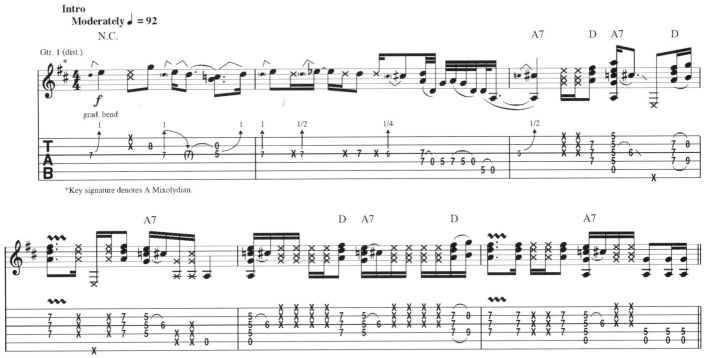

*Key signature denotes A Mixolydian.

Get Ready

Performed by Rare Earth
From *Get Ready* (1969)

Rare Earth was one of the few white bands signed to the Motown label to score a hit record, with their 1969 debut, *Get Ready,* shooting to #12 on the charts. The success was largely due to the #4 single of the same name, which was penned by Smokey Robinson and first recorded by the Temptations in 1966, where it hit #29. The band recorded another Temptations number for *Ecology* in 1970, "I Know I'm Losing You," which hit #7 and helped send the album to #15. Switching to their self-titled Rare Earth label for 1971's *One World,* they continued their streak, with the album reaching #28 on the strength of the #7 classic "I Just Want to Celebrate." That would mark the end of their starlit run, however, as they failed to crack the Top 40 again.

Although Rare Earth went through seemingly countless band members throughout the years, it was Rod Richards (born Rod Cox) that played on the famous, side-long, 21 minute live version of "Get Ready." Although very little has been documented about his gear (and video footage is scarce), it sounds like humbuckers on the album (to me, at least), so a safe bet would be a Les Paul. The amp is most likely a tweed Fender or a Marshall with the volume set moderately, because the breakup is fairly mild.

"Get Ready" makes use of one of the most ubiquitous scale patterns in all of blues and rock. We're in the key of D here, and the notes on strings 4 and 3 are all from the D minor pentatonic scale (D–F–G–A–C). However, instead of sticking strictly to the scale's notes at the end of the riff, you simply lay your third finger down flat when fretting the G note at fret 12, allowing it to catch the B note on string 2 at the same fret. This is the major 6th of the key, and it lends a D Dorian color to the phrase. In essence, the B is harmonizing (a 3rd above) with the G, as the A is harmonizing (a 3rd above) with the F that follows. This type of move was second nature to players like Hendrix and Stevie Ray, among countless others. The other attractive element of this riff is its question-and-answer format. Notice that the rhythm is almost identical in each measure, but the harmonized 3rds in measure 2 function as an "answer" to measure 1's question phrase.

Get Ready

Words and Music by William "Smokey" Robinson

Gimme Three Steps

Performed by Lynyrd Skynyrd
From *Pronounced Leh-Nerd Skin-Nerd* (1973)

Southern rock heroes Lynyrd Skynyrd shot out of the gates guns-a-blazin' on their first album, reaching #27 and producing several of the band's best-known songs. Known predominantly for the epic Southern rock anthem-to-end-all-anthems, "Free Bird," which peaked at #19, *Pronounced Leh-Nerd Skin-Nerd* also included the classics "Simple Man," "Gimme Three Steps," and "Tuesday's Gone." They didn't let up after that either, enjoying a string of Top 20 albums and singles throughout their 1977 album *Street Survivors,* which was released only three days before the tragic plane crash took the lives of singer Ronnie Van Zant, guitarist Steve Gaines, backup vocalist Cassie Gaines (Steve's sister), the assistant road manager, and both pilot and co-pilot. Completely grief-stricken, the band dissolved shortly thereafter, although the remaining members formed the Rossington-Collins Band, releasing two albums in the early 1980s. In 1987, however, the surviving original members teamed up with Johnny Vant Zant (Ronnie's younger brother) on vocals for a reunion/tribute tour that yielded the double-live album *Southern by the Grace of God.*

Allen Collins kicks off "Gimme Three Steps" with a signature riff in D major that plugged his trusty Gibson Explorer into a 50W Marshall stack and cranked it up nearly all the way. (It wasn't until about 1976 that Skynyrd began using the Peavey Mace amps.) Beginning with a first-inversion D chord shape in seventh position, Collins creates a motif by alternating the 5th/root (A/D) dyad on strings 4–3 with the 3rd (F♯) on string 5. In measure 2, he expands on this with a second motif in which he precedes the 3rd with the 2nd (E). This entire riff is transposed almost verbatim down to open position for the A chord (V) in measures 3–4. The only notable differences are the inclusion of the open fifth string (since it is the root of the A chord, might as well include it) along with strings 4 and 3 and the bluesy C to C♯ move in measure 4 (although this is followed later in the same measure with the expected B to C♯ move). Although the tempo moves along at a nice clip of 132 bpm, it's no problem attacking all these notes with downstrokes, because this helps with digging in and achieving the overdriven (but not full-on distorted) tone heard on the recording.

Gimme Three Steps
Words and Music by Allen Collins and Ronnie Van Zant

Girl U Want

Performed by Devo
From *Freedom of Choice* (1980)

The first thing that comes to mind when many people hear Devo's name is electronic music filled with synths and drum machines. Granted, they were one of the pioneers of synthesizers and made frequent use of them, but their earlier albums (which contain most of their classics) are also bursting with guitars and real drums. Although drummer Alan Myers was phenomenally steady and could certainly sound like a machine. It's unfortunate that they've been pigeon holed as a one-hit wonder, because they produced plenty of noteworthy music other than "Whip It." Their third album, *Freedom of Choice* (#22), epitomized the band's sound, showcasing an effective blend of synths, guitars, and drums, aptly demonstrated on the aforementioned "Whip It" and "Girl U Want," among others.

The main riff from "Girl U Want," which drives most of the song, exemplifies Devo in so many ways. If you were to replace the major 7th note (D♯) with a ♭7th (D), slow down the tempo, and play it with swung eighth notes, it would sound like a fairly convincing blues rock riff. But as is, it's quirky, robotic, and incredibly memorable. Making use of only two different notes (D♯ and E) — albeit the E note appears in two octaves — Bob Mothersbaugh (Bob 1) sputters out a syncopated, synthlike riff in the low register that grooves surprisingly hard for such a stiff-sounding phrase. Note that the riff is comprised of the same five-note sequence (D♯–E–E–D♯–E) played twice. However, the rhythm is altered significantly to make this almost unrecognizable at first. It's a brilliant example of how the same notes can be recycled with interesting results just by shifting things around within the measure. Don't neglect the *"let ring"* indications in the music — those ringing E notes help thicken up the riff considerably.

To create the tone, Mothersbaugh used his famous Ibanez "Spud" guitar, which was custom-made for him in 1979 based on his own drawing. It was meant to look like a potato (and be brown like one), but for some reason Ibanez produced a blue guitar that looked almost more like a cloud. Nevertheless, Mothersbaugh played it and played it often. It's long been retired and only makes an appearance for the most special of occasions. Mothersbaugh ran through an Acoustic amp, which he claims was basically a Mesa/Boogie clone with a graphic EQ. He also cranked the midrange on the guitar, which has active electronics, and he "made designs" with the EQ sliders on the amp.

Girl U Want

Words and Music by Mark Mothersbaugh and Gerald Casale

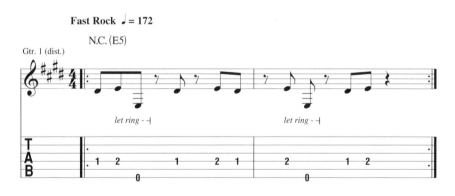

Girls, Girls, Girls

Performed by Mötley Crüe

From *Girls, Girls, Girls* (1987)

After the darker, pseudo-evil sound and imagery of *Shout at the Devil* (1983), the Crüe lightened up a bit and highlighted the sleazier side of their personas for *Theatre of Pain* (1985). The move paid off commercially when the album hit #6, and their cover of Brownsville Station's "Smokin' in the Boys Room" gave them their first Top 20 hit, peaking at #16. The piano-driven power ballad "Home Sweet Home," although it didn't chart, also enjoyed heavy rotation on MTV and became a fan favorite. Taking note of this formula's success, the band leaned even farther to the sleazy side with their next album, 1987's *Girls, Girls, Girls,* and it paid off yet again. The album just missed the tip top of the charts, peaking at #2, while the title track danced all the way up to #12 — both top accomplishments for the band thus far.

Mick and the boys tinged their metal with a slight blues-infected swagger on "Girls, Girls, Girls," coming off like a cross between Van Halen's "Panama" (pre-verse riff) and Aerosmith's brand of sassy hard rock. To lay it down, Mick turned to his custom Kramer Telecaster and a blend of Marshall and Soldano amps. After dipping a sustained G5 chord with the whammy (not shown), he kicks off the song's intro riff proper, which begins with Van Halen-style sliding 4th double stops (D/G–E/A–D/G) on strings 5 and 4. Using the low open E string to shift positions, he slides a low G5 down a half step to F♯5 before bottoming out on the low E for measure 2, pecking out E5 dyads on the open top two strings alternated with low, palm-muted versions of the same on strings 6 and 5. After repeating measure 1's material for measure 3, he pays tribute to the Aerosmith side of things, alternating his low E5 chords with a bluesy G–G♯ move. Make sure you're not rushing this one; it needs to groove hard for maximum effect!

Girls, Girls, Girls

Words by Nikki Sixx
Music by Mick Mars, Tommy Lee and Nikki Sixx

Godzilla

Performed by Blue Öyster Cult
From *Spectres* (1977)

After experiencing their first massive commercial success with 1976's *Agent of Fortune,* which contained the timeless classic "Don't Fear the Reaper," Blue Öyster Cult found themselves exactly where they wanted to be. However, they seemed a bit shellshocked on 1977's *Spectres*, as if they were unsure how to respond to their newfound fame. The album is a bit scattered in its focus and finds the band experimenting with a few new surprising sounds. Regardless, this album is mostly remembered for the novelty rock of "Godzilla," which, along with "Don't Fear the Reaper" and "Burnin' for You," remains among of the band's most well-known songs and a staple in concert. All things considered, *Spectres* would probably be considered a better album if hadn't followed their crowning achievement, *Agent of Fortune*.

Working with his Gibson SG (or possibly a Les Paul) through his 100W Marshall, Buck Dharma kicks off this ode to the Japanese movie appropriately with big, lumbering power chords. His guitar (which is doubled for bigness factor) is also treated to some studio delay to add to the immensity. Working out of the key of F♯ minor, he keeps it simple, technique wise, and basically creates a melody that happens to be voiced in power chords. After making the tonal announcement in measure 1 with two big quarter-note F♯5 chords, he establishes the key with the iv (B5) and v (C♯5) chords and, moving down a 4th, uses a G♯5 — which could be viewed as from the F♯ Dorian mode — to approach the A5 in measure 2 by half step. In an interesting twist, he continues in measure 2 by using D♯5 (♯VI) to lead into E5 (♭VII) by half step, again dropping down a 4th to B5, which marks the end of the two-measure phrase.

The rhythm is half the appeal here, because the deliberate downbeats on F♯5 and A5 perfectly portray Godzilla stomping and smashing the city's treasured buildings (models though they were), while the three-eighth-note chain of chords at the end of each measure aptly depict the footsteps necessary to reach his next target. Although the song is obviously tongue in cheek and can't be taken too seriously, it's interesting to note that even novelty songs can contain intelligent musical devices that help paint the appropriate auditory picture.

Godzilla
Words and Music by Donald Roeser

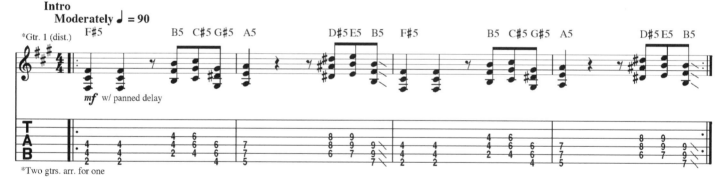

Hangar 18

Performed by Megadeth

From *Rust in Peace* (1990)

A newly-sober Dave Mustaine rounded up some fresh blood in drummer Nick Menza and guitarist Marty Friedman for 1990's critically acclaimed *Rust in Peace* album. The title of the album came to Dave after he saw a bumper sticker that read "May all your nuclear weapons rust in peace." It hit #23 on the charts with the help of singles "Holy Wars… The Punishment Due" and "Hangar 18," the latter of which was nominated for a Grammy in the Best Metal Performance category. Anti-war and government conspiracy themes run through most of the album's lyrics, and "Hangar 18" was inspired by Menza's fascination with the alleged government cover-up scandal of alien life in 1947.

"Hangar 18" begins with an all-out chord assault, with both Dave Mustaine and Marty Friedman strumming away on stinging, upper-string triads (not shown). Although the verse to the song doesn't begin for 40 measures, all the harmonic material used throughout the intro is heard in the first eight measures of the song. In a clever use of arranging and reworking old material to make it sound new, the guitar team plow through a basic eight-measure progression of Dm–B♭/D–B°/D–C/D (each chord lasting two measures) six times (counting the repeat shown below), but they arrange it four different ways. Before the riff that's shown below, they've already been through two different sets of strummed triads and an arpeggio workout, never leaving a dull moment through the intro.

The riff seen here is the final incarnation of the progression and serves as the backdrop to the verse. In another brilliant stroke of arranging, the harmonic rhythm doubles here, with each harmony lasting only one measure, which gives the song a welcome nudge after the intro and freshens the progression once again. In this riff, they highlight the most important tones of this progression — the common root (D) and the chromatically rising note that subsequently transforms each chord into the next (A to B♭ to B to C). Mustaine cleverly arranges these in a driving riff that begins each measure with the lower tone on string 3 (starting with A in measure 1 for the Dm, B♭ in measure 2 for B♭/D, etc.) and slides up to the high tonic at fret 7, supported in between by chugging palm mutes on the open D string. To provide an extra bit of color, Friedman harmonizes this riff a 3rd above the melody (not shown). Altogether, it's quite an impressive display of guitar arranging!

Hangar 18

Words and Music by Dave Mustaine

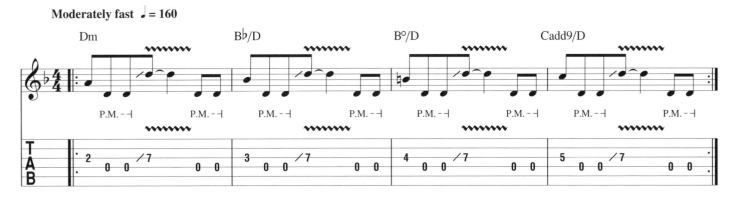

A Hazy Shade of Winter

Performed by the Bangles
From the *Less Than Zero* soundtrack (1987)

The Bangles arrived on the scene with a 1960s British pop sound as can be heard on their 1984 debut, *All Over the Place*. But their follow-up, *Different Light* (1986), presented a much more polished sound and image, and it paid off commercially. With four Top 20 hits, including the #1 "Walk Like an Egyptian" and #2 "Manic Monday" (written for the band by Prince), the album hit #2 and made the band megastars. With great success, however, came great strife, as the media began to single out Susanna Hoffs as the shining star. Their #2 cover of Simon & Garfunkel's "A Hazy Shade of Winter" in 1987 helped bandage the internal wounds. "Eternal Flame" from 1988's *Everything* hit #1, but the band's days were numbered. They broke up shortly after *Everything*'s release.

Originally performed by Paul Simon in the key of D minor on a 12-string acoustic, guitarist Vicky Peterson and the gals transposed the tune up a minor 3rd to F minor to better suit their voices; they also goosed up the tempo a bit to make it rock a bit harder. It's possible Vicky used a capo while recording this song in the studio, as she has been known to do so when playing live with the reformed band, but in videos from the late 1980s, she played it without, so no capo position is indicated in the sheet music. Although she endorsed Carvin guitars in those days and could be seen playing them in videos, she most likely tracked the song using her Gibson Les Paul through a Fender Deluxe or Super Reverb.

There are numerous position shifts in this riff. At the beginning, Peterson works right out of the F minor pentatonic scale form in eighth position, which has its root on string 5, fret 8. At the end of measure 1, she shifts down to sixth position for the syncopated E♭ note and remains there throughout measure 2 for the power-chord-framed riff. In measure 3, she uses what could be thought of as a shift fingering for D♭ major pentatonic, shifting from fourth position on the D♭ note up to sixth position for the following F, A♭, and B♭ notes. She gives the latter a bluesy whole-step bend and release for effect and remains in sixth position to grab the low C note at the end of the measure with her third finger. In measure 4, it's a matter of quickly shifting back a fret to fifth position for the G and C notes. The B♭ on string 4 can either be played by your pinky or third finger if you don't mind a slight stretch.

A Hazy Shade of Winter
Words and Music by Paul Simon

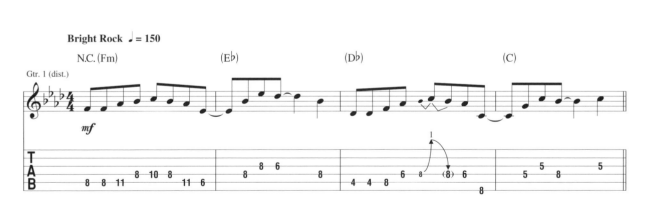

Heaven

Performed by Los Lonely Boys
From *Los Lonely Boys* (2004)

After releasing two self-distributed albums in Nashville, the Garza brothers — Henry (guitars, vocals), Jojo (bass, vocals), and Ringo (drums, vocals) — moved back home to Texas to record an album in Willie Nelson's studio in Austin. Originally released independently by Or Music, *Los Lonely Boys* (2004) got picked up by Epic Records and reached #9 on the charts thanks to the #16 hit "Heaven." Their grip on the top rungs of the charts began to slip with each subsequent release, however, with 2011's *Rockpango* topping out at #70.

Garza mainly uses Strats through Fender Twins and 100W Marshalls, and, taking a cue from Stevie Ray Vaughan, uses .013–.056 gauge strings and tunes down a half step (most of the time). "Heaven" is a classic example of his Strat/Twin combination. The tone is on the cleaner side of things, with a hint of break-up, and not too bright. A remarkably fluent and soulful player, he's received his share of criticism for wearing the Stevie Ray influence on his sleeve. In all fairness, though, what blues player coming out of Texas since the late 20th century hasn't been influenced by Vaughan? Besides, Stevie Ray made no secret of his infatuation and admiration of several giants — most notably, of course, being Hendrix — and he certainly did his fair share of gear-copping in that regard.

The intro (and most of the song, in fact) takes place over a basic I–ii vamp in the key of G, which translates to G and Am. Although Henry kicks off this tune all by his lonesome on the guitar, his theme clearly outlines the harmony that's heard beneath him on the repeat. Working exclusively on the top two strings, he plays diatonic 3rd dyads in syncopated fashion, beginning in measures 1 and 2 with root position voicings (root/3rd) on bottom and moving up to first inversion (3rd/5th), relative to each chord change. After reaching the high C/E pair at the end of measure 2 over Am, he works his way back down stepwise through G with B/D to reach A/C for Am, dancing up to the first-inversion voicing once again in measure 4 and descending quickly stepwise to reach the starting point for the repeat again.

Heaven
Words and Music by Henry Garza, Joey Garza and Ringo Garza

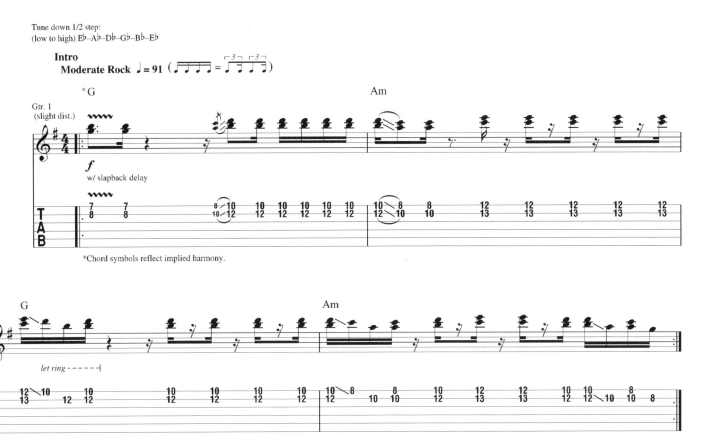

Hells Bells

Performed by AC/DC
From *Back in Black* (1980)

Although AC/DC came close to calling it quits after the untimely death of their original lead singer, Bon Scott, they soldiered on. Granted, they'd experienced some commercial success with the 1976 US release of *Dirty Deeds Done Dirt Cheap* (#3) and 1979's *Highway to Hell* (#17), but nothing could have prepared them for what lay next. On the surface, *Back in Black* doesn't seem all that spectacular. It was a hit album, for sure, reaching #4 and containing two Top 40 singles in "You Shook Me All Night Long" and the title track. But lots of albums have accomplished that feat. Very few, though, enjoy the staying power it takes to become the second (or third — it jockeys for position with Pink Floyd's *The Dark Side of the Moon*) best-selling album of all time.

After the ominous bell introduction, Angus kicks off the *Back in Black* album with the famous "Hells Bells" riff. Giving his Gibson SG and the tubes in his Marshall Super Lead stack a good workout, he crafts a memorable part using the open A string as a pedal tone (a constant note among others changing). He begins in seventh position and works exclusively on strings 4 and 3 with a series of staggered dyads culled from the A minor pentatonic scale (A–C–D–E–G) that descend from A/E at their highest down to G and C at their lowest before working their way back up (along with the open string 5 sounding in between). Notice that he's not simply moving a 5th dyad down two frets each time; instead, each "melody note" on string 3 is given its own, independent supporting note on string 4 — either A or G. After working almost all the way through a repeat of the proceedings, he abandons ship for the last two beats of measure 4 and descends through a low-register C5–G/B–A5 chord riff to inject new life for the repeat.

Although chord symbols are provided, which reflect the tones present in relation to the root A note, the effect is not really that of a chord progression. It sounds closer to a hard rock version of a classical counterpoint structure, because the tones seemingly leapfrog over and under one another. And after triumphantly using the word "leapfrog" while describing an AC/DC song, I'll bring this analysis to an end.

Hells Bells

Words and Music by Angus Young, Malcolm Young and Brian Johnson

Her Strut

Performed by Bob Seger & The Silver Bullet Band
From *Against the Wind* (1980)

Sometimes criticized for the softer sound of 1980's *Against the Wind* album, Bob has made it very clear through interviews that he and the Silver Bullet Band were on a mission with that album; they wanted a #1. They got it with *Against the Wind.* Since his debut in the late 1960s, he'd toiled on in relative obscurity (compared to what lay ahead) until his first taste of success when *Live Bullet* (1976) gave him his first Top 40 album. It was *Night Moves* that same year (which was actually recorded before *Live Bullet*), however, that made him a household name. Along with the title track, which hit #4, the album *almost* featured two other Top 40 singles: "Main Street" (#24) and "Rock and Roll Never Forgets," which just missed it at #41. The 1978 follow-up, *Stranger in Town,* outdid its predecessor with three singles well within the Top 40 umbrella; it peaked at #4 as well. With a clear view of the summit, Seger and company set out to finally conquer the #1 spot with 1980's *Against the Wind,* succeeding in style with three Top 20 singles: "Against the Wind" (#5), "Fire Lake" (#6), and "You'll Accompany Me" (#14).

Bob has also stated in several interviews that one of the many reasons he's particularly fond of *Against the Wind* is that it represented a period of growth for him as a player, with him performing more guitar duties (including solos) than ever before. In fact, he played all the guitar parts on "Her Strut." For the song's signature riff, Bob plugged a Les Paul into a Marshall, cranked her up, and let her strut. A mid-tempo rocker in the key of E, Bob crafts an interesting amalgamation of a riff for this one. Somewhat similar to the classic, open-position E riffs of Orbison's "Pretty Woman" or the Beatles' "Day Tripper," the song uses similar materials but in a different way. The most stock feature of Seger's riff here is the minor to major 3rd move (G to G♯, in this case) but the rest of the notes — E on string 4 and D, C♯, and B on string 5 — would normally be replaced by chords in this type of riff. The result is a catchy, singable hook that's both fun to play and also fills up a good amount of space without getting muddy. Taken together, it suggests a basic E7 tonality, although the repeated C♯ notes hint at a brief IV (A) tonality.

Her Strut
Words and Music by Bob Seger

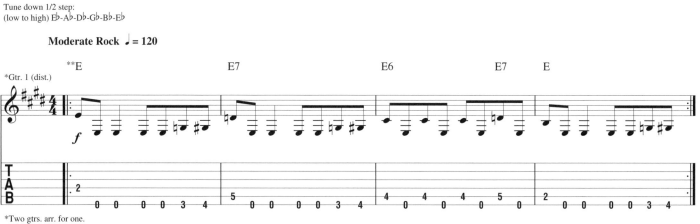

Hit Me with Your Best Shot

Performed by Pat Benatar

From *Crimes of Passion* (1980)

Pat Benatar came right out of the gates on her 1979 debut, *In the Heat of the Night,* with "Heartbreaker" as the lead track, leaving no doubt that she could rock with the big boys. That #23 track, along with the #27 "We Live for Love," helped the album reach #12. The latter song was written by newly acquired member of the team, Neil Giraldo, who was suggested to Pat's team by producer Mike Chapman. Halfway through the follow-up album *Crimes of Passion,* Neil took over the producer's chair for good. Obviously he knew what he was doing, as the album hit #2 and produced two Top 20 singles: "Hit Me with Your Best Shot" (#9) and "Treat Me Right" (#18).

Neil used custom-made BC Rich Eagle guitars in those early days with Benatar and ran them through a Marshall JMC800 series Model 4211 combo amp. This was a two-channel amp with a 2x12 speaker configuration. "Hit Me with Your Best Shot" is in E major and begins with the famous chord riff shown below. Note that one of the reasons the riff sounds so full and clear is that Neil double-tracked the part and panned them separately left and right. Instead of using two similar sounds, though, he used one distorted tone and one fairly clean tone, providing power on one side and clarity on the other. It's a really nice studio trick that many players have gone on to exploit, including Stevie Ray Vaughan.

The riff is built from four diatonic chords in E: E (I), A (IV), C#m (vi), and B (V). In measures 1–2, a I–IV–vi–V progression kicks things off in a fairly straightforward manner, with the first three chords cut short for dramatic effect before sustaining the B chord at the end of the phrase. In measures 3–4, after beginning in a similar way with the E and A chords, Neil throws the riff into overdrive with a continuous stream of syncopated chords played in eighth notes. Although this serves as a hook of its own, it also provides a great burst of momentum going back into the repeat — almost like a rollercoaster takes a big dip to pick up speed in order to make another ascent up the track.

Hit Me with Your Best Shot

Words and Music by Eddie Schwartz

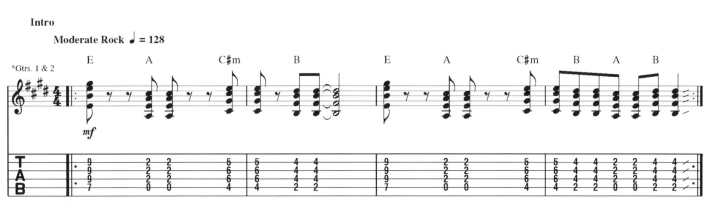

*Gtr. 1 (slight dist.); Gtr. 2 (clean)

Hocus Pocus

Performed by Gary Hoey
From *Animal Instinct* (1993)

Along with Joe Satriani and Steve Vai, Gary Hoey is one of the few to maintain a fairly successful career as an instrumental rock player in the wake of the grunge takeover. With his 1993 major label debut for Warner Bros., *Animal Instinct,* he managed to enter the fray at a very dismal time for shredders. Nevertheless, thanks largely to his cover of Focus's "Hocus Pocus," the album became a minor hit, reaching #9 on the Heatseekers chart. And thanks mostly to a successful string of Christmas albums — *Ho! Ho! Hoey!* in 1995, with *Vol. 2* and *Vol. 3* arriving in 1997 and 1999, respectively — he managed to stay relevant throughout the 1990s, earning a devoted following in the process. In the new millennium, he's continued to release albums and found success as a Fender clinician as well.

Although Gary has stated that he had over ten amps to choose from when recording *Animal Instinct,* he's a known Rocktron endorsee, and he created presets on the Chameleon 2000 digital preamp that he claims he used for many songs on the album, including "Hocus Pocus." Perhaps he used some of both; the specifics aren't documented. At any rate, the cabinet was mostly likely a Marshall 4x12, and the power amp could have been a VHT, which is what appears in his rack currently (as of January, 2012). Although he's been playing Fender Big Apple Strats for awhile now, back in the early 1990s, he played mostly Hamers.

The riff shown below appears at approximately the 0:55, after the extended three-measure drum fill. Measures 1–3 are comprised of notes entirely diatonic to the A minor scale. Beginning at the high E, Gary simply works down the scale in melodic 3rds (E–C–E, D–B–D, etc.), applying vibrato to each sustained note on string 1, and coloring the entire phrase with his Dunlop wah pedal. Although the chord symbols show all power chords (because that's what was played on the track), the implied harmony of the chord progression in measures 1–3 can be analyzed as such: Am (i)–E7 (V)–F (♭VI)–Cmaj7 (♭III)–Dm (iv)–C. In measure 4, he outlines the II–V progression, B–E, by arpeggiating up the B chord's root (B) and 3rd (D♯) and resolving to the root (E) of the E chord on beat 3 for a half cadence — a phrase that comes to rest on the V chord.

Hocus Pocus
Words and Music by Thijs Van Leer and Jan Akkerman

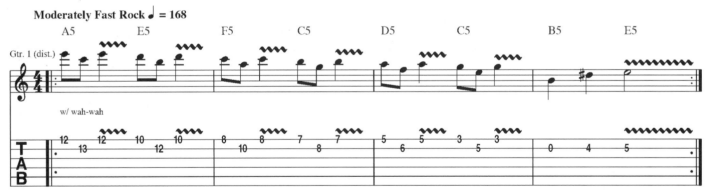

Hold On Loosely

Performed by .38 Special

From *Wild-Eyed Southern Boys* (1981)

After releasing a few full-fledged southern rock albums in the late 1970s with relatively little commercial success, .38 Special began to mix in elements of arena rock in the early 1980s to produce the sound for which they would ultimately become known. *Wild-Eyed Southern Boys* (1981) is a prime example of this new recipe. Their first bona fide hit, it reached #18 on the strength of the Top 40 single "Hold On Loosely," which, along with the #10 "Caught Up in You" (*Special Forces,* 1982), became one of the band's signature songs.

Thanks to Jeff Carlisi's very informative personal website, I know precisely what equipment he used to achieve the classic tones on "Hold On Loosely." However, it's unclear as to whether he, Don Barnes, or Donnie Van Zant played the intro riff below. On the video, Don kicks it off, with Jeff and Donnie joining in for chord accents (not shown), so I'm going to assume that's the way it was done on the album. Don Barnes used a Gibson Les Paul Jr., which had been routed out to house a humbucker, and played through a Peavey Mace amp, as did Jeff Carlisi. The Peavey Mace was a 160W amp with a tube power section (it used 6 6L6 power tubes) and solid state preamp section that was primarily designed to sound like a Marshall. Speaker cabinets used were Marshall 4x12's with 25W Celestions. Although Jeff predominantly used a 1969 Les Paul Deluxe for his solos (as he did for the classic one in this song), he made use of his custom-made Rhyne Explorer for his primary rhythm guitar in the studio.

"Hold On Loosely" is the key of E major and opens with a I–V–♭VII–IV progression: E–B–D–A. By way of clever voice-leading, however, power chords are alternated with first-inversion chords (E5–B/D♯–D5–A/C♯) to generate a riff that slowly moves down the fretboard with a chromatically descending bass line: E–D♯–D–C♯. While palm muted low notes keep the rhythm in steady eighth notes, the chords are sounded in syncopated punches, which are accented by the full band on the repeat upon its entrance at the end of measure 4.

Hold On Loosely

Words and Music by Jeff Carlisi, Don Barnes and Jim Peterik

Hot Blooded

Performed by Foreigner
From *Double Vision* (1978)

After a brief stint in the Leslie West Band and some time spent as an A&R man, Mick Jones began assembling what would become Foreigner in the mid-1970s. The vocalist, Lou Gramm, quickly became his songwriting partner, and the two set off writing the material for what would become the band's eponymous debut in 1977. Based off the strength of the #4 arena rock hit "Feels Like the First Time" and the sleek, progressive sound of the #6 "Cold as Ice," the album easily hit #4 and established the band firmly. By the time *Double Vision* arrived in 1978, the Jones/Gramm partnership was in full swing, and the album produced three Top 20 singles on the way to hitting #3 on the charts: "Hot Blooded" (#3), "Blue Morning, Blue Day" (#15), and the title track (#2). The band continued their commercially successful streak through 1987, earning a #1 album along the way (*4*, 1981), before splitting up to pursue other interests. Jones has reunited many times with several members (at points including Gramm) and continues to tour today.

Mick Jones has long been a Les Paul and Marshall man, and those are the tools of his choice for "Hot Blooded." Unlike many others back in the day, though, Mick used Hiwatt cabs with Fane speakers, stating he felt he could get "more expression with them." Most likely, the guitar on the track is his favorite '62 Black Les Paul Custom with three pickups, from which he removed the middle pickup, among other modifications. This would eventually become the inspiration for his signature Gibson model.

"Hot Blooded" is in the key of G and starts off rocking — with four measures of a G5 power chord. After the key and beat are established, Mick launches into the song's signature riff. A clever use of sus4 chords, Mick answers the Gsus4–G progression in measure 2 with the opposite on the IV chord: C–Csus4. This creates an inner melody of C–B (over the G chord) and E–F (over the C chord). To make the riff speak clearly, Jones employs hybrid picking, using the pick for the low notes on strings 6 and 5 and his fingers for the dyads on strings 4–3 (on the G chord) and 3–2 (on the C chord). Taken altogether, the riff is extremely hooky and singable; in fact, it doubles the vocal melody of the chorus!

Hot Blooded
Words and Music by Mick Jones and Lou Gramm

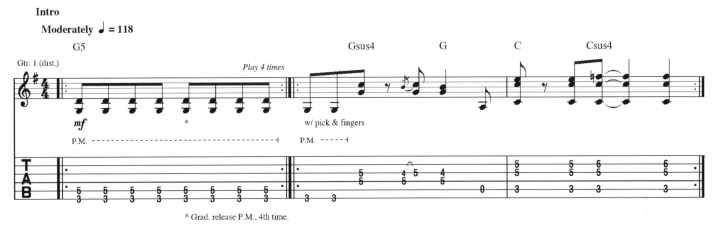

* Grad. release P.M., 4th time.

The House of the Rising Sun

Performed by the Animals
From *The Animals* (1964 U.S. Version)

Leaning more toward the R&B side of things than rock, the Animals were immensely influential among the first wave of British Invasion bands. Although they did achieve considerable success with many songs, including "We Gotta Get Out of This Place" and "Don't Let Me Be Misunderstood," their signature song is most definitely "The House of the Rising Sun." Although it had been recorded over a dozen times before, the Animals' version was unlike anything else and has been described as the first true folk rock recording. Interestingly, the song was only included on the U.S. version of the band's debut album in 1964, although it was released as a single in both England and the U.S. The song hit #1 in both countries; one of the earliest trans-Atlantic hits of the decade to not be associated with the Beatles.

The song kicks off with one of the most immediately recognizable intros of the decade. Hilton Valentine begins with his famous arpeggio riff, accompanied only by Chas Chandler on bass, which spells out the song's chord progression and 6/8 meter. Running through a Selmer amp, he performed it on his early 1960s Gretsch Tennessean guitar, which he'd used as a member of his previous band, the Wildcats.

Although the transcription here accurately portrays what's on record, take it with a grain of salt and concentrate more on the intended effect rather than dissecting it beat by beat. Clearly, Valentine is using a pattern of ascending and descending arpeggios in which he ascends up from the root of the chord voicing (either string 5, 4, or 6) and descends from the highest string, played with the same rhythm throughout. Beats where two notes are identified are likely incidental, because the riff is deceptively harder than it appears. Notice also that Valentine has the habit of lifting his fret hand off the strings during the last eighth note of each measure in preparation for the next chord, which results in the open G string played as the last note.

The House of the Rising Sun

Words and Music by Alan Price

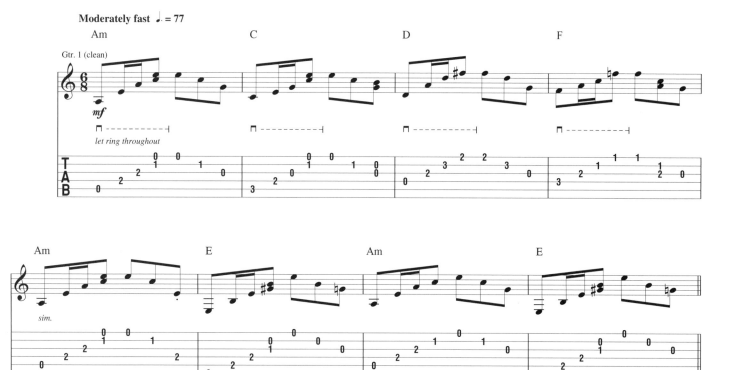

I Feel Fine

Performed by the Beatles
Single Released in 1964

The list of Beatles' firsts runs long. "I Feel Fine" contains the first use of feedback on a record. John, who wrote the song and performed the famous riff on a Gibson J-160E, which had been fitted with a P90 pickup and plugged into a Vox AC30, leaned his guitar against the amp after a take before heading into the control room for a listen. As amplified acoustic guitars are prone to do, especially in such close proximity to the speaker, it began to feed back. The band, always eager to expand their sonic arsenal, asked George Martin if they could leave the sound on the record. Martin agreed, and, after a bit of tape editing, the sound appeared at the front of the song's final take.

The song's intro riff is one of the most famous Beatles riffs of all, and it's also one of the most difficult. In the key of G, the song begins on the V chord (D7) with the standard E-form barre chord shape in tenth position. After playing a common blues box-sounding riff in measure 1 that moves 1–♭7–5 (D–C–A), Lennon moves up to string 3 for the sus4 (G) and 3rd (F♯) in measure 2. That all lays nicely in tenth position, but he follows the 3rd with the 2nd (E), which is found on string 4 at fret 14, before nicking the 3rd again. This is a bit of a stretch, but considering the size of the frets in tenth position, it's certainly manageable. However, this same two-measure phrase is transposed down a whole step to C in eighth position for measures 3–4 and — the killer — down to G in third position for measures 5–8. You'll find the move considerably harder on the G chord than it was up on the D chord for sure!

I Feel Fine
Words and Music by John Lennon and Paul McCartney

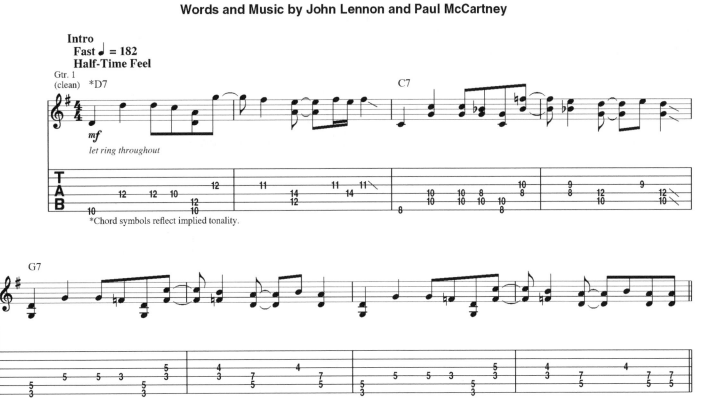

I Love Rock 'n Roll

Performed by Joan Jett & The Blackhearts

From *I Love Rock 'n Roll* (1981)

Joan Jett almost stood alone in the 1980s. Sure, there were other females who rocked as hard as she did, such as Pat Benatar (at times) and the Wilson sisters of Heart (in their earlier days). But she was a leather-wearing guitar-slinger with a "don't give a damn" attitude that really stood out. After making a name for herself with her major label debut, *Bad Reputation* (#51) in 1981, Joan recruited a back-up band, the Blackhearts, for her next album. With a focused, harder sound, the change proved to be a successful one, as *I Love Rock 'n Roll* shot to #2, thanks to the hard-rocking #1 title track and the cavernous melodrama of the Tommy James & The Shondells cover, "Crimson and Clover" (#7).

Although Joan played during this intro as well, she was playing higher register chords (not shown) to thicken the sound using her Gibson Melody Maker and Music Man amp. The signature riff shown below was played by Eric Ambel using his Gibson Les Paul. Although a live video from the era shows Eric with a Peavey backline, it was a lip-synched performance and therefore not a good indicator of what was actually used in the studio. The song is in the key of E and is an all-and-out rockfest in the most basic sense. There's no showboating here — just straightforward hard rock.

Making use of the most basic of harmonic ingredients — the I, IV, and V chords — the riff includes two important elements that draw attention to themselves: rests and syncopation. In big sounding rock 'n' roll like this, silence is a powerful thing. The contrast between a full-volume power chord and nothing at all is quite an attention-grabber, and this riff leaves a big hole on beat 2 in each measure (which happens to be where the snare cracks). The syncopation comes into play in beat 4 of each measure with a G note (bent a bluesy quarter step) on the "e" (counting sixteenths as "1 e & a, 2 e & a," etc.). It's interesting to note that, although you will play the same exact note both times, it sounds different because of the context. At the end of measure 1, it sounds as if it wants to resolve upward to the A, whereas at the end of measure 2, it sounds as if it wants to be followed by the low E. It's often said that simplicity rules when it comes to rock, and this riff demonstrates this as well as any.

I Love Rock 'n Roll

Words and Music by Alan Merrill and Jake Hooker

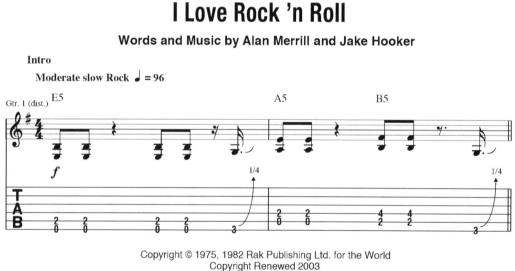

Iris

Performed by the Goo Goo Dolls
From *Dizzy Up the Girl* (1998)

Sounding much more punk-influenced in the early days, the Goo Goo Dolls' first few albums featured bassist Robby Takac on lead vocals. Gradually, they began incorporating Johnny Rzeznik's vocals and songwriting more and more, which resulted in the band shifting its focus from the punkier side of things to the poppier side. When "Name" hit #5, it gave the band their first Top 40 album, sending *A Boy Named Goo* (1995) to #27. Approached afterward to write a song for the *City of Angels* soundtrack, Rzeznik responded with "Iris," a Top Ten hit that sent the band's popularity into the stratosphere and made *Dizzy Up the Girl* (1998) one of the biggest albums of the decade.

Johnny Rzeznik has been a longtime fan of Guild acoustics (although he's used a few Gibsons as well), and he most likely employed his D-55 for the tracking of "Iris." As is common in many Goo Goo Dolls tunes (including "Name"), "Iris" features a totally unique tuning. From standard tuning, this is what you would do:

1. Tune the sixth string down from E to B
2. Tune the fifth string down from A to D
3. Leave the fourth string as is, tuned to D
4. Tune the third string down from G to D
5. Tune the second string up from B to D
6. Tune the first string down from E to D

Obviously, if you do this with a standard guitar, you're going to end up with some floppy stings (and one really tight B string). Therefore, a custom set of strings is used with different gauges to compensate for the drastically altered string tension.

With five strings tuned to D, there's going to be a lot of "letting the tuning do the work" on this one. For the first measure, Johnny plays a melody on string 4 while allowing the top three strings (all D notes) to drone away. The sound is quite lush, to say the least. In measure 2, he plays 7th intervals (though they look like 6ths and 5ths to standard tuning players) against the open first and third strings: a major 7th for the Gmaj7 and a minor 7th for the Dadd9/F#. Even though the final chord symbol says "D5," this is a bit misleading, because there's no 5th present; it's all D notes. However, because we don't have a chord symbol to represent just one note, we use D5, as it's the closest thing to it.

Iris

Words and Music by John Rzeznik

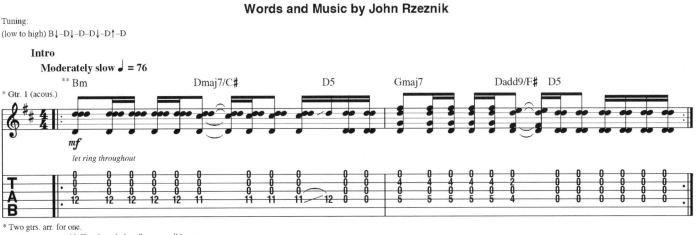

* Two gtrs. arr. for one.

** Chord symbols reflect overall harmony.

Iron Man

Performed by Black Sabbath
From *Paranoid* (1970)

After establishing the standard of heavy metal with their eponymous debut in 1970, the boys in black returned with *Paranoid,* considered by many to be the finest metal album of all time. Although radio play was practically nonexistent, both "Paranoid" and "Iron Man" nearly hit the Top 40, which helped send the album up to #12 in that golden era of AOR (album oriented rock). Although Tony Iommi, citing his well-documented sheet metal factory injury as the catalyst, began tuning down to C♯ with *Masters of Reality* in 1971, he performed all the bludgeoning riffs on the first two albums in standard tuning. As he was never able to get the tone from them that everyone else was, Tony eschewed the Gibson Les Paul in the early days for the SG, and he's been one of the guitar's biggest proponents of the instrument ever since.

His amp of choice in those early days was a Laney LA 100BL — one of the first amps that then-upstart Lyndon Laney had built. Iommi liked how easily he was able to overload the input with the help of his Rangemaster treble boost. Iommi ran the SG through it and straight into the Laney, setting all of amp's controls on 10 except for the bass, which was set to 0. In the classic intro, Tony begins with a rather unusual move. He prebends the low E string up a whole step to F♯, plucks it, and then gradually allows it to return down to pitch. After three times, he begins the immortal: working exclusively from the key of B minor, Iommi creates the most memorable power chord melody of all time. In typical Iommi fashion, he remains on strings 6 and 5 throughout, sliding up as far as fifteenth position to maintain tonal continuity.

Iron Man

Words and Music by Frank Iommi, John Osbourne, William Ward and Terence Butler

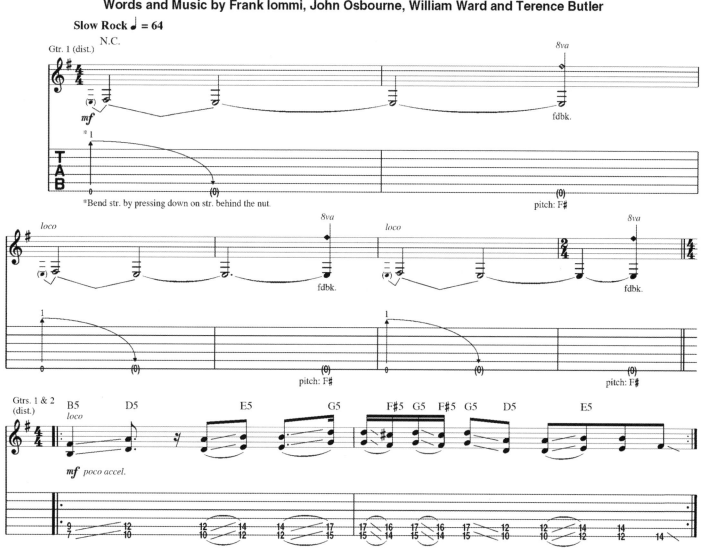

Is This Love

Performed by Bob Marley & The Wailers

From *Kaya* (1978)

Bob Marley, for the most part, set aside his political musings on *Kaya,* the laid back 1978 album from the Wailers. To anyone familiar with Marley's habits, this would make sense, as the word "kaya" is synonymous with marijuana in Rastafarian culture. Of course, Marley had been known to partake of the drug long before this namesake collection of mellow songs revolving around the timeless themes of love, spirituality, and…well…drug use. Although he received a bit of criticism at the time and was accused of going soft or backing down (with regards to his politically charged earlier work), these were ill-informed attacks, which were cleared up with subsequent releases *Survival* (1979) and *Uprising* (1980).

"Is This Love" is a brilliant composition that seems to have its footing equally in F♯ minor and the relative A major. Although the song begins with the famous F♯ minor riff shown here, it often cadences on the A chord, resulting in a beautiful ambiguity that only serves to deepen the lovely mood achieved by Marley and company. The main intro riff is stated by at least three guitars, including two clean-tone electrics and one twelve-string acoustic — the latter a stroke of genius, because it lifts the tone of the riff to sublime. The electric tones are most likely Junior Marvin's Fender Strats through a Roland JC-120, while Marley made use of Marvin's Guild 12-string on the track.

After a syncopated riff from F♯ minor pentatonic sets the pace in measures 1–2, it's altered slightly in measure 3 to fit the D harmony and followed in measure 4 with a dyad-driven hook over the A chord consisting of a D/F♯ shape that's pulled off to a C♯ on string 3. You can think too hard about the fingering in this riff, but if you simply remain in fifth position, fretting the A and C♯ notes with your third and second fingers, respectively, you can barre the D/F♯ dyad with the flattened third finger. When you pull this shape off, it's actually easy to accidentally mute the E note on the second string, which ends up being exactly what's needed here. After repeating the first portion of the riff in measures 5–7, the intro concludes with a descending 6ths riff in quarter-note triplets played hybrid picking style (with pick and fingers), which outlines the A to E chord change.

Is This Love

Words and Music by Bob Marley

Jack and Diane

Performed by John "Cougar" Mellencamp
From *American Fool* (1982)

John Mellencamp — then performing under the stage name John (originally "Johnny") Cougar — had released five albums prior to his commercial breakthrough in 1982. After making few dents with his first few albums, things started looking up in 1979 when the *Johnny Cougar* album spawned his first Top 40 hit with "I Need a Lover." He gained even more momentum with 1980's *Nothing Matters and What If It Did,* breaking the Top 30 with "This Time" and "Ain't Even Done with the Night." The stage was set for his sixth album, and *American Fool* delivered with "Hurt So Good" (#2) and his signature song, "Jack and Diane," which spent four weeks at #1, easily sending the album to the #1 spot as well. The hits continued for Mellencamp throughout the 1980s as his stature among the critics grew, and he became a well-respected and dedicated advocate for the American farmer, organizing Farm Aid with fellow songwriting giants Neil Young and Willie Nelson.

Mellencamp has revealed that the characters in "Jack and Diane" are completely made up, although there have been many rumors to the contrary throughout the years. Interestingly, the song's somewhat disjointed production was actually a product of the band's inability to really gel on the song's feel. Mellencamp has stated that, although the song sounded good to him when he played it acoustically, the band could never really follow him that well. Obviously, the album version worked on some level, because the song remains the biggest hit of his career.

The famous riff shown here occurs after the first verse and actually serves as one of many guitar hooks decorating the song. John performs the A major riff on his Gibson acoustic throughout, using the open A string as a drone beneath various chord voicings on strings 4–2. The harmonies mostly consist of A, D/A, and E/A, the latter of which is ingeniously decorated with a C♯ note on string 3 to form the briefly notated harmony of C♯m/A. The magic of this riff lies in the way the rhythmic hooks — supplemented and augmented by a few well-placed muted strums for effect — combine with the internal melodies created by the different voicings. It's a truly inventive rhythm guitar part that demonstrates the possibilities of acoustic guitar strumming.

Jack and Diane

Words and Music by John Mellencamp

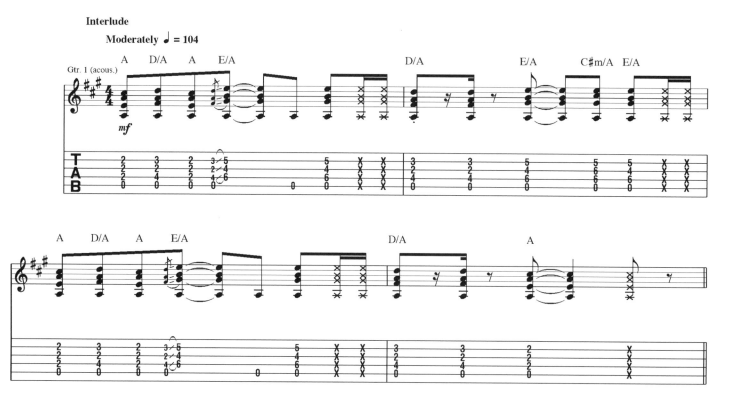

Jailbreak

Performed by Thin Lizzy
From *Jailbreak* (1976)

Although Thin Lizzy toiled through the early 1970s with little commercial success, they continued to develop their signature twin-guitar sound with each album. After successful American tours in support of Bob Seger, Status Quo, and Bachman-Turner Overdrive in 1975, the band's profile increased considerably in the States, and the time for their breakthrough was at hand. They seized the opportunity by recording *Jailbreak* in 1976, which was produced by John Alcock. Bassist/frontman/songwriter Phil Lynott made the decision, in conjunction with Alcock, to employ several session musicians on the album in order to lend a more polished sound. The decision paid off, because *Jailbreak* became the band's commercial breakthrough, producing two hit singles — "Cowboy Song" and "The Boys Are Back in Town" (#12) — the latter is one of the band's signature songs and their biggest hit of all. The album peaked at #18 — a feat they would not top throughout the remainder of their career, which basically ended with their disbandment in 1983.

Lynott, the first commercially successful black Irishman in the world of hard rock, succumbed to drug and alcohol abuse and died of sepsis in 1986. Several tribute incarnations of the band appeared throughout the years, but they've not managed to approach the success of the original band. Although Thin Lizzy remains underappreciated for their contributions to the hard rock genre, they influenced countless musicians on both sides of the pond and played a pivotal role in heightening the stature of guitar slinger extraordinaire Gary Moore, who played with the band briefly in the late 1970s and collaborated often with Lynott on various projects throughout the years.

"Jailbreak" is a major-key rocker, which was slightly uncharacteristic in the hard rock of the day. The main riff is built on almost nothing but I (A5), V (E5), and vi (F#5) power chords, but its myriad elements, including syncopation, dead strums, and a nifty pull-off from the F#5 chord to the open low E string, all combine to create a memorable riff that seriously rocks. The tone, crafted from Brian Roberston's and Scott Gorham's no-nonsense approach of the famed Les Paul/Marshall combo, is not overly distorted. Rather, it's mildly overdriven with a supreme power tube crunch. Remember to keep that first A5 short and staccato!

Jailbreak
Words and Music by Philip Parris Lynott

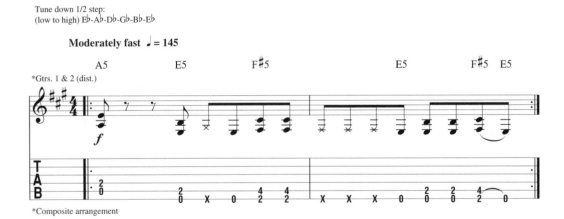

Killing Floor

Performed by Howlin' Wolf

Released as a Single in 1964

Along with B.B. King and Muddy Waters, Howlin' Wolf stands as one of the most widely influential Chicago electric blues performers of all time. With some of the most timeless and widely covered songs in blues history, including "Smokestack Lightning," "Killing Floor," "Commit a Crime," "Back Door Man," and "Spoonful," among many others, his legacy is unquestionably solidified for generations to come. With a voice that roared like a locomotive, grinded like a buzz saw, and bayed like his namesake wolf, he created a musical world all his own and remains one of the most original artists in all the blues genre — truly a legend.

From 1955 until Wolf's death in 1976, his right hand man on guitar was Hubert Sumlin. Although a bit more understated than his employer, Sumlin was nearly as original in the world of blues guitar. Unlike Wolf, he was formally educated in music, studying for six months with a private instructor who taught him to read music and the basics of music theory. Originally a pick player, Sumlin shed his plectrum shortly after joining Howlin' Wolf's band, a move that proved instrumental to his inimitable sound. An economic player who rarely played chords, Sumlin knew "when to get in and when to get out" and decorated countless Wolf hits with his trademark single note riffs.

"Killing Floor" is a 12-bar blues in A, and Sumlin's signature riff is one of the greatest in all of blues guitar. Working with various triads on the top three strings, he creates a descending chordal hook for each chord, which he answers with a single-note ascending bass melody containing the root, 3rd, 4th, and 5th of each chord. Although the chord forms can be a bit tricky at first if you're not familiar with them, the riff is transposed note-for-note relative to each chord, so once you've got it down for the I chord (A7), it'll easily fall into place for the IV (D7) and V (E7) chords. As is commonplace in many 12-bars, the turnaround concludes with a ♭VI–V (F7–E7) move, voiced with three-note dominant chords on strings 5–3. Throughout most of his career, Sumlin played a mid-1950s Les Paul through a Louis Electric Model HS M12 amp, which was similar to a 1959 Fender tweed Twin. Remember to ditch the pick for an authentic Sumlin vibe!

Killing Floor

Words and Music by Chester Burnett

Kryptonite

Performed by 3 Doors Down
From *The Better Life* (2000)

Formed in the late 1990s in Mississippi, 3 Doors Down shot out of the post-grunge gates in 2000 with instant commercial success. *The Better Life* (#7), containing the hits "Kryptonite," "Loser," and "Be Like That," achieved quadruple platinum status in its first year, making the band's name and setting the stage for fairly consistent success throughout the decade. With a sound that resides somewhere between alternative metal and southern rock, the band carved out a nice little niche for itself, along with similar acts Collective Soul, Creed, and Nickelback. The hits continued on 2002's *Away from the Sun* (#8), which contained two top 10 hits in "Here Without You" (#5) and "When I'm Gone" (#4), allowing the band to easily navigate the dreaded sophomore slump.

Amazingly enough, vocalist/drummer Brad Arnold wrote "Kryptonite" at age 15 in math class — one of the first songs he wrote. The band recorded a demo of the song and submitted it to a local radio station in hopes of regional airplay. The strategy worked, because the station fell in love with the single and gave it plenty of airtime, which provided the band with a huge regional following and led to their eventual signing with Republic Records.

Rhythm guitarist Chris Henderson kicks off the tune with its signature riff shown below. In the key of B minor, "Kryptonite" makes use of one the most common minor-key chord progressions in all of rock: the ♭VI–♭VII–i. In B minor, this translates to Bm (i), G (♭VI), and A (♭VII). However, Henderson employs several devices to lend a fresh perspective to this tried-and-true musical move. With his PRS running straight into a Mesa Boogie and Marshall cabinet, Henderson arpeggiates through voicings on strings 6–2 to sound the harmony. He employs several open strings throughout, allowing them to ring together and create a seamless transition from chord to chord. Note the open G string at the end of measure 1 and 3 as an example. For the A chord, he elects to eschew the standard A major voicing in favor of Asus2. This not only accentuates the open, hollow sound of the song's harmonic palette, but it also affords the use of the open B string, which he allows to bleed into the following B minor chord.

Kryptonite
Words and Music by Matt Roberts, Brad Arnold and Todd Harrell

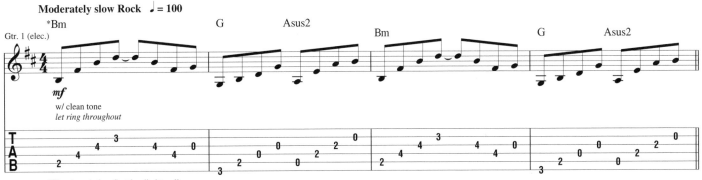

*Chord symbols reflect implied tonality.

La Bamba

Performed by Ritchie Valens
Released as a Single in 1958

Originally a Mexican folk song, "La Bamba" was adapted by Richie Valens and released it in 1958 as the backside to his single "Donna." The traditional song is a staple of weddings in Veracruz. Though Valens' recording career spanned just over eight months, he scored five charting singles in 1958–59, including the #2 smash "Donna" and his signature tune "La Bamba," which reached the #22 spot. Sadly, Valens didn't live to enjoy the massive and enduring success of his musical legacy, because he was on board the ill-fated plane that crashed in 1959, taking along with it the lives of superstars Buddy Holly and J.P. "The Big Bopper" Richardson. Completely self-taught, Valens quit high school after signing with Del-Fi Records under the tutelage of label president Bob Keane. His first full-band recording, which featured Carol Kaye on bass, was "Come On, Let's Go," which nearly cracked the Top 40, peaking at #42. With the time constraints of school lifted, Valens took to the touring circuit, performing on Dick Clark's American Bandstand in October of 1958 and soon sharing the stage with many of his idols, including Buddy Holly, Chuck Berry, The Everly Brothers, and Duane Eddy. During a tour of the Midwest in early 1959, Valens, Holly, and Richardson shared the flight that would end their promising careers and influence Don McLean to immortalize the event in his classic, "American Pie." February 3 has ever since been known as "the day the music died."

Ritchie plowed through the signature "La Bamba" riff with his Harmony H44 Stratotone, which he had sanded down and painted green in his high school shop class. The amplifier was likely one that belonged to the studio and was probably a small Fender tube amp, such as a Princeton or a Deluxe. Valens played the song in the key of C, and like countless other songs, it's built on the I (C), IV (F), and V (G) chords. After an ascending run up from the low G on string 6 to the tonic C on string 5, Valens works an arpeggio motive in measure 1 through the chords, employing double stops in ascending string sets that highlight chord tones of each respective chord. In measure 2, he turns things around again with a V chord run that begins with an ascending G7 arpeggio and concludes with a descending run back to the tonic C.

La Bamba

By Ritchie Valens

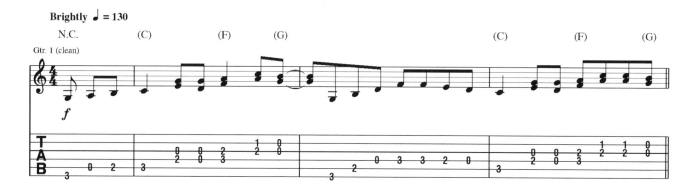

La Grange

Performed by ZZ Top

From *Tres Hombres* (1973)

ZZ Top has spent the past 40-plus years carving out their own instantly recognizable brand of blues rock. At times it's leaned more toward the blues, and other times more toward rock, but it's always been heavily laced with the band's inimitable charm and sense of humor. You only need to peruse a few song titles, such as "Pearl Necklace," "Jesus Just Left Chicago," "Tush," and "Tube Snake Boogie," for evidence that these fellows don't take themselves too seriously. However, they do take their music seriously.

After experiencing a bit of success with the Moving Sidewalks in the late 1960s, including a famous touring stint with Jimi Hendrix, Billy Gibbons formed the Top in 1969 in Houston, Texas. The group built its fan base steadily with their first two albums (back when bands were afforded the time to do such a thing), but it was 1973's *Tres Hombres* that broke the band on a national scale. On the string of the #41 hit "La Grange" and the fan favorite "Jesus Just Left Chicago," the album peaked at #8 and led to a string of sold-out shows on their ensuing tour. Their momentum continued to build with *Fandango* (1975), which reached #10 riding on the … ahem … coattails of the greasy blues hard rock of "Tush" (#20). After treading a bit of water, relatively speaking, with *Tejas* (1976), *Degüello* (1979), and *El Loco* (1981), the Top boys sprung back in a huge way with *Eliminator* (1983). Heavy on the synthesizers, drum machines, and danceable tempos hovering around 120 bpm, the album was a bit of a gamble for the boys that paid off in world domination. They practically lived on MTV throughout 1984 and enjoyed multi-platinum sales. Although the band has yet to match the commercial summit of their mid-1980s period (1985's *Afterburner* also sold 5 million copies), they haven't really had to. After earning the rights to go where the music leads them, they record the albums that they want to and still play to dedicated fans around the world.

An obvious homage to John Lee Hooker, the "La Grange" riff is often mistakenly attributed only to ZZ Top by rock guitarists that haven't done their blues homework. Working from a barred A5 shape, Gibbons employs hybrid picking to peck out the syncopated chords, adding the occasional bluesy notes of G and C on strings 4 and 3, respectively, giving the latter that ever-so-slight quarter step bend that's so ubiquitous in the world of blues guitar. Although predominantly a Gibson/Marshall man throughout the years, Gibbons peeled off this gem with a 1955 Strat and a brownfaced Fender Deluxe in the studio.

La Grange

Words and Music by Billy F Gibbons, Dusty Hill and Frank Lee Beard

Layla

Performed by Derek and the Dominos
From *Layla and Other Assorted Love Songs*

Eric Clapton has been part, and perhaps the leading light, of many legendary bands. First he made a name for himself with the Yardbirds, then he blew everyone's mind with John Mayall & The Bluesbreakers. After that, he was part of the uber-supergroup Cream when barely in his 20s. After Cream disbanded in 1968, Clapton made one more go of the supergroup concept with Blind Faith, which called it quits after one album and a supporting tour. Clapton then assembled Derek and the Dominos in an attempt to take the spotlight off him, hoping to blend into an ensemble role. After becoming infatuated with George Harrison's first wife, Pattie Boyd, and subsequently rejected by her, Clapton found nearly all the inspiration he needed for the songs on *Layla and Other Assorted Love Songs,* which was released in 1970. The album hit the #16 spot, mainly on the strength of the Top Ten title track.

"Layla" begins in the key of D minor, and though the verse modulates to a different key, it returns to D minor for the chorus. The famous intro riff is articulated with three guitars — two playing in the lower octave and one doubling an octave higher. After a pickup phrase from D minor pentatonic, which is played by all three guitars, Gtrs. 1 and 2 sustain the tonic D note (an octave apart from each other) while Gtr. 3 articulates the harmony with a clever, highly syncopated riff built mostly on power chords. The i (D5), ♭VI (B♭5), and ♭VII (C5) chords are embellished with several subtle touches, including a slide from D5 to C5 and a two-note pattern (A–G) used as a pivot melody of sorts. The riff concludes with a repeat of the pentatonic pickup phrase, setting up a repeat. Although rumors have abounded for years about Clapton recording this track with a Tweed Fender Champ, producer Tom Dowd has revealed in several interviews that Clapton indeed played his famous Browine Strat through a brand new (at the time) Silverfaced Champ.

Layla
Words and Music by Eric Clapton and Jim Gordon

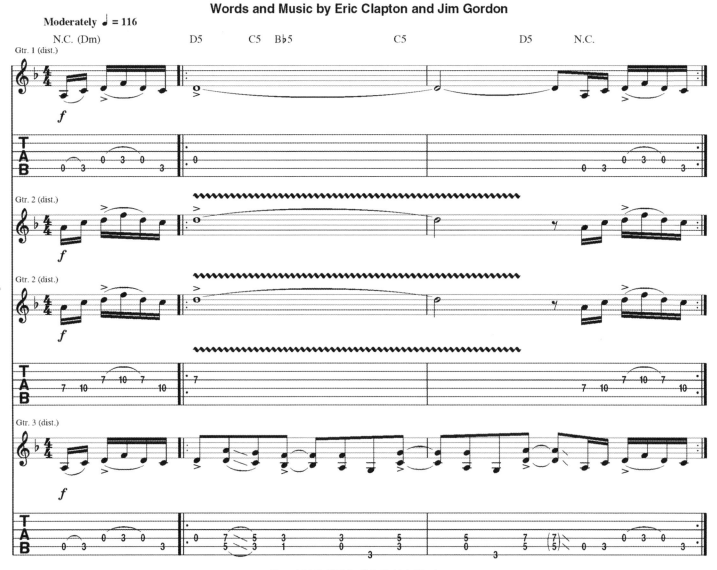

Le Freak

Performed by Chic

From *C'est Chic* (1978)

Although they were a bit late to the disco party, Chic nonetheless knew how to do it up right. Session musicians Nile Rodgers (guitar) and Bernard Edwards (bass) founded the band in 1976, filling out the lineup with stellar musicians they'd met through their studio connections. After recording the demo single "Dance, Dance, Dance (Yowsah, Yowsah, Yowsah)" and shopping it, the small label Buddah released the song as a 12" single in 1977. Atlantic stepped in quickly after the song exploded on the club scene, rereleased the song to a larger audience, and it shot up the charts to #6, putting Chic on the disco map. The band quickly capitalized on the momentum by releasing their self-titled debut album, which included another hit in "Everybody Dance."

It was their follow-up album, *C'est Chic* (1978), however, that made the band a national name and one of the biggest disco acts in the world. The colossal #1 smash "Le Freak" spent weeks on top of the charts, selling over four million copies and becoming Atlantic's best selling single in history at that time. (The song held that title until it was dethroned by Madonna's "Vogue" in 1990.) As a result, *C'est Chic* achieved platinum status — a rarity in the disco world. The band continued their domination with *Risqué* (1979), which also went platinum thanks to the infectious grooves of "Good Times" — another definitive track of the genre. With the end of the disco movement at the end of the decade, and a greater concentration on producing by Rodgers and Edwards, the band dissolved in 1983.

"Le Freak" was conceived by Rodgers and Edwards after the two were denied entrance to the elite Studio 54 club in New York. (Though they had been invited by Grace Jones, she failed to notify the doormen.) The song is in A minor and spends most of its time vamping between Am and D chords, briefly alluding to C before the return to Am. The riff here is pretty much funk guitar 101; it's played entirely in fifth position and consists of syncopated dyad voicings on strings 1–3 (essentially broken chord shapes), a few single-note stabs on string 4, and several muted dead strums for a percussive effect. To achieve the classic funk tone heard on the album, Rodgers plugged his Strat directly into a Neve console, applied some compression, and blended in a bit of miked amp — most likely a Fender Twin or Super Reverb. Take note of the staccato markings; they're essential to the proper feel.

Le Freak

Words and Music by Nile Rodgers and Bernard Edwards

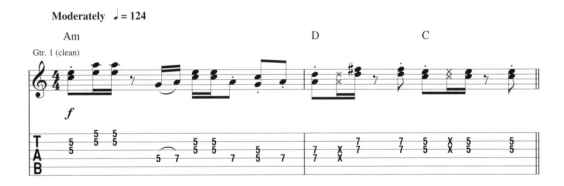

The Lemon Song

Performed by Led Zeppelin

From *Led Zeppelin II* (1969)

Led Zeppelin wasted no time entrenching themselves on the top of the hard rock mountain with the release of *Led Zeppelin* in 1969. Although the album didn't contain a Top 40 single, it's heyday was the age of AOR (album oriented rock), and that meant it didn't have to have a hit single in order to be successful and reach #10 on the charts, which it did. While on tour that year, Led Zeppelin managed to sneak away between dates and record *Led Zeppelin II* at various studios in the UK and North America. "The Lemon Song" was tracked in Hollywood, California, at Mystic Studios and produced by Jimmy Page, as was the whole album.

As happened with Zeppelin several times during their career, a copyright issue arose with "The Lemon Song." While on tour in support of *Led Zeppelin,* the band often performed Howlin' Wolf's classic blues gem "Killing Floor" (at the time, the song was only five or six years old). Over the course of the tour, they reworked it a bit, and Page began to improvise some new lyrics. While recording *II*, they laid down their version of it and called it "The Lemon Song." Zeppelin was sued in 1972 by Arc Music, the publisher that owned the rights to Wolf's "Killing Floor," and the parties settled out of court.

For the recording of *II*, Page began to use the gear for which he would become famous — namely, the classic Les Paul and Marshall combo. He owned three Les Pauls at the time, one of which he'd purchased from Joe Walsh, and it's likely he used one of them for the solo of "The Lemon Song." The intro riff, however, sounds more like single coils and is most likely his Telecaster. (Although Page has mentioned in various interviews that he only used the Les Paul while recording *II*, there are some parts that really do sound like single coils.) The amp is either a Marshall 100-watt or a Vox UL4210, which was a hybrid amp with a solid state preamp section and tube power section.

Zeppelin performs "The Lemon Song" in E, as opposed to Wolf's "Killing Floor," which was in A. Page employs a hybrid picking technique here, picking the ascending notes on string 6 and plucking the open B string with his finger. The notes on the low E string essentially echo the "Killing Floor" riff, although the combined B string adds a thickness and sophistication to the sound that sets it apart. After climbing up to the 5th (B) on string 6, Page grabs the "Hendrix Chord," E7#9, to cap off the phrase in measure 2.

The Lemon Song

**Words and Music by Chester Burnett, John Bonham,
Jimmy Page, Robert Plant and John Paul Jones**

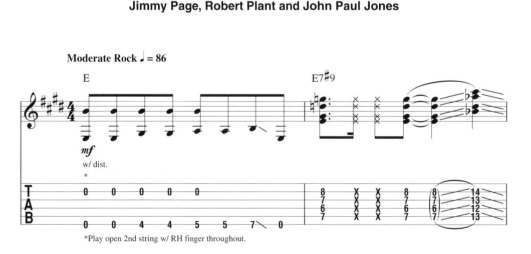

*Play open 2nd string w/ RH finger throughout.

Life in the Fast Lane

Performed by the Eagles
From *Hotel California* (1976)

In terms of album sales and recognition, the Eagles led the dream life. Their first two albums (*Eagles,* 1972 and *Desperado,* 1973) were commercially successful, but they weren't *phenomenally* successful, which meant that they were able to ease into the culture shock of rock stardom. Their stature increased steadily with the next two albums. *On the Border* (1974) produced the band's first #1 hit with "Best of My Love," shoving the album to the #17 spot, and *One of These Nights* (1975) made them bonafide stars with three Top Ten hits and their first #1 album ranking.

With the release of *Hotel California* in 1976, however, they became bonafide megastars. The album spawned three Top Ten singles — "Hotel California" #1, "New Kid in Town" #1, and "Life in the Fast Lane" #11 — sending it to the #1 spot, where it remained there for eight weeks in 1977. The first album to feature new member Joe Walsh, *Hotel California* has gone on to sell over 16 million albums in the U.S. alone. The band continued its chart domination with the follow-up three years later: 1979's *The Long Run,* which hit #1 and again contained three Top Ten singles, but by that point, tensions within the band had become unbearable, and after *Eagles Live* was released in 1980, the band split up.

Glenn Frey has mentioned that the idea for "Life in the Fast Lane" came to him after hearing a drug dealer use the phrase and later hearing Joe Walsh play the famous intro riff onstage before a show. On the recording, Walsh plugged a Fender Strat straight into a tweed Fender Deluxe amp for the intro riff and cranked it up to nearly wide open. This song is a classic example of a tone that's not *nearly* as distorted as most people remember it being. It's a common neophyte mistake to use insane amounts of preamp distortion when playing classic songs that contain actually only fair to moderate amounts of tube break-up. The notes are all derived from E minor pentatonic, but the phrase is dressed up with some grace-note descending slides and bluesy half-step bends on string 6 from G up to G♯. Another touch of rhythmic brilliance occurs at the end of measure 3, when the repetition of the riff begins a beat early — on beat 4 instead of beat 1 — turning the beat around briefly.

Life in the Fast Lane
Words and Music by Don Henley, Glenn Frey and Joe Walsh

Look-Ka Py Py

Performed by the Meters
From *Look-Ka Py Py* (1969)

If Memphis had Booker T. & The M.G.'s, New Orleans had the Meters. Although they didn't receive the attention of the M.G.'s, the Meters performed the same function in a different city, leading the way in creating each respective locale's definitive funk tone. The senior statesmen of the group, Art Neville, assembled the band after his brief stint with the Hawketts and a short solo career. Soon the band was plucked by producers Allen Toussaint and Marshall Sehorn to be the house band for their label Sansu Enterprises. In 1969, they released their eponymous debut for Sundazed Records, which contained the minor hit "Cissy Strut." The tune put their name on the map, reached #23 in the pop charts, and eventually became one of the band's signature songs.

With the follow-up, 1970's *Look-Ka Py Py,* the Meters expanded their fan base with more of the same instrumental "N'Awlins" funk for which they had become known. The title track reached #11 on the R&B charts. They managed to hold their ground for several more albums in the early 1970s, but with the rise of disco, their sound began to lose favor with the public, and they called it quits by 1977.

There seems to be some contradictory information floating around with regards to Leo Nocentelli's gear. In one article, he mentions that he used a Gibson 175 for all the early Meters stuff, while in another he claims it was a Tele. The amp was most likely a blackface Fender Twin Reverb or Super Reverb with the volume set low enough to maintain a clean tone. After an ever-so-cool harmonized vocal intro, Leo brings the band into the main G7 riff with the three-note pickup D–F–D. What follows is basically a tutoring session in New Orleans funk guitar. Both the hammered minor to major 3rd (B♭ to B, in this case) and the descending octave minor pentatonic riff on beats 1 of measures 1 and 2, respectively, are textbook funk licks, while the syncopated G7 fragments (dyads) on strings 2 and 1 are clipped so staccato that the notes are sometimes even hard to make out. Also note the question-and-answer structure that's in effect, with measure 1 posing the "question" in the higher octave and measure 2 "answering" with the descent into the lower octave. Everything about this riff oozes groove, and it's made even more powerful by the counterpoint provided by George Porter on bass, Art Neville on organ, and Joseph Modeliste on skins. To play this riff by itself gives only half the story; you owe it to yourself to hear the whole ensemble.

Look-Ka Py Py

Words and Music by Leo Nocentelli, George Porter, Arthur Neville and Joseph Modeliste

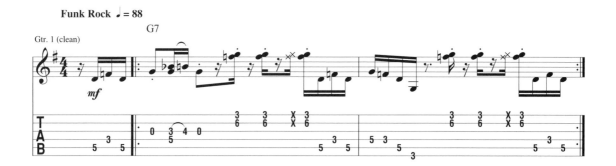

Love Song

Performed by Tesla
From *The Great Radio Controversy* (1989)

Bluesier and grittier than most other 1980s metal bands, Tesla stood out against the glam and glitter. Although they certainly fell into the pop metal category, they sounded as though they wanted to cling to the earthier rock of the 1970s, whereas most bands were content to leave it behind — or at least cover its roots with enough makeup to make it undetectable. (Guitarist Frank Hannon often sported a double-neck Gibson SG on stage, Jimmy Page-style.) This more grounded approach to their sound allowed Tesla to hang on a bit longer than most bands when the grunge reaper arrived in the early 1990s, although they too eventually succumbed to the changing winds.

Combining a dual guitar attack and a streetwise sentiment in much of their lyrics, the band joined the metal party a bit late but still made a respectable entrance with 1986's *Mechanical Resonance.* Featuring the two minor hits "Modern Day Cowboy" and "Little Suzi," the album hit #32 and provided them the opportunity to stretch out a bit on their follow-up. *The Great Radio Controversy* (1989) confirmed for the world that they were indeed the real deal. Much more sprawling in songwriting scope and sound than its predecessor, the album "resonated" much more than *Mechanical Resonance,* reaching #18 and producing their first Top Ten hit in the free love-tinged, decidedly non-power ballad, "Love Song." Afforded additional leeway from the label, Tesla really took a left turn with *Five Man Acoustical Jam* — a pre-MTV Unplugged acoustic live album containing a mixture of originals and a few classic covers from the 1960s. The gamble paid off with their highest charting album yet (#12) and another Top Ten hit with their cover of "Signs." *Psychotic Supper* (1991) performed well at #13, but the metal parade was leaving town, and the group disbanded shortly after 1994's *Bust a Nut* (#20), but they reformed in 2000 and have continued to release albums since.

Although not present on the single version, the album version of "Love Song" features an mini-orchestra of acoustic guitars, all overdubbed by Frank Hannon. It begins sparsely enough, however, with the two-voice contrapuntal phrase shown here. Plucking his Gibson Jumbo acoustic, Frank outlines the I–V–vi–IV progression (D–A–Bm–G) in D with single bass notes on bottom and a combination of melodies and arpeggios on top. The flashy legato move at the end of measure 1 helps to dress up the basic melodic contour, as does the arpeggio in measure 3. Fingerstyle is best here, but you'll need to use at least a hybrid picking approach (both pick and fingers) if you refuse to put down the plastic.

Love Song
Words and Music by Jeffrey Keith and Frank Hannon

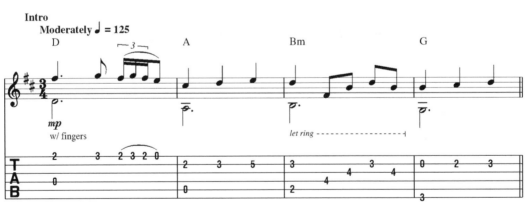

Mama, I'm Coming Home

Performed by Ozzy Osbourne

From *No More Tears* (1991)

Ozzy's always loved working with great guitar players, and the tragic death of Randy Rhoads left some huge shoes to fill. Jake E. Lee certainly played some impressive stuff on *Bark at the Moon* (1983) and *The Ultimate Sin* (1986), but it wasn't until he discovered Zakk Wylde for 1989's *No Rest for the Wicked* that Ozzy seemed to feel a true sense of kinship with a guitarist again. Zakk wasted no time making believers out of the guitar world on that album, heavily stamping its tracks with his trademark pinch harmonics and pentatonic shredding. Although the album failed to produce a hit single, it peaked at #13 and achieved gold sales within the year. It has since sold over 2.5 million copies.

The new Ozzy band returned in 1991 with *No More Tears.* The sound had shifted a bit to a grungier metal (notably in the title track), and certain tracks, such as "Mama, I'm Coming Home" even leaned ever so slightly toward a southern rock feel. This was likely Zakk's influence, as he's certainly been known to dabble in the southern sides of hard rock and metal.

A song for Ozzy's wife/manager, Sharon Osbourne (nicknamed "Mama"), "Mama, I'm Coming Home" begins with a southern, pedal steel lick in E right out of the Lynyrd Skynyrd playbook. Played on an acoustic — most likely Zakk's Gibson Dove — the brief pickup phrase gives way to the intro riff proper, which is an arpeggio line built on the idea of a descending E major scale on string 3 played against the ringing open strings 1 and 2 as drones. When doubled by a 12-string, this creates a huge, lush sound reminiscent of some of the Eagles' trademark acoustic moments. Although there are chord symbols provided, the effect is really more of a riff than actual chord changes. The phrase can easily be played pick style or hybrid style, although with the former, you may want to experiment with pick directions to find a pattern that works best for you. Remember to tune down a half step if you want to play along to the recording!

Mama, I'm Coming Home

Words and Music by Ozzy Osbourne and Zakk Wylde

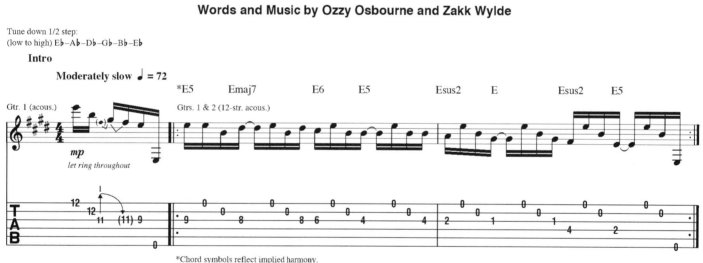

*Chord symbols reflect implied harmony.

Man in the Box

Performed by Alice in Chains

From *Facelift* (1990)

Though much of the country thinks grunge took over the airwaves instantly with Nirvana's *Nevermind* in 1991, that's not the case. Several other Seattle grunge bands, including Soundgarden and Alice and Chains, had already been creeping into the mainstream on major labels. Alice in Chains were signed to Columbia Records in 1989 shortly after Soundgarden signed their major label deal with A&M in 1988. Columbia held Alice in high regard and made the release of their debut EP *We Die Young* (July of 1990) a top priority. After the title track showed promise with metal radio stations, the band rushed in to record their debut album, *Facelift*. Drummer Sean Kinney played the sessions with a broken hand, because there was no time to allow it to heal, and he didn't want to miss his (possibly only) big break.

Not an instant success, *Facelift* sold only 40,000 copies in the first six months. However, after MTV placed "Man in the Box" in regular rotation, sales increased dramatically, and it became the first grunge album to go platinum, even though it only peaked at #42 on the *Billboard* chart. Guitarist, co-vocalist, and songwriter Jerry Cantrell has stated that it was the song "Man in the Box" that really helped Alice in Chains find their unique sound. Indeed, the track is one of the band's signature songs. The song begins with the famous riff, which consists of two separate but equal parts. On the one hand, you have the rhythm part (Gtr. 2): a syncopated, grinding riff created by playing a D5 power chord on strings 5 and 4 above the open low E string. This voicing, when played through the distorted tones of his Bogner Fish preamp, Mesa Boogie power amp, and Marshall 4x12 cabinet, produces a thick, grinding wall of sound that was almost surely doubled (or more) in the studio for maximum effect. On top of this, Gtr. 1 lays down the Hendrix-inspired wah-laden E minor pentatonic melody that sounds a bit like "Voodoo Chile" after it's taken some steroids. Cantrell ran his G&L Rampage through his Dunlop Crybaby for this track, but it was also blended with a talk box in the studio to achieve the final product. The two guitars come together at the end for the pentatonic hammer-on lick in seventh position. Taken together, the riff is powerful, and memorable one that announced the arrival of Alice in Chains in a big way.

Man in the Box

Written by Jerry Cantrell, Layne Staley, Sean Kinney and Michael Starr

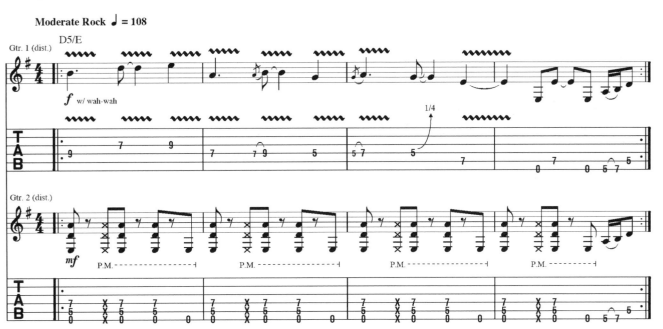

Tune down 1/2 step:
(low to high) Eb–Ab–Db–Gb–Bb–Eb

Moderate Rock ♩ = 108

Man on the Silver Mountain

Performed by Rainbow

From *Ritchie Blackmore's Rainbow* (1975)

As Ritchie Blackmore became increasingly dissatisfied with the R&B and soul elements that crept into the music of Deep Purple through the likes of vocalist David Coverdale and bassist/vocalist Glenn Hughes, he decided to record a solo project with the help of various members of Elf, Procol Harum, and ELO in 1974. Originally intended as only a single ("Black Sheep of the Family" b/w "Sixteenth Century Greensleeves"), Blackmore decided to turn it into a full album. With the formation of his new band, Rainbow (named after the Rainbow Bar and Grill in Hollywood), he decided to leave Deep Purple in 1975.

The new album, billed as *Ritchie Blackmore's Rainbow,* featured Ronnie James Dio as vocalist, co-writer of music, and sole lyric writer. As expected, the lyrics dealt with medieval themes and mysticism, and the music contained a classical edge through Blackmore's influence. The album featured a minor radio hit in "Man on the Silver Mountain" and peaked at #30 on the *Billboard* chart but failed to become a big commercial success. Over the ensuing years, the band's roster would rotate more frequently than a volleyball team, and they eventually called it quits for the first time in 1984. The band surfaced again in the mid-1990s, with Blackmore as the only member from any past incarnation.

Wielding his 1973 Strat and a 200 watt Marshall stack, Blackmore opens the song with a riff that sounds strikingly similar to "Smoke on the Water." The tempo is much faster, but both songs are in the key of G and involve 4th dyads moved in parallel. Working first within the third-position G minor pentatonic scale exclusively, the riff takes a bit of an unexpected turn at the very end, when Blackmore descends down to the first-position dyad of B♭/E♭, which is derived from the G Aeolian mode (minor scale): G–A–B♭–C–D–E♭–F. It's important to realize that a 4th interval is simply a 5th interval turned upside down. Therefore, 4ths can be power chords too; this is illustrated by the chord symbols, in which the final chords of the riff (in measure 4) are labeled G5–F5–E♭5. Another aspect of this riff's sounds lies in the fact that Blackmore employs hybrid picking — the low G notes are played with the pick, and the double stops are played with the second and third fingers — to keep the double stops tight and controlled, allowing each note to sound with equal volume.

Man on the Silver Mountain

**Words and Music by
Ronnie James Dio and Richard Blackmore**

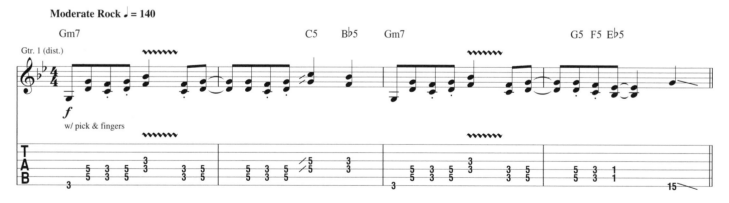

Message in a Bottle

Performed by the Police
From *Reggatta de Blanc* (1979)

After making their mark with the nervous-sounding punkish rock of their debut, *Outlandos d'Amour* ("Outlaws of Love"), in 1978, the Police returned to the same studio/producer combination to record the follow up, 1979's *Reggatta de Blanc* ("White Reggae"). Because that debut had been successful, the band felt little pressure from the record company and were able to do things the way they saw fit. Because Sting was a bit short on material upon entering the studio, the band contributed to the writing and they cannibalized bits of older songs to fill out the album. "Bring on the Night" and "The Bed's Too Big Without You" began as Last Exit (one of Sting's previous bands) songs, and the title track originated from improvisations on stage during "Can't Stand Losing You" on the previous tour.

Although the album performed exceptionally well and topped the charts in the U.K. and Australia, with both "Walking on the Moon" and "Message on the Bottle" reaching the #1 spot, the band was still growing on the U.S., where the album peaked at #25. Eventually Police's domination would spread worldwide, firmly entrenching them among the top bands of the world in the 1980s. Their albums included 1980's *Zenyatta Mondatta* (#5), 1981's *Ghost in the Machine* (#2), and their swan song high note *Synchronicity* (#1) in 1983.

Andy Summers had an affinity for 20th Century composers and therefore often relied upon sounds other than the triad to flesh out his riffs. "Message in a Bottle" is a perfect example. Sounding in the key of C♯ minor, the famous riff is built entirely upon a moveable sus2 voicing that consists of two consecutively stacked perfect 5th intervals. Each chord is built root–5th–9th (2nd) from low to high. Each chord — C♯sus2, Asus2, Bsus2, and F♯sus2 — in the i–♭VI–♭VII–v progression is arpeggiated low to high, with only the first C♯sus2 sounding on the beat in nonsyncopated fashion. Andy played his famous modified 1961 Telecaster (which he bought from a student for $200) on this track through two 100 watt Marshall half stacks, both of which were set with the volumes only halfway up. Contrary to popular belief, he did not use a chorus pedal to achieve his thick tone. Instead, he used an Electro-Harmonix Electric Mistress flanger pedal. He set the depth fairly shallow to achieve a subtle widening effect and also made use of an MXR Dyna Comp pedal to even out the attack.

Message in a Bottle

Music and Lyrics by Sting

Money

Performed by Pink Floyd
From *The Dark Side of the Moon* (1973)

There are successful albums, and then there's *The Dark Side of the Moon,* which stands at the top of the heap with a *very* select few. At a first glance of the facts, you might not think so. After all, it only held the #1 spot for one week when it was released in 1973. When you consider the fact, however, that it remained on the charts for 740 more weeks, you begin to get a grip on the album's lasting dominance. If it's hard to grasp what that number means, try converting it to years: 14.25. To say it has staying power is an understatement. The band's members all can't even explain the album's enduring, unprecedented success.

Amazingly, the album only produced one big hit single, and it didn't even crack the Top Ten, much less top the charts. "Money" peaked at #13 upon the album's release, which probably makes it the only rock song in 7/4 meter to become a Top 40 hit. In retrospect, the album contains almost nothing but indisputable classics, including "Time," "Breathe," "Us and Them," and "Brain Damage." Although this album proved to be the band's commercial breakout album, they went on to reach world domination in other ways with 1979's concept album *The Wall,* which also hit #1 and produced the #1 hit "Another Brick in the Wall, Pt. 2." Even with its massive, worldwide success, *The Wall* pales in comparison to *Dark Side's* continued, unwavering performance.

After the cash register tape loop intro, "Money" settles into its lopsided 7/4 groove with Roger Waters' bass line, which is derived from a B minor pentatonic scale (B–D–E–F♯–A) and played in second position. David Gilmour doubles this line on his custom Bill Lewis guitar through most likely a silverface Twin Reverb, applying a palm mute throughout. As measure 3 illustrates, Gilmour will take occasional liberty at times, slightly varying the line with the occasional omitted or added note. Of course, to add a slight blues infection, Gilmour stretches the ♭3rd notes (D) at the end of each measure by a quarter step.

Money
Words and Music by Roger Waters

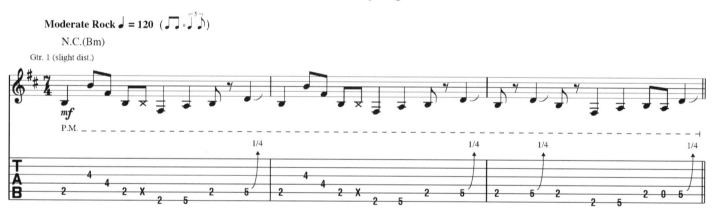

Money for Nothing

Performed by Dire Straits

From *Brothers in Arms* (1985)

Dire Straits had been steadily holding their ground since their entrance on the scene in 1978 with their eponymous debut. Peaking early, *Dire Straits* reached #2 on the strength of the #4 hit-turned-classic "Sultans of Swing" and introduced the world to Mark Knopfler's tasty, understated fingerpicking. Subsequent albums, although containing fan favorites such as "Telegraph Road," "Romeo and Juliet," and "Tunnel of Love," failed to match the debut in terms of sales or relevance. *Brothers in Arms,* released in 1985, changed all that, however. Containing three Top 20 hits in "Money for Nothing" (#1), "So Far Away" (#19), and "Walk of Life" (#7), the album spent nine weeks at #1 in the U.S. and has gone on to sell over 30 million copies worldwide.

Although initially appalled at the idea of creating the music video for "Money for Nothing" with then-state-of-the-art computer animation, Knopfler eventually relented and allowed the director free rein to make the video he imagined. The video won Video of the Year in 1986, the song became a #1 smash, and the rest is history.

Mark has stated that his goal with the song was to recreate Billy Gibbons' tone; he even called Gibbons asking for specifics. Although Gibbons revealed nothing to him, they happened upon a classic tone all their own almost through accident. Knopfler plugged a Les Paul Jr. into a Laney amp for the recording session. There were three mics set up haphazardly from the night's previous session (none of which were pointing directly at the amp), and when they turned on the channels at the console, the band was amazed at what they heard. They made no adjustments and recorded the track right away. Knopfler kicks off the song with a gritty riff derived from the G minor pentatonic scale. Combining double stops, muted dead notes, legato moves, and a few strategically placed harmonics, the riff undulates in varied peaks and dips, mostly suggesting a G tonal center, but briefly coming to rest with a B♭5–C5 and F5–G5 cadences in measures 4 and 8, respectively. Of course, fingerstyle is a must for authenticity!

Money for Nothing

Words and Music by Mark Knopfler and Sting

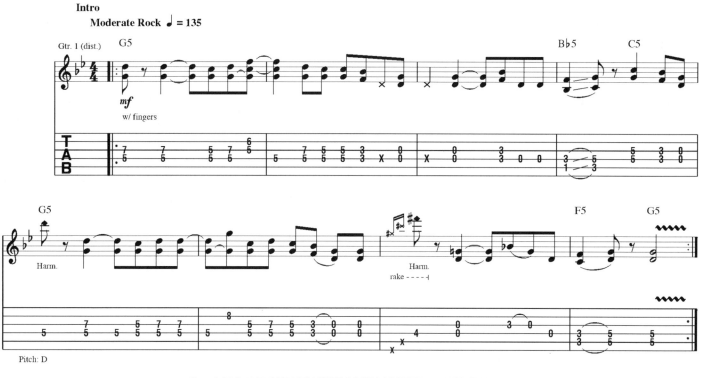

Monkey Wrench

Performed by Foo Fighters

From *The Colour and the Shape* (1997)

While touring with Nirvana in the early 1990s, drummer Dave Grohl would occasionally write songs by himself in hotel rooms to pass the time. Intimidated by Kurt Cobain's songwriting prowess, Grohl chose to keep his songs to himself. By the time Cobain died in 1994, Grohl had amassed over 40 songs. Instead of joining another band on drums (he was invited to join Tom Petty & The Heartbreakers), he decided to book some studio time and record some songs. Save for one guitar part, he performed every instrument and vocal by himself and began handing out cassettes of the finished product to friends to hear what they thought. He chose the name "Foo Fighters" for the project to maintain anonymity in the early days. Through the grapevine, several labels became interested, and Capitol Records signed the band and released the eponymous album in 1995. Mainly on the strength of the single "Big Me," the album reached #23.

For the follow-up, Grohl brought a full band into the studio. The result, *The Colour and the Shape,* was released in 1997 and proved to be their commercial breakthrough. Containing "Monkey Wrench," "My Hero," and "Everlong," the album cracked the #10 spot and remains the band's best seller, with over two million copies sold. The band has since released a steady stream of albums — no worldwide smashes, but nearly all critically acclaimed and more than capable of sustaining a substantial fan base.

Inspired by the break-up of Grohl and ex-wife Jennifer Youngblood, "Monkey Wrench" is a fast and furious hard rocker that barely lets up. It kicks right into high gear from the beginning with two prominent guitar parts. Gtrs. 1 and 2 double up on a power chord riff in drop D tuning, working its way down the neck through the main I–V–IV progression in B, alternating quickly between E5 and D5 (♭III) at the end. Atop that is a stinging melodic part that pits a descending B major melody on string three against constant, droning open B and E strings. This creates a frantic, huge sound that covers a massive sonic landscape. Grohl makes use of numerous guitars when recording, but the tones on this track were most likely created with either a Gretsch White Falcon or Gibson Les Paul through a Hiwatt 100 watt stack.

Monkey Wrench

Words and Music by David Grohl, Nate Mendel and Pat Smear

More Than a Feeling

Performed by Boston

From *Boston* (1976)

Before hitting the scene with his band Boston, MIT graduate Tom Scholz was working at Polaroid as an engineer. He met vocalist Brad Delp (as well as other future members of Boston) while still attending MIT, where he had played keyboards with various bands. Using his earnings from Polaroid, Scholz put together a home studio in his basement consisting of a 12-track Scully recorder and a Dan Flickinger console, as well as many devices he'd invented himself, including the now-famous Rockman guitar preamp. The recordings he made there resulted in a record deal with Epic. After some sleight of hand from producer John Boylan, which was necessary to hide from Epic the fact that most of the final recordings (save for Delp's vocals) were made in a home basement, *Boston* was released in 1976. On the strength of the two hits "More Than a Feeling" (#5) and "Peace of Mind" (#38), the album reached #3 and went on to become the best-selling debut in history up to that point. It still resides in the #2 spot behind Guns N' Roses' *Appetite for Destruction*.

Armed with little more than a cheap Yamaha 12-string acoustic, an EV RE16 dynamic mic, and a Dsus4 chord, Tom Scholz created one of the most famous guitar intros of the 1970s for "More Than a Feeling." After decorating the D chord in measure 1 with a suspended 4th (G) that's resolved to the major 3rd (F♯), he rounds out the phrase in measure 2 with a tried-and-true ♭VII (C)–IV (G) move. Notice, however, that the D chord on string 2 is held through the C chord, creating a Cadd9. (You could also technically call this Csus2, since the major 3rd (E), which would normally appear on string 4, is not played.)

Scholz plays a great rhythmic hook in measure 2, repeating the three-note ascending arpeggio figure (C–G–D) with the bass note lowered a half step to B, creating a G chord in first inversion (G/B). He finishes off with a one-beat pattern of G–D to round off the measure. There's one more bit of brilliant symmetry in this riff as well. Notice the intervallic structure of the three-note treble melody in measure 1 (G–F♯–D): a half step down followed by a major 3rd down. Now take a look at the bass melody in measure 2 (C–B–G): it's the same thing transposed down a whole step (and an octave). This may not be a conscious move on Scholz's part (although he is quite clever at math, so you never know!), but it certainly lends a great cohesion to the riff!

More Than a Feeling

Words and Music by Tom Scholz

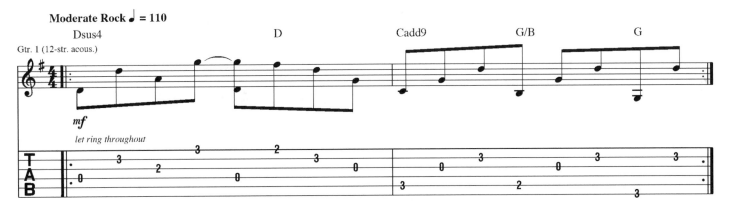

More Than Words

Performed by Extreme
From *Extreme II: Pornograffitti* (1990)

Extreme made a decent splash when they arrived on the scene with their eponymous debut in 1989, with Nuno Bettencourt making waves in the guitar world. They sounded heavily influenced by Van Halen on the album, and it peaked at #80. Their popularity increased with a feature placement of "Play with Me" in the film *Bill and Ted's Excellent Adventure,* which showcased Bettencourt's virtuosity in full force. It wasn't until their sophomore effort, however, that they experienced commercial success on a large scale. Released in 1990, *Pornograffitti* expanded on their sound, blending strong elements of funk, R&B, and even jazz into a signature brand of metal. However, the most unrepresentative songs on the album caught on. The Beatles-esque acoustic ballad "More Than Words," the majority of which was written by Bettencourt while in the bathroom, became a surprise #1 smash and sent the album to the #10 spot and double platinum status. Another acoustic number, "Hole Hearted," which fell a little closer to Supertramp in style, reached #4. A lot of fans that bought the album looking for more of the same mellow, acoustic-laden numbers. The follow-up, *III Sides to Every Story,* came out after the grunge bomb had exploded, and, though the album peaked at #10, it failed to produce a hit single. By the time 1995's *Waiting for the Punchline* arrived, the metal train had left town.

Wielding his Washburn acoustic, Nuno crafted this signature song's riff in the key of G. Played fingerstyle, it's an excellent example of the backbeat percussive technique. Most of the chords are plucked in block chord style (as opposed to arpeggiated), but notice that on every beat 2 and 4, there are "Xs" marked in the music. These are percussive "dead" notes that are achieved by forcefully planting your plucking-hand fingers onto the strings, which creates a "tick" sound. This is an especially effective technique when the guitar is the sole accompaniment, because it simulates the snare drum backbeat and can really set up a nice groove, as demonstrated by Nuno. Notice also how he keeps a common G note on top of almost all the voicings, which lends continuity and smoothness to the changing harmony. Remember to tune down a half step if you want to play along to the original recording.

More Than Words
Words and Music by Nuno Bettencourt and Gary Cherone

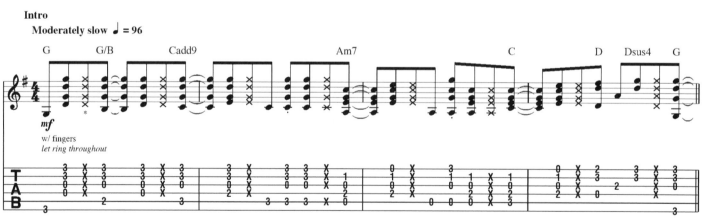

*Plant R.H. fingers forcibly onto strings, creating a percussive sound

My Girl

Performed by the Temptations

From *The Temptations Sing Smokey* (1965)

The Temptations had already made a name for themselves with a few hits under their belt — most notably "The Way You Do the Things You Do" — by the time they released *The Temptations Sing Smokey* in 1965. (And, in fact, they had already "sung Smokey" with the aforementioned hit, as well as "I'll Be in Trouble" and "Since I Lost My Baby.") But it was the #1 hit, "My Girl," that made the band superstars; it was also their signature song. The song marks the debut of a lead vocal by David Ruffin — a decision made by writer/producer Smokey Robinson after he witnessed Ruffin's solo spot on tour. The Temptations' penchant for recording Smokey compositions would continue for years to come with tracks like "Get Ready" — a collaboration surpassed only by the one with songwriter Norman Whitfield, whose pen provided (or co-provided in some instances) more hits for the band than you could shake a stick at.

Robert White of the Funk Brothers played his Gibson L5 archtop on this track to create its signature riff, which has become one of the most recognizable guitar riffs in history. The amp is most likely a Fender Deluxe or Twin. Genius in its simplicity, the riff contains five different notes (the tonic is played an octave higher as well). Put frankly, it's just an ascending C major pentatonic scale. But the rhythm, as well as the tone and the feel that White injects, turns it into one of the greatest guitar hooks of all. It's also a great example of a moveable major pentatonic pattern. These notes could very easily be played in one position (either second or fifth position), but it wouldn't sound quite the same. Although it's not shown here, note that White transposes this same lick down to first position for the IV chord, F. With this type of riff, the most important thing is remaining in the pocket, which is something White knew a thing or two about. He also reportedly used his thumb to pick all the notes, which results in a mellower tone than when playing with a pick.

My Girl

Words and Music by William "Smokey" Robinson and Ronald White

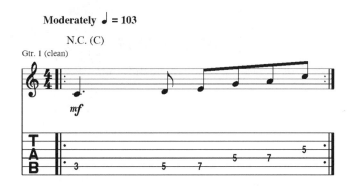

No One Knows

Performed by Queens of the Stone Age
From *Songs for the Deaf* (2002)

After the dissolution of his former band Kyuss, guitarist/singer/songwriter Josh Homme resurrected the ashes with a few members to form Queens of the Stone Age — the name an obvious homage to his affinity for stoner rock. After making a name for themselves with 1998's *Queens of the Stone Age* and 2000's *Rated R,* the band experienced their first big commercial breakthrough with *Songs for the Deaf* in 2002. It was commonplace for Homme to feature numerous guest musicians on his albums, but *Songs...* featured Dave Grohl on drums, which no doubt helped boost their profile in more ways than one. Singles "No One Knows" and "Go with the Flow" cracked the Top Ten on the Modern Rock Tracks chart, sending the album to #17 and earning the band their first gold album.

To conjure the deep, heavy feel on "No One Knows," Josh Homme and company tuned down two whole steps for a tuning of, low to high, C–F–B♭–E♭–G–C. If you want to make a habit of doing this, you should consider using a higher gauge string set than normal, because the tension on the neck is much less in C tuning than it is with standard tuning. Homme is very secretive in terms of his gear, but he often favors Ampeg tube amps, such as the high-wattage VT-22, and solidbody Ovation GP guitars, which were high-quality Les Paul replications. In the video for "No One Knows," Josh is playing a Mason Mastersound MS520, but it's unclear as to whether he used this guitar to record the song.

Although the music is written in E minor, and therefore will be referenced as such, remember that it sounds in C minor due to the slackened tuning. The main riff is a thundering, aggressive chordal hook that makes fresh use of a sus4 chord. Although sus4 chords are often used to decorate major chords (D to Dsus4 is an extremely common example), they're used less often in conjunction with minor chords the way they are here. Consequently, whereas you'd normally be able to barre the ninth fret and grab the A note on string 3 with your second finger, that fingering won't work, because you need to pull off the A note to the G note that lies on the eighth fret. Therefore, a low to high fingering of 2–3–4 is suggested for the sus4 voicing here. Remember also to notice the staccato markings throughout; they're essential for providing the riff's lumbering, heavy-handed feel.

No One Knows

Words and Music by Mark Lanegan, Josh Homme and Nick Oliveri

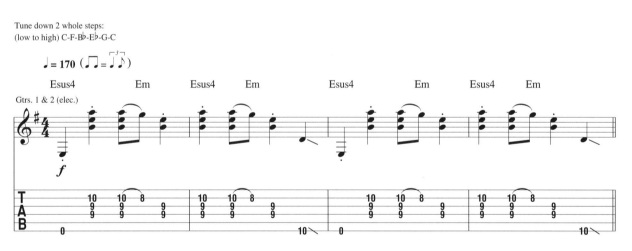

Norwegian Wood
(This Bird Has Flown)

Performed by the Beatles
From *Rubber Soul* (1965)

The Beatles entered the studio on October 18th, 1965 to begin recording sessions for what would become *Rubber Soul*. The label wanted them to have something new out for the Christmas market that year, so they recorded, mixed, and released the entire album in a little over a month and a half — not bad for an album that's #5 on *Rolling Stone* magazine's list of the Top 500 Albums of All Time. As was par for the course for the Fab Four, the album easily shot to #1 and was loaded with classics, including "In My Life," "Got to Get You Into My Life," "Norwegian Wood (This Bird Has Flown)," "Drive My Car," "Nowhere Man," and "Michelle."

Written about an affair that Lennon was having, the first two takes of the song at the October 21st recording session in 1965 were in the key of D major. Then the band decided to try it a whole step higher in E major for take three. Lennon accomplished this by simply placing a capo on fret 2 of his Gibson J-160E and playing the same exact thing. Although the chord symbol simply reads D for almost three measures (or E, when considering the sounding key), this notation is quite deceptive, because there's a whole lot more going on than simply strumming a D chord. This riff is a prime example of what I like to call the melodic strumming technique. It involves strumming mostly chords while weaving a melody into the pattern as well, which can be on top, in the middle, or on the bottom of the chord. (For another fine example of this style from the Beatles, check out "Here Comes the Sun.")

In this case, the melody starts as an inner voice with the note A (on string 3 in the D chord) and slowly moves down to become the bass voice by the end of the phrase. Notice that, although the melody moves from G at the end of measure 1 (open third string) to F♯ on string 4 at the beginning of measure 2, Lennon allows the open G string to ring through the second measure. This creates a dense minor 2nd between the F♯ and G, which ultimately becomes part of this riff's charm. It wouldn't sound nearly as interesting if he'd fretted the A note on string 3. If you've never played in this style before, it'll take a bit of getting used to, because it requires a good bit of precision in the pick hand to bring out the melody. But it's a great technique to get down, because it can really liven up a stale strumming part.

Norwegian Wood (This Bird Has Flown)
Words and Music by John Lennon and Paul McCartney

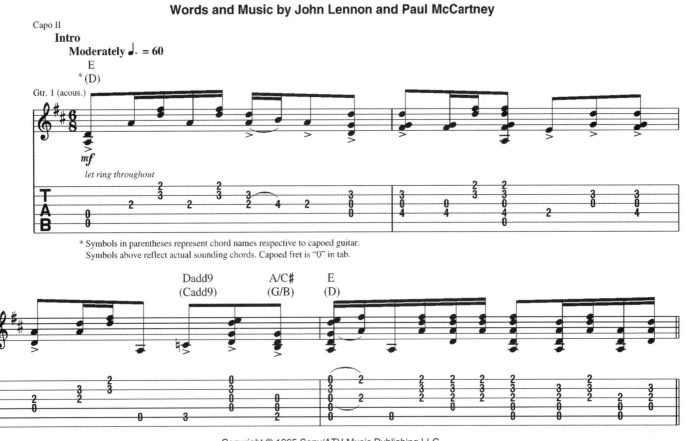

Oh, Pretty Woman

Performed by Roy Orbison
Released as a single in 1964 and included on *Orbisongs* (1966)

Roy Orbison was a hit-making machine in the early 1960s, racking up no less than 20 Top 40 hits by 1965. Highlights along the way include "Only the Lonely" (1960, #2), "Running Scared" (1961, #1), "Crying" (1961, #2), and "In Dreams" (1963, #7. "Oh, Pretty Woman," which topped the charts in 1964, would be his last huge hit — his career quickly deteriorated afterward. The late 1960s were full of tragedy for Orbison;, he lost his first wife in a car accident and his two of his three sons in a house fire.

It wasn't until the late 1980s that his career experienced a full revival, first spurred on by the prominent use of "In Dreams" in David Lynch's film *Blue Velvet.* Shortly afterward, he rerecorded many of his hits and released *In Dreams: The Greatest Hits.* He was inducted into the Nashville Songwriters Hall of Fame the same year, with Bruce Springsteen giving the induction speech. Several months later, Orbison was joined by Springsteen and several other stars, including Jackson Browne, Elvis Costello, Tom Waits, Bonnie Raitt, and T-Bone Burnett for a Los Angeles concert, which was filmed and released as *Roy Obrison and Friends: A Black and White Night.* In 1988, Orbison found himself back on top of the charts as a member of a supergroup, the Traveling Wilburys, alongside legends Jeff Lynne, Tom Petty, Bob Dylan, and George Harrison. Sadly, Orbison wouldn't be around too long to enjoy his reenergized career, because he died from a heart attack on December 6, 1988 at the age of 52.

Though three guitarists — Jerry Kennedy, Billy Sanford, and Wayne Moss — are credited with playing guitar on "Oh, Pretty Woman," it was Billy Sanford who kicked off the song with the immortal riff. The details on the gear he used are sketchy, because Sanford had just arrived in Nashville and evidently played a borrowed guitar on the track. This riff became the blueprint for countless riffs to follow, including the Beatles' "Day Tripper" and Dwight Yoakam's "Fast as You." After climbing up through an E7 arpeggio (E–G#–B–D), the riff takes an unexpected turn on top by nicking the 9th (F#) before coming back down the root and ♭7th. This inclusion of the 9th is what separates it from the typical blues bass line pattern that's heard in countless 12-bar songs. giving the riff a bit of sophistication and distancing it from the blues, though it certainly borrows heavily from the blues language.

Oh, Pretty Woman
Words and Music by Roy Orbison and Bill Dees

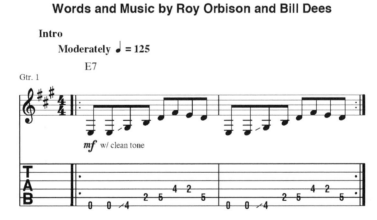

Outshined

Performed by Soundgarden
From *Badmotorfinger* (1991)

The first of the Seattle grunge giants to sign with a major label, Soundgarden would have to slug it out to achieve the worldwide success that Nirvana did in 1991. After its 1988 debut *Ultramega OK* (SST Records) got the band's foot in the door of the hard rock scene, the band signed with major label A&M for its follow-up, 1989's *Louder Than Love.* It charted at #108 and seemed an overall step in the right direction, but trouble lay ahead for the band. Bassist Hiro Yamamoto left one month before they were scheduled to tour in support of the album, and the band scrambled to find a replacement, with Jason Everman filling in. On the day the band returned from the road, Cornell's roommate, Andrew Woods (lead singer of Mother Love Bone) died from a heroin overdose. The band soldiered on and, with bassist Ben Shepherd replacing Everman, released *Badmotorfinger* in 1991, which became the commercial breakthrough they'd been looking for. Reaching #39 on the charts, it eventually went on to sell over two million copies and spawned two of the band's most well-known songs in "Rusty Cage" and "Outshined."

Most likely playing his trusty Guild S-100 (which looks like the Gibson SG) through a Mesa Boogie Dual Rectifier, Thayil opens "Outshined" with the famous, ultra-heavy riff in drop D tuning (D–A–D–G–B–E), which is doubled (if not tripled) to achieve the massive sound heard on the album. Consisting of all power chords save for one strategically-placed C note, which is treated to a thick vibrato, the riff rolls along heavy-handedly in 7/4 meter — uncommon for most bands but not so much for Soundgarden, who regularly employ odd meters like 7/4, 6/4, and 5/4 without much thought. One of the benefits of drop D tuning is that it affords the "one-finger power chord" technique, and Thayil certainly exploits that here. All the chords are derived from the D minor pentatonic scale (D–F–G–A–C), with the exception of A♭5. The root of that chord (A♭) is derived from the D blues scale, whereas its 5th (E♭) is actually the ♭2nd of the key. It's likely not intentional, but is simply a result of harmonizing the A♭ as a power chord. The tempo here is slow enough that you could move one finger around to play all the chords if you'd like, but at faster tempos, power chords played in drop D tuning are often performed by flattening out the second, third, and sometimes fourth fingers to form mini-barres, just the way the first finger often does.

Outshined

Words and Music by Chris Cornell

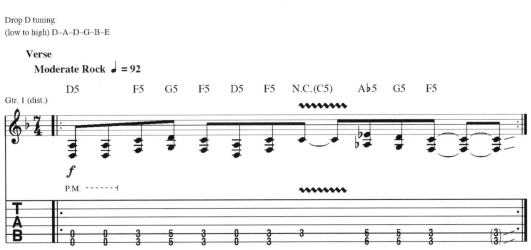

Owner of a Lonely Heart

Performed by Yes
From *90125* (1983)

After becoming one of the biggest progressive rock acts of the 1970s, Yes split in 1980 after several members decided to pursue their own interests. In 1982, Yes reformed when bassist Chris Squire and drummer Alan White joined South African guitarist Trevor Rabin (formally of Rabbit). Yes keyboardist Tony Kaye was also on board for a spell, and Trevor Horn (also a brief member of Yes in the early 1980s) was brought in as a potential vocalist, instead becoming the band's producer. Horn and Kaye clashed, and Kaye left after about 6 months of rehearsals and recording. After Squire ran into Yes vocalist Jon Anderson at a party and played him some demo tapes, Anderson jumped on board as the vocalist. At the suggestion of the label, the band renamed itself as Yes, and *90215* was released in 1983. The album was a huge comeback for the band, reaching #5 on the charts largely on the immense popularity of the #1 single, "Owner of a Lonely Heart." Because the band's sound had shifted dramatically toward pop rock and shed nearly all of its progressive tendencies, the album divided fans dramatically. It eventually went on to sell over 6 million copies and remains the band's best-selling album by far.

On "Owner of a Lonely Heart," Rabin turned to his old standby guitar at the time — a 1966 Strat that had been completely "bastardized" (in his words). All three pickups are stacked humbuckers, and the tail piece has been blocked off so there's no tremolo. He plugged into an Ampeg 120 amp, which he describes as "warm and clean," and achieved the distorted, compressed sound with mostly MXR stomp boxes, which heavily dominated his pedal board at the time. (He made famous use of the MXR Pitch Transposer as well for the solo of the song.) After a few drum hits, Rabin kicks off the tune with the song's signature power chord riff in the key of A minor. This is a prime example of using the A Dorian mode, because the riff simply walks power chords up the scale: A5–B5–C5–D5. Whereas an A natural minor mode would contain the note F, the B5 chord here contains the note F♯, which comes from A Dorian. During the second part of the phrase (measure 4), Rabin quickly jabs at G5, which cycles the riff back around again. His tone is severely compressed here and extremely trebly, which is the result of EQing the signal on the board. When the band kicks in (not shown), Rabin resorts to a more typical, full-bodied tone.

Owner of a Lonely Heart

Words and Music by Trevor Rabin, Jon Anderson, Chris Squire and Trevor Horn

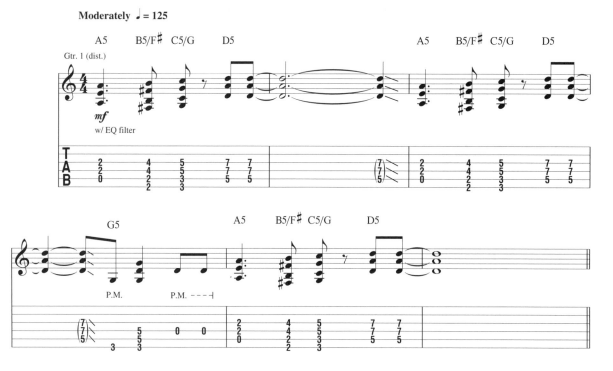

Panama

Performed by Van Halen
From *1984* (1984)

Van Halen spent the late 1970s and early 1980s becoming the biggest band in the world. Tired of fighting with producer Ted Templeman and vocalist David Lee Roth regarding the increasing prominence of synthesizers in the band's sound, Eddie Van Halen began building his own studio in his backyard after the release of *Diver Down* (1982). The new studio (named 5150) allowed him to work in relative solitude and flesh out the songs as he saw fit. Although *1984* spawned three Top 20 singles ("Jump" #1, "Panama" #13, and "I'll Wait" #13), it missed the top spot on the charts by one, peaking at #2.

Roth said he was inspired to write "Panama," which is about a car, after reading a review that stated he only wrote lyrics about sex, women, and cars and realizing that he actually hadn't ever written about a car. The song begins with one of many prototypical riffs of the 1980s. In this case, it's the alternation of dyads or triads with palm-muted pedal tone bass notes on the lower strings. This riff is one of the more adventurous of the type, because it uses more than one bass note and mixes major and minor modes — an Eddie Van Halen staple. (Riffs often used only the open E or A strings as pedal tones and stuck with the minor mode only.) Van Halen loved to play with rhythm in their riffs, and this song is a great example of that. The beginning has thrown more than a few bands off, because it begins on the "and" of beat 1. Upon first hearing the song, the listener takes several beats to get acclimated and find where the downbeat actually is. Notice also the three-against-four rhythmic pattern at work, in which the chord/bass note/bass note pattern is played in straight eighth notes, creating a highly syncopated feel.

Harmonically speaking, Eddie mixes several major triads — E, B, D, and A — in various inversions on strings 2–4 along with a few sus4 chords — Esus4 and Dsus 4 — to create an interesting harmony pattern that complements the syncopation nicely. Notice that measure 3 is essentially a repeat of measure 1, only down a whole step. He rounds off the four-measure phrase with a characteristic whammy bar dive. Ed created the smooth-yet-crunchy tone on *1984* with his custom-built Kramer (a prototype for a signature model that never came to be) running through his 1967 Marshall 1959 Plexi Super Lead. This amp was 100 watts, and Eddie lowered the voltage to 89 volts with his variac to increase the gain at lower volumes.

Panama

Words and Music by Edward Van Halen, Alex Van Halen and David Lee Roth

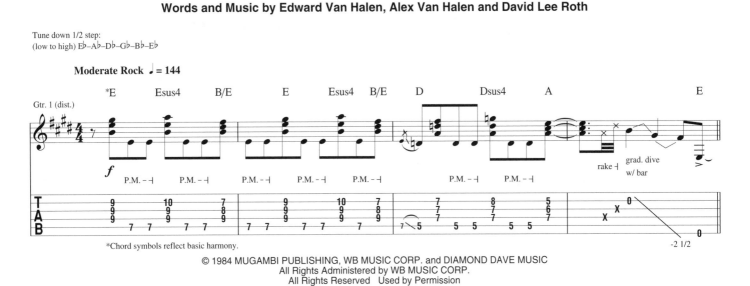

Paperback Writer

Performed by the Beatles
Released as a single in 1966

For years, EMI did their best to stave off the Beatles' ever-growing desire to experiment with unusual techniques in the studio. In 1966, the band's former engineer, Norman Smith, left to pursue music production, and the young-and-upcoming Geoff Emerick stepped in to fill the slot. Emerick had a knack for disregarding the strict polices of EMI with regards to mic placement and signal levels, and that's likely the reason he was chosen by the band as a replacement. By the time they entered the studio in 1966 to record *Revolver*, no one was going to stand in the way of their experimentation. Fortunately, the album easily shot to #1, produced a hit single ("Eleanor Rigby," #11), and is almost always placed in the top ten of any "Greatest Albums of All Time" list. During the sessions for the album, the band also recorded the single "Paperback Writer" (b/w "Rain"), which hit #1 and had the distinction of being one of the first Beatles' hit single that didn't center around a romantic relationship.

Although it's unclear who exactly played what on "Paperback Writer," McCartney claims to have played the song's famous intro riff on an Epiphone Casino through either a blackface Fender Showman (with 1x15 cab) or a Vox 7120 amp. Although photos from the session show George Harrison playing a bass, it's generally believed that McCartney went back and overdubbed the bass part heard on the record. The intro riff is classic and typical of the Beatles' style. It's built on familiar elements, like a G barre chord in this case, but they add their own unique spin. Framing within the E-form G barre shape in third position, McCartney works from the G minor pentatonic scale (though the minor 3rd is never actually played) to craft a tough, syncopated riff that kicks off the song in style. According to engineer Geoff Emerick, a great deal of the guitar sound's presence is owed to the way in which they recorded it. With a Neumann U47 tube mic about 12 to 18 inches away from the speaker, they ran the signal through a Fairchild 660 limiter en route to the console. Emerick has stated that, even if the signal is not loud enough to trigger the limiter, the fact that it's running through the Fairchild's circuitry simply does wonders for the sound.

Paperback Writer

Words and Music by John Lennon and Paul McCartney

Paranoid

Performed by Black Sabbath
From *Paranoid* (1970)

Black Sabbath are generally credited with the invention of heavy metal on their 1970 eponymous debut. Certainly, other bands had flirted with the style's aggression and subject matter, but never before had all the genre's salient traits so firmly coalesced as with *Black Sabbath.* The tones, riffs, lyrics, image, and mystique were all present from the beginning. And Black Sabbath remains the most influential heavy metal band of all time. After turning the world on its ear with their debut, the band released its masterpiece only eight months later in *Paranoid.* Although the album suffered near nonexistent airplay, it muscled its way to #12 on the backs of the singles "Iron Man" (#52) and "Paranoid" (#61), along with the now-standard among metal repertoire, "War Pigs." Tony Iommi continued to pave metal's distant future with *Masters of Reality* in 1971, which marked the beginning of his experimentation with tuning down a minor 3rd to C#. This innovation was the direct result of accidentally cutting off the tips of his second and third fingers while working in a sheet metal factory. The lower tension of the slackened strings was much easier on his prosthetic replacement finger tips.

Although Tony Iommi is one of the biggest Gibson SG proponents in the world, he actually recorded "Paranoid" with a Gibson Les Paul. In fact, this was the only song he ever recorded with a Les Paul. He ran the Les Paul through a modified Rangemaster treble boost on the way to his Laney LA 100BL amp, which had all the controls dimed except for the bass, which was set to 0. Besides the fact that Laney amps (then an upstart company) were free, Iommi used them because he was able to coax the desired tones out of them by overloading the input. The opening riff of "Paranoid" is a lesson in simplicity. Based in twelfth position, out of the E minor pentatonic box, it's composed in a question-and-answer format. The first measure contains three E5 chords in a syncopated rhythm — each time with the 5th (B) preceded by a grace-note hammer-on from the 4th (A). You'll need to barre strings 6 and 5 with your first finger for the hammer-on. The second measure "answers" this chordal "question" with an eighth note hammer-on riff that's played twice nearly verbatim — the only difference is the final note. Although this riff seems minor pentatonic in nature, the minor 3rd (G) is never actually played; only the root (E), 4th (A), 5th, (B), and ♭7th (D) tones are used.

Paranoid

Words and Music by Anthony Iommi, John Osbourne, William Ward and Terence Butler

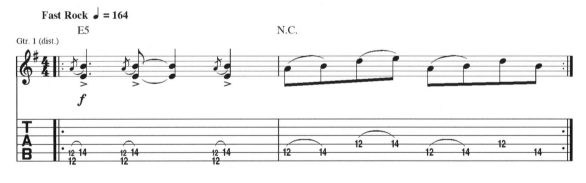

Personal Jesus

Performed by Depeche Mode

From *Violator* (1990)

Although Depeche Mode are often thought of as an all-electronic band, you realize that's not the case once you listen a bit more closely. After experiencing their worldwide commercial breakthrough with *Some Great Reward* in 1984, which hit #54 largely on the strength of the #13 hit "People Are People," the band's sound began to subtly shift with each subsequent album, becoming more layered and sophisticated. Briefly experiencing a stumble with 1986's *Black Celebration,* they began to regain their stride with *Music for the Masses* (1987, #35) and *101* (1989, #45). The band had been more popular in Great Britain than in America, but with the release of *Violator* in 1990, that distinction all but disappeared. On the strength of the massive hits "Personal Jesus" (#28), "Enjoy the Silence" (#8), and "Policy of Truth" (#15), the album soared to #7 and sold more than 3 million copies in the U.S. alone. The album was produced by Flood, the same British producer that had engineered U2's *The Joshua Tree* and co-produced Nine Inch Nails' *Pretty Hate Machine*. Although the band (and producer Flood) felt confident that they'd made a great album, none of them dreamed that it would reach the levels of success that it did.

Martin Gore most likely ran his Gretsch White Falcon direct for the recording of "Personal Jesus," possibly running through the Zoom 9030 multi-effects processor. With most Depeche Mode songs after the first few albums, the guitars play a supportive role, usually doubling a synth line or providing an additional layer in the background. In this song, guitar is more prominent than is typical for the band, and the bluesy guitar riff all but fuels the intro and verses. Firmly rooted in the F# minor pentatonic box in second position, Gore takes two notes, F# and A, and creates a swaggering, shuffling groove that wouldn't be too out of place in a blues outfit, given the appropriate tonal adjustments and a few quarter-step bends here and there. As is the case with all repetitive patterns like this, maintaining a steady groove and relaxing deep into the pocket is paramount. The effectiveness of these types of hypnotic grooves can be totally ruined by excessive rushing.

Personal Jesus

Words and Music by Martin Gore

*Composite arrangement
**Chord symbols reflect implied harmony.

Peter Gunn

Performed by Duane Eddy
From *Especially for You* (1959)

When asked by Chet Atkins how he got so commercial, Duane Eddy replied, "By not playing over their heads, Chet!" Although he didn't dazzle with lightning chops or intricate fingerstyle arrangements, Duane has all the guitar virtuosos beat in one regard; he's sold over 100 million albums, and that makes him the best selling instrumentalist of all time. As the acknowledged "master of twang," Eddy gave the instrument its first truly distinctive voice. Duane's instrumentals were a perfect marriage of sound and song.

Eddy arrived at his signature sound by taking a "what not to do" approach — specifically, he didn't want to do what the other guys were doing. So he eschewed the grinding double-stop licks of Chuck Berry and intricate fingerpicking arrangements of Chet Atkins, instead focusing on the muscular, lower range of the guitar with an emphasis on melody. Right out of the gates, Eddy scored four Top 40 hits in 1958 with his debut album, *Have Twangy Guitar – Will Travel*. He fared equally well with his follow-up, 1959's *Especially for You*, which climbed its way to #24 on the strength of its two Top 40 hits, "Yep" (#30) and "Peter Gunn" (#27). For the latter, he won a Grammy award for Best Rock Instrumental.

To create the legendary twang in those early days, Eddy relied on a 6120 Gretsch through a modified Magnatone combo amp (it had a 5" tweeter installed in addition to the standard 15" speaker). To achieve the trademark echo on early tracks like "Peter Gunn" and "Rebel Rouser," producer Lee Hazelwood fed the guitar signal into an empty 2,000 gallon water tank with a microphone at the opposite end. For "Peter Gunn," you'll need to tune *up* a half step to match the pitch of the recording. Duane begins with some Gretsch tremolo bar manipulation, depressing the bar a half step, picking the open low E string, and allowing it rise up to pitch in rhythm. It'll take a bit of practice to achieve Eddy's precision here, so don't get discouraged right away. At measure 3, he kicks into the main theme on the sixth string, adding a harmony part via overdub that's a perfect 5th higher. Essentially, it's like playing the same riff in B minor instead of E minor.

Peter Gunn
Theme Song from The Television Series
By Henry Mancini

Plush

Performed by Stone Temple Pilots
From *Core* (1992)

Though critics panned it ferociously, calling the band grunge imitators, the record-buying public quite enjoyed STP's debut, *Core* (1992), sending it to #3 and pushing it into multi-platinum status. "Plush," "Creep," "Wicked Garden," and "Sex Type Thing" all scaled the Modern Rock and Mainstream Rock charts with ease, and the band's brand of grunge-tinged stadium rock found itself all over the radio and MTV. With their follow-up, *Purple,* in 1994, the critics eased up just a bit, because the band had made a conscious effort to distance themselves from the grunge sound by infusing the songs with bits of psychedelia and British rock. The gamble worked and the album peaked at #1 and became another multi-platinum smash while amassing even more fans. *Tiny Music…Songs from the Vatican Gift Shop* continued to diversify their sound and again proved to be a commercial success, but serious troubles began in the form of vocalist Scott Weiland's heroin addiction. Weiland would continue to battle his drug demons for years to come, which made it difficult for the band to maintain a strong momentum.

Dean DeLeo makes use of many guitars for different songs, but it's a good bet that he recorded "Plush" with one of his Les Pauls. For amplification, DeLeo ran into a rare Demeter TGP-3, which is a three-channel tube guitar preamp, and a VHT classic power amp for his crunch tone. However, he blended that with a Vox AC30, which was set a bit cleaner and had a slight chorus applied via a Boss CE-3 pedal. This dual setup allows him to achieve a thick, distorted sound while still maintaining the clarity heard on the album. DeLeo often uses a similar setup when playing live. The main riff in "Plush" makes use of a few nontypical voicings for a hard rock song. Working exclusively on the top three strings, DeLeo maintains a pedal tone tonic G note on the top string throughout, varying the notes on strings 2 and 3 to imply a progression of G5–Bb°7–C6–G. Besides the common high G, the other most notable aspect is the chromatically descending line that's formed on string 2: D–Db–C–B. As if milking that idea even further, DeLeo then ascends through those notes, B–C–C#, at the end of the phrase to arrive back at the G5 for the repeat. Another hook of this riff has to do with the rhythm. The rests on beat 2 of each measure should be dead silent, so that the only thing you hear is the crack of the snare drum.

Plush

Words and Music by Scott Weiland, Dean DeLeo, Robert DeLeo and Eric Kretz

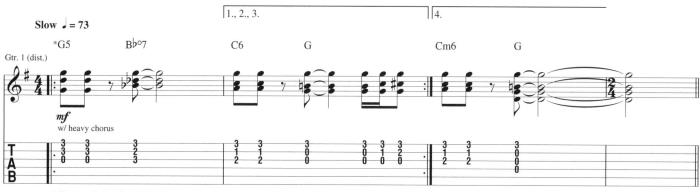

*Chord symbols reflect implied harmony.

Pride and Joy

Performed by Stevie Ray Vaughan and Double Trouble
From *Texas Flood* (1983)

With the release of Stevie Ray Vaughan's debut, *Texas Flood,* in 1983, the blues guitar world was changed forever. Never before had such authoritative chops been paired with such unbridled passion on the instrument. Stevie Ray had enormous hands, but his sound was even bigger. Backed by the deeply rooted groove of Tommy Shannon (bass) and Chris "Whipper" Layton (drums), the album made clear from the beginning that Stevie was the real deal and climbed to #38 largely due to the minor hit single "Pride and Joy," which would go on to become his signature song. Throughout the decade, he continued to stretch the boundaries of blues guitar, although he battled a drug addiction that plagued him for years. Ironically, only a year after getting clean and sober for his masterful, Grammy-winning *In Step* (1989), his life was cut tragically short in a helicopter crash in Wisconsin. *Family Style*, an album he recorded in the spring of 1990, was released in October of that same year and began a long series of posthumous releases. Vaughan was only 35 years old.

In perhaps the most famous blues guitar intro of the 1980s, Stevie Ray kicks off "Pride and Joy" unaccompanied, playing four measures of attitude-soaked blues nuggets to set the tone for the onslaught to come. First is the unison E line, which has him playing the fifth fret of string 2 along with the first string open, creating a big, fat, tonic E note. Notice, however, that he begins on the "and" of beat 1, gracing into the fifth fret from a whole step below for effect. In measure 2, he shifts up to seventh position for the "train whistle lick," which is accomplished with a dyad of G (♭3rd) and B (5th), the former being treated to a quarter-step bend. After recapping measure 1 in measure 3, Stevie beckons the band to enter with a masterfully-executed bending phrase from the open-position E blues scale. Stevie and Double Trouble recorded the *Texas Flood* album in Jackson Browne's studio over the course of three days in 1983 (although the first day consisted almost solely of setting up equipment). On hand were Stevie's "Number One" Strat, a pair of Fender Vibroverbs (he played through both, but only one was miked), and a Dumble that was borrowed from Browne. His only "effect," which can be heard during the solos on "Pride and Joy," was an Ibanez Tube Screamer.

Pride and Joy
Written by Stevie Ray Vaughan

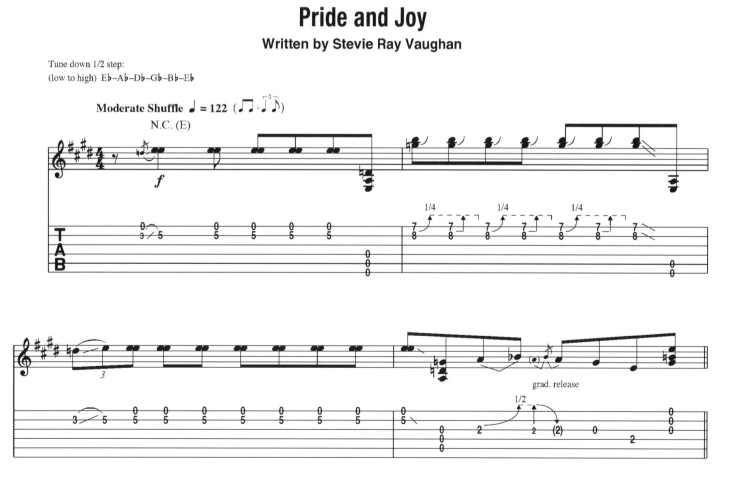

Raining Blood

Performed by Slayer
From *Reign in Blood* (1986)

After working through a fairly lackluster debut, *Show No Mercy* (1983), Slayer quickly made a name for themselves with *Hell Awaits* in 1985. Although it was still a bit rough around the edges production-wise, the complexity of material had clearly begun to take shape, and the band earned a devoted following. With their third album, however, their thrash metal vision came fully into focus. Working for the first time with producer Rick Rubin, who'd never worked with a metal band before, the band's sound became leaner, meaner, and more concentrated than ever. *Reign in Blood* (1986) clocks in at only 29 minutes, with the average song lasting little over three minutes — a far cry from the seven- and eight-minute opuses that populated the genre at the time. With no radio airplay, the album still managed to reach #94, paving the way for a successful stream of Top 40 albums that began with 1990's *Season in the Abyss* and continues to this day. But more importantly, the album is now looked at as one of the definitive, undisputed masterpieces of the genre.

Following the ominous drum intro, augmented by howling feedback and other eerie sound effects, Kerry King and Jeff Hanneman kick into the intro riff at the brisk (but not terribly brisk for Slayer) tempo of 178 bpm. Although the riff is somewhat based on an E tonal center, due to the first three chugs on the open low E string, it's entirely chromatic in nature, moving a prominent half-step motive on string 4 down fret-by-fret (B–B♭, A♯–A, A–A♭), as well as single notes on string 5 in measure 2 (F♯–F). In fact, although the band doesn't do this, if you perform the entire riff in sixth position, beginning with your second finger for the E at fret 7, the riff makes quite a nice fingering exercise. After two repetitions, the guitars split into harmony, with the higher part tracking in perfect 4ths above the main riff (not shown). While King worked his trusty B.C. Rich with EMG pickups and Hannemen his ESP or Jackson (both with EMGs), both players ran through MXR 10-band EQs en route to their Marshall JCM-800 amps with Celestion-loaded cabs. At the suggestion of producer Rick Rubin, very little reverb was added to the guitars (or any other instrument for that matter), resulting in an in-your-face sound that became the thrash metal template for years to come. Remember to tune down a half step if you want to play with the original recording.

Raining Blood

Words and Music by Jeff Hanneman and Kerry King

Rebel, Rebel

Performed by David Bowie
From *Diamond Dogs* (1974)

After ruling the glam rock world through the first few years of the 1970s and creating a virtual cult with his alter ego Ziggy Stardust, David Bowie retired his old ways with 1974's *Diamond Dogs*, briefing taking up residence in the new persona of "Halloween Jack." It resulted in a #1 album and #1 hit ("Rebel Rebel") in the UK and #5 album in the U.S., surpassing his previous achievements in the States and helping to prime America for his next venture — the R&B-fueled "plastic soul" of *Young Americans* (1975). Peaking at #9, that album contained Bowie's first #1 hit Stateside in the greasy funk of "Fame," while the uptempo, uptight rock of "Young Americans" hit #28.

Session guitarist Alan Parker, called in to help on a few tracks, played the famous "Rebel Rebel" riff on a Les Paul through a Fender amp — most likely a Deluxe Reverb, Princeton Reverb, or something similar. (Parker only says "Fender Reverb amp" in several interviews.) The fact that the tone has significant break-up tends to suggest one of the lower-wattage models. (He also specifically mentions that the amp had a single Wharfedale speaker, which rules out the Twin Reverb, Super Reverb, and Pro Reverb.) Parker recalls that Bowie came to him with about 3/4 of the riff written and stating he wanted it to have a Rolling Stones vibe. They certainly achieved that — the riff could easily pass for the Stones to the untrained ear.

The key of the song is a bit ambiguous and could be viewed as A major or E Mixolydian; both contain the same set of scale tones. The riff can basically be broken down as moving from D to E, with a quick passing A chord occurring just before the E. I tend to view this as a IV (D) and V (E) in the key of A, but others view E as the tonic and thus view the chords as ♭VII (D) and I (E). Parker voices the D as Dsus2, using the top two strings to create a descending melody of E–D. The C♯ note (string 2) of the A chord continues the descending melody and leads down to B, the inner voice of the first inversion E voicing at the end of measure 1. After a few syncopated jabs on the E triad, a descending pull-off arpeggio figure of C♯–B–G♯–E leads smoothly back to the open D string, setting up the riff's repetition.

Rebel, Rebel
Words and Music by David Bowie

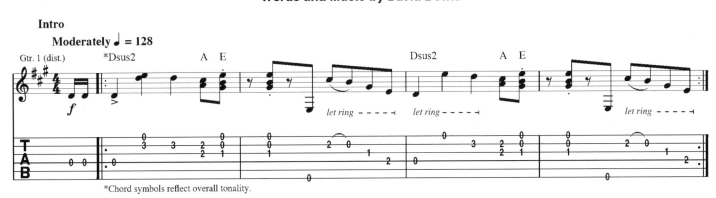

*Chord symbols reflect overall tonality.

Rebel Yell

Performed by Billy Idol
From *Rebel Yell* (1983)

Billy Idol scored a sizeable hit on his eponymous debut in 1982 with "White Wedding," thanks especially to an ultra-popular video on MTV, pushing the album to #45 and introducing the U.S. to his dance pop hard rock. It was his follow-up, however, 1983's *Rebel Yell,* that made Idol a household name. On the backs of the title track (#46), "Flesh for Fantasy" (#29), "Eyes Without a Face" (#4), and "Catch My Fall" (#50), the album screamed (yelled?) its way to #6, introducing the guitar world to the pyrotechnic guitar stylings of Steve Stevens in the process. Although Idol's next offering, *Whiplash Smile* (1987), performed admirably at #6, his reckless lifestyle began to catch up with him, and he slid slowly down the charts and out of the public's favor.

Guitarist and co-writer Steve Stevens claims that the famous intro riff, which sounds freakishly close to a synth, came as a direct result of being tired of hearing so many synths in those days. Setting out to prove that the guitar could handle those duties as well, he got rid of the pick and plucked the notes fingerstyle, emulating the simultaneous, immediate attack of a keyboard. Running his Kramer through a late 1960s Marshall plexi and vintage cabinet with 25-watt Celestions, the amp was miked with both a Shure SM57 and a Neumann U 87 to form the final composite tone. They also made use of Electric Lady studios' reverb tank on all the guitars; no digital reverbs were used at all. Stevens doubled all his rhythm parts and panned them left and right.

For the famous intro riff, Stevens barres the top two notes, A and D, which act as the ♭7th and ♭3rd of Bm7, with his pinky, using his index and ring fingers for the melody on the bottom. Again, fingerstyle technique, or hybrid picking (pick and fingers), is required to keep the parts separate and to achieve the keyboard-like attack. Don't neglect the staccato markings on the double stops; those should be kept short, while the bass melody is allowed to ring out, which aids in the distinction between the two parts. Although it's not shown, the song also famously contains Stevens' "ray gun" effect during the guitar solo, which was created with a Lexicon PCM 41.

Rebel Yell
Words and Music by Billy Idol and Steve Stevens

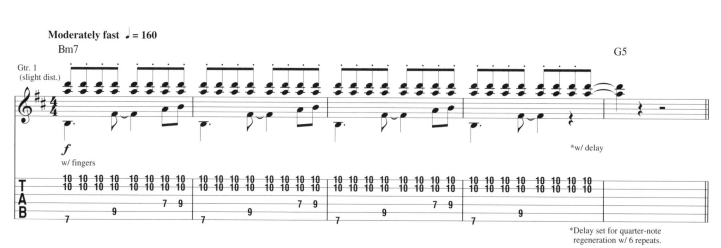

Refugee

Performed by Tom Petty & The Heartbreakers
From *Damn the Torpedoes* (1979)

After a respectable showing on *Tom Petty & The Heartbreakers* (#55), which contained some would-be staples of classic rock radio, including "American Girl" and "Breakdown," Petty and company treaded a bit of water with a follow-up two years later. *You're Gonna Get It* (1978) managed to reach #23, but much of the album felt like filler or leftovers from the stronger debut. After a business struggle with MCA records (the new owners of Shelter Records) drove Petty to bankruptcy, things were looking fairly bleak. However, that all began to change with 1979's *Damn the Torpedoes.* Containing no less than four standout classics of the Petty repertoire — "Refugee," "Here Comes My Girl," "Even the Losers," and "Don't Do Me Like That" — the album peaked at #2 and expanded the band's audience significantly.

Hard Promises followed suit in 1981, with "The Waiting" (#19) and "A Woman in Love (It's Not Me)" both charting, which sent the album to the #5 spot. The band treaded water a bit with 1982's *Long After Dark* (#9), but they were upwardly mobile once more with 1985's *Southern Accents,* which hit #7 on the strength of the huge hit and MTV staple, "Don't Come Around Here No More" (#13)).

After their first album, which was recorded entirely with Mike Campbell on a Broadcaster and Tom on a Strat through a tweed Deluxe and Fender Super Six, the Heartbreakers began their gear-collecting phase; they now own hundreds of vintage amps and guitars. Therefore, it's difficult to pinpoint specifics on every song. However, Mike Campbell most likely played "Refugee" on one of his Les Pauls through a vintage Fender — quite possibly the tweed Deluxe. The Heartbreakers are famous for their classic, half-dirty tone, and this track is dripping with it. To sound the song's main riff, which moves F#m–A5–E, Campbell mixes full chords (for F#m and E), a power chord (A5), and connective single-note phrase (F#–G#) between the F#m and A5. The effect is a memorable, yet powerful riff that's become one the band's signature moments.

Refugee

Words and Music by Tom Petty and Mike Campbell

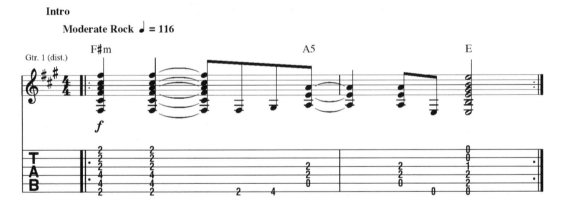

Rhiannon

Performed by Fleetwood Mac
From *Fleetwood Mac* (1977)

Fleetwood Mac's first several albums might come as a surprise. Originally under the leadership (predominantly) of British blues guitarist extraordinaire Peter Green, the band began its life as a blues band. It wasn't until after Green's departure (fueled by mental instability resulting from drug abuse), that the band began to resemble the pop icons they are. In fact, it took several albums and increasing contributions by keyboardist/vocalist Christine McVie and guitarist Bob Welch to shed the blues vestiges of the old band, with 1972's *Bare Trees* (the band's seventh album) hinting at what lay ahead. *Penguin* (1973), *Mystery to Me* (1973), and *Heroes Are Hard to Find* (1974) all made subtle progress forward, but it was the band's eleventh album, 1975's *Fleetwood Mac,* where it all changed. With the addition of the California wonder team Lindsay Buckingham and Stevie Nicks, nothing was the same for the band ever again. With three Top 20 singles in "Rhiannon" (#11), "Say You Love Me" (#11), and "Over My Head" (#20), the album shot to #1 — a position the band would soon visit again with *Rumours* in 1977.

Buckingham kicks off the classic "Rhiannon" with this unaccompanied intro lick, which is doubled on the recording and panned left and right for a wide, stereo image. Running his cream Les Paul Custom through what is probably a Hiwatt, he lets his fingers do the talking for this masterful riff in A minor. It's neatly divided into two distinct parts: the bass notes on bottom, and the double stops (dyads) on top. Very simply, the thumb plucks the bass notes, and the first and second fingers pluck the double stops. With the exception of the E/A in the middle of measure 2, the dyads are all 3rd intervals harmonized from the A minor scale. The bass notes consist of only A (measures 1 and 2) and F (measures 3 and 4), implying the Am (i)–F (♭VI) progression. Notice that Buckingham maintains a specific two-bar rhythmic pattern in the bass, even though the dyads on top change rhythms throughout. This coordination will take a while to develop if you've not messed with fingerstyle playing very much. Buckingham is one of the masters at this and has always played with his fingers, so cut yourself some slack if you don't have it down in five minutes!

Rhiannon
Words and Music by Stevie Nicks

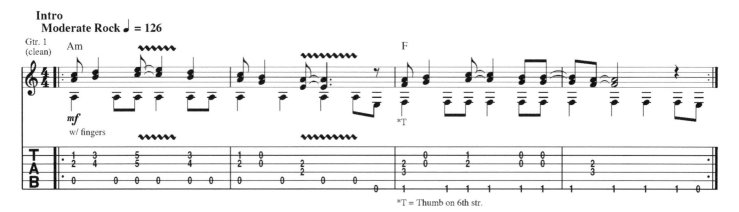

*T = Thumb on 6th str.

Rock and Roll Hoochie Koo

Performed by Rick Derringer

From *All American Boy* (1973)

Most famous for his string of hits in the 1970s, first with the Edgar Winter Group and then on his own, at that point Rick Derringer actually had already experienced a healthy dose of success in the music business. In 1965, at the tender age of seventeen, he recorded the #1 smash hit "Hang On Sloopy" with the McCoys (which featured his brother Randy on drums), and the band enjoyed another Top Ten hit with their cover of "Fever" (#7) that same year. After several years, Rick joined Johnny Winter to form Johnny Winter And, following that with stints in Edgar Winter's White Trash and the Edgar Winter Group, where he served as producer and played various instruments on *They Only Come Out at Night* (1972), *Shock Treatment* (1974), and *Jasmine Nightdreams* (1975). While still part of the Edgar Winter Group, he released his first solo album, 1973's *All American Boy.* Sporting a Top 40 hit with his version of "Rock and Roll Hoochie Koo" (the song had also been featured on the *Johnny Winter And* album in 1970), the album reached #25, but subsequent albums through the 1970s and 1980s failed to chart well.

Derringer's version of "Rock and Roll Hoochie Koo" is a bit faster and rocks a little harder than the original version with Johnny Winter, although both possess their own unique charm. The main riff shown here is basically identical in both versions, although in Winter's, the descending lick in measures 2 and 4 is occasionally harmonized for a bit of ear candy. Rick most likely played his Gibson ES335 on this track through a Marshall non-master volume model, cranking the amp enough to get some nice power tube break-up. The song is in the key of A minor, and the main riff is built upon a framework of alternating syncopated chord stabs (measures 1 and 3) with a descending lick down the A blues scale. The i, ♭III, and iv chords provide all the harmony, all voiced as power chords (A5, C5, and D5). Also notice the subtle question-and-answer technique at play here. Whereas the first blues lick (measure 2) ends on the higher octave A note (string 4, fret 7), the second one (measure 4) ends on the low octave (string 6, fret 5). It's this kind of attention to detail that can really add another layer of sophistication to a track.

Rock and Roll Hoochie Koo

Words and Music by Rick Derringer

Rock Lobster

Performed by the B-52s

From *The B-52s* (1979)

The B-52s were pretty strange when they arrived on the scene, and that's saying something when you consider what "normal" was during the new-wave era. Formed in Athens, GA, in 1976, the band recorded their first single, "Rock Lobster," for DB records two years later. The song caught on with the underground market and eventually led to a deal with Warner Bros. in 1979, who released their eponymous debut (which contained a rerecorded version of "Rock Lobster") that same year. The album charted at #59, with "Rock Lobster" hitting the #56 spot. After steadily gaining ground over the next few years, the band took a year's hiatus and reconvened for the recording of 1986's *Bouncing Off the Satellites.* During the sessions, founding member and guitarist Ricky Wilson died of AIDS-related complications, devastating the band. Grief-stricken and unsure of their direction, the band cancelled plans for a supporting tour and took an indefinite break. During this time, former drummer Keith Strickland began writing on guitar, and these new songs convinced the band to start writing again. 1989's *Cosmic Thing* proved to be their biggest success yet, reaching #4 on the charts and eventually achieving quadruple platinum sales. It remains their most successful album to date.

In one of the most classic new wave/surf/punk guitar intros of the era, Ricky Wilson kicks off "Rock Lobster" with his super catchy riff in E minor. Working exclusively from the E minor scale, he implies the chords Em, C–B with a walking bass-style phrase that moves along at the healthy clip of 178 bpm. There was nothing typical about the way Wilson played guitar. First of all, he usually played with the two middle strings removed completely, leaving a "four-string" guitar. Then, to complicate things further, he would tune his four remaining strings in all sorts of ways, depending on the song. This was all done in extremely nontechnical fashion; he wouldn't even write down the tunings.

On "Rock Lobster," Wilson played his trademark Mosrite guitar through most likely a Fender Twin reverb to attain his surf-approved tones. Note the oddball tuning shown in the music; you'll need to tune your fifth and sixth strings down a minor 3rd if you want to play along with the original. (The top strings are not used for this riff, so you can leave them where they are if you only want to play this riff.) As the tone is particularly thick sounding, it's a good bet that Wilson used thicker gauged strings than normal.

Rock Lobster

Words and Music by Kate Pierson, Fred Schneider, Keith Strickland, Cindy Wilson and Ricky Wilson

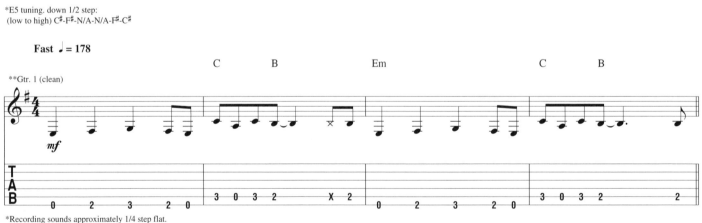

Rock You Like a Hurricane

Performed by the Scorpions
From *Love at First Sting* (1984)

One of the heavyweights of the 1980s metal scene, the Scorpions actually began life in the late 1960s and released their debut album, *Lonesome Crow,* in 1972. The musical climate was quite different at that time, and bands were usually given a good bit more time to develop a following. Through the following decade, the band did just that, all the while shuffling members (including guitarists Uli Roth and Michael Schenker along the way) before establishing their classic lineup with lead guitarist Matthias Jabs in 1978. The following album, *Lovedrive* (1979), which did contain some contributions from Michael Schenker as well, reached #55 and won the band their biggest audience yet — especially in the United States. They increased their momentum with 1980's *Animal Magnetism* ("The Zoo," "Make It Real"), but it was 1982's *Blackout* that brought them their first true taste of success. On the strength of the hit "No One Like You" (#65), the album climbed to #10 and helped poise the band for superstardom.

The band seized the opportunity with *Love at First Sting* (1984), which hit #6 and sported the band's biggest hit of the eighties in the metal anthem "Rock You Like a Hurricane" (#25) — not to mention the classic rocker "Big City Nights" and textbook power ballad "Still Loving You." After the ultra-polished *Savage Amusement* in 1988, the band stripped things down a bit more for 1990's *Crazy World,* which resulted in their highest charting single of all, "Winds of Change." Ironically, the musical winds changed soon afterward, ushering in the grunge era and effectively shutting the door on the hair metal world.

"Rock You Like a Hurricane" contains the prototypical power chord riff. It's simple, direct, and to the point — and it seriously rocks. Balanced between powerful downbeats and syncopated upbeats, the riff stutters along in a way that constantly maintains interest and forward momentum. It's in the metal-approved key of E minor, and after the initial E5 (i) in seventh position, Rudolph Schenker spends the next two measures using his Gibson Flying V and Marshall JCM800 to scale his way back up through G5 (♭III), A5 (iv), C5 (♭VI), and D5 (♭VII), en route to the E5 to start over again. Be sure to honor the rests in the music, as the intermittent silence adds power to the riff, and dig the slide down from the E5 as well.

Rock You Like a Hurricane

Words and Music by Rudolf Schenker, Klaus Meine and Herman Rarebell

Saturday Night's Alright
(For Fighting)

Performed by Elton John
From *Goodbye Yellow Brick Road* (1973)

By the time Elton John released *Goodbye Yellow Brick Road* in 1973, he was in the middle of an unprecedented stream of six #1 albums between 1972 and 1975. In retrospect, however, *Goodbye…* is widely regarded as his finest album of all. A sprawling double album of more than 76 minutes, it covers much stylistic ground and aptly demonstrates the diversity of the John/Taupin songwriting team. With two Top 20 hits — the title track (#2) and "Saturday Night's Alright for Fighting" (#12) — the album easily shot to #1, where it remained for eight weeks. It also sported several other John classics, including "Bennie and the Jets" and "Candle in the Wind," the latter becoming a #6 hit in 1987 on *Live in Australia*.

Along with the drums, guitarist Davey Johnstone kicks off one of Elton's fiercest rockers with the classic riff that's reminiscent of the Rolling Stones. In fact, it's built on Keith Richards' favorite barre chord form — stripped down to strings 4–2, which are common to standard tuning and Keith's favorite open G tuning. This barre formation is moved around to several positions, each one adorned with notes hammered-on in alteration with the core chord. Richards would normally alternate the 5th of the chord (on string 4) with the 6th, along with the 3rd on string 2 alternated with the 4th, to create an entirely different chord in inversion. Johnstone, however, instead of alternating the 5th with the 6th, alternates the root (string 3) with the 2nd. Taken in conjunction with the 4th, this creates a sus2/4 sound, which, though similar in effect, sounds quite different than the typical Richards riff. It may not be obvious at first, but when you play the two methods back to back, it's quite clear.

With his 1962 goldtop Les Paul — sounding as though it's plugged straight into the board with a fuzz pedal — Johnstone puts this riff concept through its paces at three different pitch levels in the key of G: G (I), F (♭VII), and C (IV) — typical classic rock vocabulary. Along with the slight variation with regards to rhythm, he also interjects some life into the riff with variances in articulation, mainly via the use of staccato. This adds an uptight energy to the riff that serves the song well — especially considering the subject matter.

Saturday Night's Alright (For Fighting)
Words and Music by Elton John and Bernie Taupin

Say It Ain't So

Performed by Weezer

From *Weezer* (1994)

Weezer is certainly not your typical rock band success story. Rarely has a band been so critically acclaimed and despised within such a short time (in some cases, by the same people). With the release of their eponymous debut in 1994 (retroactively named "Blue"), the band were labeled posers, and the critics did their best to write them off. But their infectious blend of power pop, 1970s arena rock, and post grunge couldn't be discounted so easily. At Weezer's core lay the intelligent hook-writing of Rivers Cuomo and skillful lyrics that at once sounded absurdly funny yet naked and sincere. After the album became a huge success, reaching #4 on the backs of "Undone (The Sweater Song)," "Buddy Holly," and "Say It Ain't So," Cuomo returned to Harvard to finish up his studies and begin writing the follow-up. The resulting *Pinkerton* (1996) became a misunderstood, forgotten gem of its day. Luckily, Cuomo didn't have to wait as long as Lou Reed did with the Velvet Underground for the fans (and critics) to come around, and the album became celebrated despite Cuomo remaining in a self-imposed exile for over a year. The rest is history, and Weezer reemerged back on top with 2001's *Weezer* ("Green"), kicking off the second and ongoing phase of their successful career.

With one of the definitive guitar intros of the 1990s, Rivers kicks off "Say It Ain't So" in glorious, understated fashion. Plugging either a 1950s Gibson Les Paul Junior or 1960s Fender Jaguar (both belonging to producer Rick Ocasek) directly into his Mesa Boogie Mark I head, which drove a tall Marshall cabinet, Cuomo creates a dynamic mix of strumming, arpeggiation, and ornamental chording to sound the i–V–♭VI–♭III progression in C♯ minor. Of note is the ultra-cool G♯add♯9 voicing, which is created by lifting the would-be first finger barre from a stand G♯ chord and allowing the open second string (B, notated here as A𝄪) to ring against the fretted B♯. In the second measure, he approaches the A barre chord form from a half step below, sliding from D♯ to the chord's 5th (E), and rounds out the two-measure phrase with a Hendrix-approved hammer-on from the E chord's 2nd (F♯) to 3rd (G♯) on string 5 beneath the B/E dyad on strings 4–3. Measures 3–4 repeat this, with the only difference being the resolution: a full, open-position E chord.

Say It Ain't So

Words and Music by Rivers Cuomo

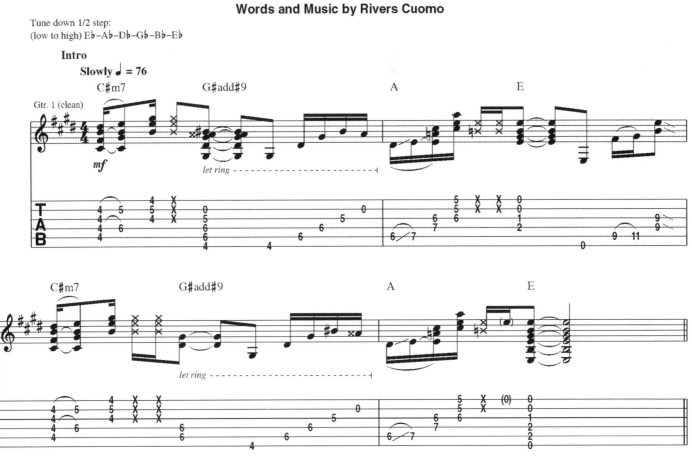

School's Out

Performed by Alice Cooper
From *School's Out* (1972)

When Vincent Furnier started his professional music career in the late 1960s, his band was called Alive Cooper. After two albums with disappointing sales, the band recruited new producer Bob Ezrin for 1971's *Love It to Death.* The move paid off big-time: the album reached #35 and catapulted Alice Cooper to the mainstream, thanks to the classics, "I'm Eighteen" and "Is It My Body." They increased their stature further with *Killer* (#21), released later that same year, but it was the follow-up, 1972's *School's Out,* that truly sent the band to the big leagues. Largely due to the #7 title track hit, the album peaked at #2, while the song's timeless message resounded across the country like wildfire. The band continued their streak with 1973's #1 *Billion Dollar Babies,* which contained the favorites "Elected" and "No More Mr. Nice Guy."

Vincent Furnier of the band Alice Cooper gave way to Alice Cooper the solo artist. After a promising start with *Welcome to My Nightmare* (1975) hitting #5 and *Goes to Hell* (1976) reaching #27, Cooper began to hit a dry spell with 1977's *Lace and Whiskey* that lasted over ten years, thanks to substance abuse battles and changing musical trends. After teaming up with producer/co-writer Desmond Child for 1989's *Trash,* however, he found himself back on top with a hit record (#20) and a Top Ten single in "Poison" (#7).

"School's Out" is about rebellion in its purest sense, and so it's fitting that the riff is straightforward and sleazy. In the key of E, Glen Buxton and Michael Bruce, both sporting Gibson SG customs and Marshalls, play out of the twelfth-position E box shape to frame the riff. As much blues rock as it is metal, it alternates lower register E5 chords on strings 6–5 with barred A and G triads on strings 4–2. After a measure and a half, a bluesy G note is sustained with vibrato, which is followed by a chromatically descending pull-off (E–E♭–D) triplet to cap the phrase. For the A chord, you'll likely need to lay your third finger flat to create the barre, which is necessary due to fretting of the E5 chord just prior.

School's Out
Words and Music by Alice Cooper and Michael Bruce

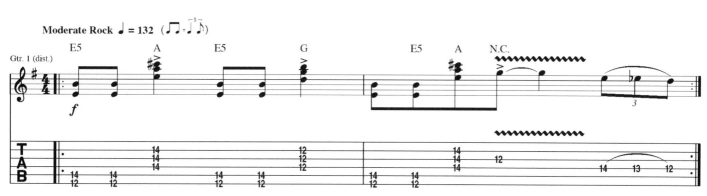

Secret Agent Man

Performed by Johnny Rivers

From ...And I Know You Wanna Dance (1966)

After relatively non-lucrative stints in Baton Rouge and Nashville as a songwriter and demo singer, Johnny Rivers' fate began to change when, in 1960 at age 18, he met fellow Louisianan James Burton. Burton was playing guitar with Ricky Nelson at the time. At Burton's suggestion, Nelson recorded one of Rivers' songs, which led Rivers to Los Angeles. There he found sporadic work as a songwriter and studio musician until 1963, when he filled in for a jazz combo at a night club. The temporary gig became a full-time one, which helped raise his profile. That same year, he was approached to record a theme song for a new television series called "Danger Man." The resulting single, "Secret Agent Man," became a #3 hit and sold over a million copies.

The next year, Rivers signed a one-year contract to open a new nightclub called the Whisky A Go Go on Sunset Strip. This resulted in a string of successful live albums recorded at the club, beginning with *Johnny Rivers Live at the Whisky A Go Go* in 1964, which reached #12 on the strength of his cover of Chuck Berry's "Memphis" (#2). In 1966, he recorded his only #1 hit, "Poor Side of Town," which signaled a change of direction to a mellower, soulful style. Rivers continued to record and tour throughout the years with varying levels of success, although he never matched his mid-1960s popularity.

With an all-Gibson lineup — his classic black 335 and a Les Paul GA-40 amp — Johnny starts "Secret Agent Man" with the immediately recognizable intro riff. Using the tonic high E string as a pedal tone, he slowly slithers up and down the G string for the chromatic B–C–C♯–C melody, ringing the open E string in between each note. Several devices are employed throughout to add character, including rhythmic syncopation (the C note is anticipated on the upbeat each time) and half-step grace-note slides from note to note on the G string. If you arrange the picking so that you're always picking an upstroke on the high E string, you'll probably make it easier on yourself!

Secret Agent Man

from the Television Series

Words and Music by P.F. Sloan and Steve Barri

Seventeen

Performed by Winger
From *Winger* (1988)

Winger were a bit more experimental compared to other heavy metal acts of the day, with a sound falling somewhere between Van Halen and Extreme. And much like Extreme, Winger showed up fairly late to the commercial reign of heavy metal. Perhaps this also accounts for the band's more adventurous nature; the same old C5–D5–E5 (or F5–G5–A5 for the A minor version, if you prefer) chord progressions were getting a bit stale by the late 1990s. Of course, Kip Winger also assembled a band of predominantly studio musicians, which generally means a high level of musicianship. The format certainly worked and the band found platinum success right out of the gate with their self-titled debut in 1988. Boasting two Top 40 singles in the Van Halen-esque "Seventeen" (#26) and the power ballad (though much more sophisticated than most) "Headed for a Heartache," *Winger* reached #21, making the band a household name and introducing the world to the newest guitar hero on the block: Reb Beach.

Back in those early days, Reb was a Kramer endorsee, tracking most of the first album with his Pacer, which was clearly seen on many guitar magazine covers of the day. And although he was also often seen endorsing Kitty Hawk amps and preamps, he claims that he never did make use of them in the studio. He ran through their preamps for live shows early on, but that was the extent of it. When recording *Winger*, he used rented Marshall 100 watt amps with 4x12 cabinets. Everything was recorded completely dry, with any echo or reverb added during mixdown via an Eventide or Lexicon unit.

After a syncopated ensemble hit, Reb kicks off the band's signature song unaccompanied for the first two measures. The riff is extremely reminiscent of Van Halen's "Panama," making use of triads on strings 4–2 that are embellished with suspended 4ths, 2nds, and the like. Although Reb makes it sound so, it's certainly not an easy riff to play with the level of precision he displays. You may have to experiment with picking directions to find something that works best for you. The syncopated three-over-four figure on beat 3 of measure 4 is a case in point. Reb's tone, although distorted, is not insanely distorted. This allows the notes to speak clearly and prevents it all from turning to mush. The double-tracking of the part adds to the bigness of the sound on the recording. And, also like Van Halen, the band is tuned down a half step, so be sure to do that when you're ready to play along.

Seventeen
Words and Music by Kip Winger, Reb Beach and Beau Hill

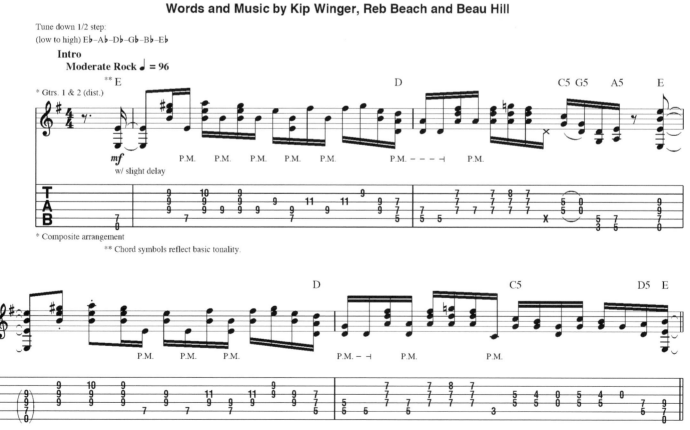

Shine

Performed by Collective Soul
From *Hints, Allegations, and Things Left Unsaid* (1994)

With their debut album in 1994, *Hints, Allegations, and Things Left Unsaid,* Georgia-based Collective Soul surfaced after the first wave of the great grunge takeover. Although they borrowed freely from the grunge sound and aesthetic, their southern-tinged sound had as much in common with Hootie & The Blowfish, filling a unique niche at the time. Based almost solely on the success of the #11 hit "Shine," the album, which was actually meant to be a demo, became a hit as well, reaching #15. The band considered the follow-up, the eponymous *Collective Soul* from 1995, to be their proper debut. Boasting the hit singles "December" and "The World I Know," it became the band's biggest album, selling over 8 million copies worldwide.

Working with his trusty Paul Reed Smith and a Sansamp, Ross Childress kicks off "Shine" with one of the most recognizable guitar riffs of the 1990s. For a riff so recognizable, it's misquoted on nearly every tab site on the internet. Most assume that Childress is in Drop D tuning down a half step — or, Drop D♭/C♯ tuning, if you prefer: D♭–A♭–D♭–G♭–B♭–E♭. This is actually the way he played the song live most often. However, if you listen closely to the recording, you'll hear a telltale sign that disproves this tuning. Near the end of measure 1, you'll hear a few A notes — a 5th above the open D string. There's not enough time for him to slide down to the A and back up to the D smoothly, and the D string is clearly ringing along with it, so that leaves two options. It's either played on the 12th fret of the A string, or he tunes the A string up a whole step and thus fingers the entire phrase two frets lower than what seems natural at first. Considering how the rest of the riff is all played on the D and G strings, the first option doesn't seem likely. So the tuning of D♭–A♭–D♭–A♭–B♭–E♭ is most logical. (Note that this was most likely just done in the studio for that main riff.)

Childress uses the D string throughout measures 1 and 2 as a pedal tone beneath the D major pentatonic melody played on the G string. Because the tempo is relatively slow, all downstrokes can be easily executed and will help to achieve the proper tone. In measure 3, he alternates the G/C dyad on strings 4–3 in syncopated rhythms against the open D string, and the same approach is applied to the D/G dyad in measure 4. Note that these 4th dyads are played differently than normal, again due to the unusual tuning.

Shine

Words and Music by Ed Roland

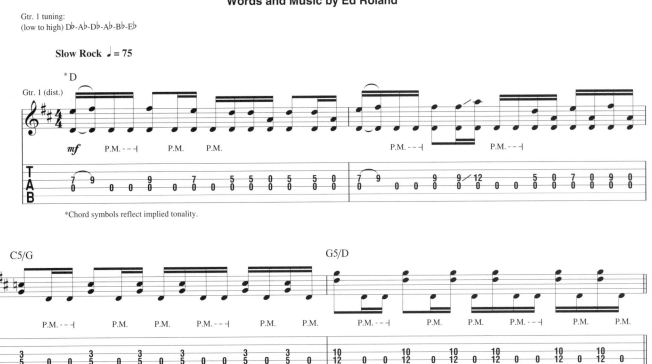

Gtr. 1 tuning:
(low to high) D♭-A♭-D♭-A♭-B♭-E♭

Slow Rock ♩ = 75

*Chord symbols reflect implied tonality.

Silent Lucidity

Performed by Queensrÿche
From *Empire* (1990)

After slugging it out on the metal scene for a good five years, Queensrÿche broke through with their sprawling concept album *Operation: Mindcrime.* The videos for singles "I Don't Believe in Love" and "Eyes of a Stranger" both received considerable airplay on MTV, helping to push the album to #50 on the charts. The album also helped establish the band's prog metal sound, which owed more to Pink Floyd than it did Van Halen. Capitalizing on their newfound clout, the band shifted to a slightly more mainstream approach for the follow-up, 1990's *Empire,* focusing on more succinct songs and arrangements with more universally appealing themes. The new direction worked on all levels, and album hit #7 largely on the strength of the acoustic-driven, Pink Floyd-esque power ballad "Silent Lucidity" (#9).

Working with an inexpensive nylon string, songwriter Chris DeGarmo begins the song with an arpeggiated riff played fingerstyle. The basic harmonic structure is G for two measures and Em for two measures, but much is done to dress it up a bit. Using the open B string as a drone throughout, Chris moves between G and Gadd9 chords by alternating between B and A notes on string 1 atop the open B string and G note on fret 5, string 4. For measures 3–4, he uses a similar method — that of alternating two top notes against two lower ones — but the low E on string 4 is the only common tone here. With F♯ and the open B string in beats 1–2, an Esus2 sound is created, giving way in the second half of the measure to D and G, which creates an Em7 tonality.

However, the rhythm is the trickiest factor of this riff. After an initial eighth note on the low G (or E) note, a three-note pattern begins that repeatedly cycles through strings 1, 2, and 3 in steady sixteenth notes. The result is a highly syncopated phrase that constantly places accents on different parts of the beat. As if this weren't enough, DeGarmo drops what would normally be the last 16th note of the measure — the open B string — resulting in the formidable time signature of 15/16! To top that, he changes to 4/4 for the final measure in anticipation of the vocal's entrance. In fact, the meters continually shift back and forth throughout the verses of the song!

Silent Lucidity

Words and Music by Chris DeGarmo

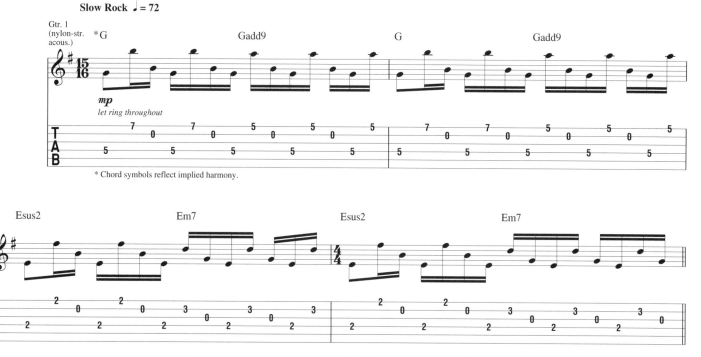

Since You've Been Gone

Performed by Rainbow
From *Down to Earth* (1979)

After quitting Deep Purple in 1975, Ritchie Blackmore started over by drafting vocalist Ronnie James Dio and most of the latter's band, Elf, to form Ritchie Blackmore's Rainbow. The band released its eponymous debut in 1975, which contained one of early metal's classics in "Man on the Silver Mountain," helping to push the album up to #30 on the Billboard charts. The personnel shuffled often, but Blackmore and Dio remained at the head of the table for the next several albums. Their brief, six-song sophomore album, *Rising* (1976), reached #48 and featured a completely new rhythm section. *Long Live Rock 'n' Roll* (1978) continued to boost the band's profile, especially in America, and Blackmore decided to make a play for a more commercially-directed approach on the following album. Dio, however, was not at all interested in such a move, and he quit the band to fill the lead singer void in Black Sabbath created by Ozzy's departure.

With the exit of Dio and after hiring of Graham Bonnet on vocals, Blackmore took the opportunity to set the band on a new course stylistically. The fantastical lyrics and themes (largely due to Dio) were almost gone, as were most of the neo-classical turns, and the sound had shifted into a more commercial direction. The move paid off in the commercial sense and "Since You've Been Gone" hit #57, and the album climbed to #66. Bonnett's tenure in the band was short-lived, though, and Joe Lynn Turner was brought in as frontman for 1981's *Difficult to Cure,* where he remained for the next two albums — practically a lifetime for a Blackmore's band mate.

"Since You've Been Gone" begins with Blackmore's unaccompanied Strat and the song's signature chordal riff. Blasting through his modified 200 watt Marshall, he states the I–V–vi–IV (G5–D–Em–C) progression in G clearly and plainly using common barre chord shapes and an open G5 voicing. Blackmore's trademark style seems to be largely absent in this song, save for the short-but-sweet melodic solo in the middle (not shown).

Since You've Been Gone
Words and Music by Russell Ballard

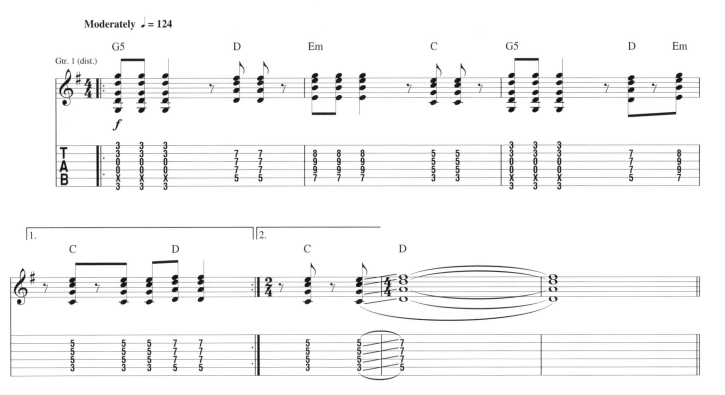

Slow Ride

Performed by Foghat
From *Fool for the City* (1975)

Foghat thrived at a time when their brand of blues-based hard rock wasn't particularly in vogue: the disco era. Wide-sweeping as disco was, there was a backlash against the scene — a counter-culture that united under the "disco sucks" refrain. Folks with that attitude focused their attention instead on bands like Led Zeppelin, Kiss, Foghat, and the like. Known in some circles as "the hardest working band in show business" (as opposed to James Brown, the acknowledged "hardest working *man*"), Foghat owed their success to relentless touring and a willingness to put in whatever work necessary to build upon their growing reputation.

After the dissolution of Savoy Brown in the early 1970s, vocalist and rhythm guitarist Dave Peverett assembled the band from several common members, and they released their eponymous debut in 1972. Scoring a minor hit with their remake of Willie Dixon's "I Just Want to Make Love to You," *Foghat* reached #67 and established their name in the world of arena rock. After making steady progress and tirelessly winning fans over the course of their next three releases, their ship came in with 1975's *Fool for the City*. On the strength of the title track, which just missed the Top 40, and the radio staple (and Foghat signature song-to-be) "Slow Ride," the album reached #23 on the charts and achieved gold sales, firmly entrenching them as major players in the rock world.

After the intro establishes the groove and key center of A, "Slow Ride" settles into its main hook, the chorus, which is driven by Peverett's famous riff. Considering that Peverett has spoken in interviews of his reverence for John Lee Hooker, the inspiration for this riff should come as no surprise. Aside from the heavier tone, achieved via his Les Paul Jr. and Marshall amp (or possibly Hiwatt), the classic riff sounds much like a slowed-down version of the typical Hooker boogie. Of course, the Hooker M.O. had already been given an update by ZZ Top on "La Grange" in 1973, in which it still appeared as a speedy boogie. But the Foghat version is straightened out to sound much closer to rock than blues. The entire riff can be played comfortably in second position, with the pinky handling the D notes, the second finger grabbing the C notes, and the first finger barring for the A5 chords. Take special notice of the rests, and don't neglect them. They help interject some breath into the riff and help give it more rhythmic propulsion.

Slow Ride
Words and Music by Lonesome Dave Peverett

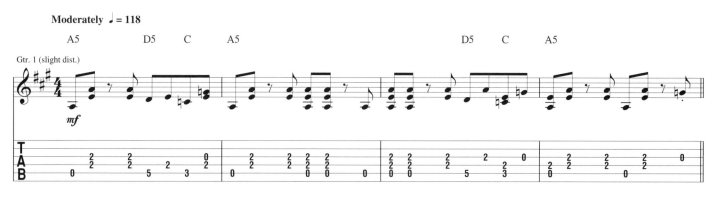

Smells Like Teen Spirit

Performed by Nirvana
From *Nevermind* (1991)

Every generation has its anthems, and the 1990s had "Smells Like Teen Spirit." With this one song, the title of which was taken from graffiti spray painted on Kurt's wall by a friend ("Kurt smells like Teen Spirit"), Nirvana drove the nails into the coffin of hair metal, ushering in the era of grunge and legitimizing its salability. Although they already had another album with Sub Pop under their belt in 1989's *Bleach,* their major label debut, *Nevermind* (1991), introduced most of the world to the band, which made their success seem much more dramatic. Geffen had originally hoped for the album to sell 250,000 copies, but it was outselling that number every week by the time it hit its stride a few months after its release. Not since Jimi Hendrix has an artist or band impacted the music world so indelibly with so little output.

Wielding most likely his Fender Mustang through a Mesa Boogie .22 Caliber amp, Kurt kicks off the biggest album of the 1990s with one of the decade's most recognizable guitar riffs. In stark contrast to the reverb-drenched, chorused-out guitar sounds that ruled the latter half of the 1980s, "Smells Like Teen Spirit" begins with a single, dry, fairly clean guitar scratching out the chords in 16th-note rhythm amid muted dead strums and incidental (yet intentional) open-string strums.

There are several interesting things about this riff, which is an otherwise i–iv–♭III–♭VI progression in F minor. The muted dead strums play just as much of a role as the actual notes do, and the riff would lose a great deal of its appeal without them. There's also a lazy, apathetic sense to the performance (fitting the song's message to a "T") that lends a certain appeal all on its own. The open strings shown at the end of each measure are simply the result of making very little effort to smoothly change from chord to chord. The hand is somewhat cumbersomely lifted off one chord to fret another, yet this is by no means an accident; it's a very real part of the sound that Kurt could have easily left out if he wanted. Also of interest are the sus4 chords: Fsus4 and A♭sus4. Whether these were included deliberately is unclear. Kurt fretted his power chords by flattening his third finger for the 5th and octave notes (strings 5 and 4, respectively, in this case). If you're not careful with this, or if you're perhaps under the influence of something, the third finger can also fret the third string, creating a sus4 chord. It certainly sounds cool, but it doesn't necessarily sound 100 percent intentional. At any rate, this sound is on the record, and the song doesn't sound quite the same with just power chords.

Smells Like Teen Spirit

Words and Music by Kurt Cobain, Chris Novoselic and Dave Grohl

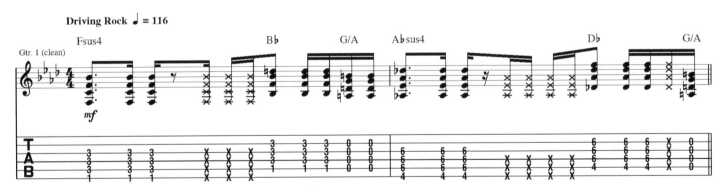

Smoke on the Water

Performed by Deep Purple
From *Machine Head* (1972)

Along with Black Sabbath and a precious other few, Deep Purple are rightfully credited with helping to shape what would become heavy metal in the decade following their debut. *Shades of Deep Purple,* released in 1968 (and predating Black Sabbath's eponymous debut by nearly two years) found success immediately, with the hit "Hush" (#4) helping to propel the album to #24. Subsequent releases, however, found the band shifting members and seemingly searching for an identity, evidenced most clearly by 1969's *Concerto for Group and Orchestra* — largely the pet project of keyboardist Jon Lord. Before too long, though, the band began to settle on its unique brand of heavy rock, drawing at times from both blues and classical influences. By 1971's *Fireball* (#32), the band had fully found its footing and was primed for their best work.

Machine Head (1972) delivered on this promise in a big way. On the strength of the opening track, "Highway Star," and the #4 anthem-to-be, "Smoke on the Water," the album reached #7 and made the band undisputed stars. In a well-known tale, "Smoke on the Water" actually tells the story of the band's experience during the Montreux Jazz Festival of 1971. While Deep Purple was recording at the entertainment complex of the Montreux Casino using the rented Rolling Stones Mobile Studio, someone shot a flare gun at the ceiling of the casino's theater during a Frank Zappa and the Mothers of Invention concert. The Deep Purple members watched the smoke from the resulting fire traveling across the neighboring Lake Geneva, prompting bassist Roger Glover to dream up the title line.

With quite possibly the most immortal of all rock guitar riffs, Blackmore opens "Smoke on the Water" unaccompanied on his Strat through his cherished, cranked Vox AC30. Firmly entrenched atop the "first five riffs you learn on guitar" list, its elegance lies in its simplicity. Working from the G blues scale, Blackmore harmonizes a line in 4ths throughout, mixing staccato and sustained articulation and alternating between downbeats and syncopated upbeats. Note that all the notes stem from the G blues scale save for the A♭ used to harmonize the D♭ note. This particular note is the ♭2nd in the key of G, which no doubt adds a sinister edge to the tonality. Although numerous tab sites show this riff being played entirely on strings 5 and 4 (as Tony Iommi may have played it, perhaps), Blackmore remains in third position in several live videos.

Smoke on the Water

Words and Music by Ritchie Blackmore, Ian Gillan, Roger Glover, Jon Lord and Ian Paice

Song 2

Performed by Blur
From *Blur* (1997)

Although Blur's debut (*Leisure,* 1991) fixed them clearly in the shoegaze pop world, they didn't stay there long. After the Seattle grunge explosion reached across the pond, several British bands began to rethink things, including Blur. For 1993's *Modern Life Is Rubbish,* the band retooled their sonic arsenal and produced a Brit pop album more reminiscent of the Kinks than My Bloody Valentine. They further explored this direction with *Parklife* (1994) and *The Great Escape* (1995), eventually realizing that they'd reached the end of the tunnel. Rival band Oasis had breached the pond and found great commercial success in the U.S., and Blur were becoming known as a second-class act in this regard.

Although the band were certified superstars in England by this point (and largely unknown in America still), creative tensions within the band were apparent, and they nearly broke up as a result. But great chaos and turmoil can create great art, and the band emerged in 1997 with *Blur.* With a newfound spirit and lust for exciting sounds, the album reflected the influence of American indie bands like Pavement. Not surprisingly, the shift in sound coincided with their first real dent in the American music scene. "Song 2" became a hit on the Modern Rock Tracks chart, reaching #6, and the album climbed to #61 on the Billboard 200.

"Song 2" is 2 minutes and 2 seconds long, has two verses, two choruses, and two bridges. Allegedly meant to be a parody of American grunge music, it was ironically embraced by the grunge audience. Guitarist Graham Coxon said in interviews, with regards to the *Blur* album, that he wanted to make music that would scare people. This is certainly what the band were aiming for with "Song 2." Coxon kicks off the song unaccompanied with the signature riff. The tone is dry and clean (yet a bit gritty), and the riff is built upon nothing but the sliding power chords notes of the F minor pentatonic scale: F5–E♭5–A♭5–B♭5–C5. He makes use of his trademark Telecaster and Marshall combo to achieve the sound and adds a few percussive dead strums to provide extra attitude. All things considered, the effect is quite similar to that of Nirvana's "Smells Like Teen Spirit," especially considering the full-blown eruption that occurs after the riff is played twice.

Song 2
Words and Music by Damon Albarn, Steven Alexander James,
Graham Coxon and David Rowntree

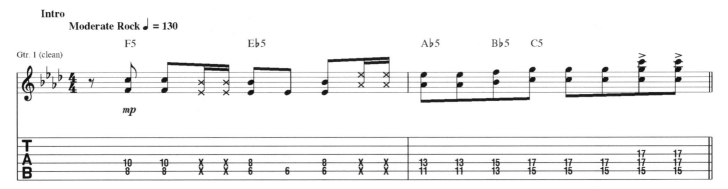

Space Truckin'

Performed by Deep Purple

From *Machine Head* (1972)

Machine Head is commonly agreed upon as Deep Purple's crowning achievement, and for good reason. Sure, it contains "Smoke on the Water," which is undoubtedly the band's signature song and by itself cements their place in rock history. But the album also represents the band at its most cohesive. Their brand of classical-tinged blues rock was never more potent, evidenced particularly in the extended solos by organist Jon Lord and guitarist Ritchie Blackmore on "Highway Star." Few bands possessed the chops to do what they did at that time, and it all coalesced perfectly on *Machine Head.* Thanks mainly to "Smoke on the Water," the album topped the U.K. charts and reached #7 in the U.S. The band certainly flirted with greatness at other times, including *Shades of Deep Purple* in 1968 (with "Hush"), *Deep Purple* in 1969 ("Bird Has Flown"), and *Burn* in 1974 (introducing David Coverdale on vocals), but never before or since has everything clicked into place as thoroughly as on *Machine Head.*

Blackmore has claimed that the main riff of "Space Truckin'" (shown here) was influenced by the Batman theme. Clearly, the common theme between the two lies in the chromatic nature of the riffs. With his Strat running through his Aiwa reel-to-reel tape recorder as a preamp boost en route to his cranked AC30, Blackmore joins keyboardist Jon Lord in a unison statement of this spiraling, chromatic riff. Framed within the A minor pentatonic box, Blackmore connects the constellation dots of the minor pentatonic shape on strings 6 and 5 with all the notes in between, resulting in the demented-sounding "scale" of A–B♭–B–C–D–E♭–E. In the riff, of course, this is presented in descending fashion (after the initial low tonic A note), which sounds like the audio equivalent of spiraling out of control and being plunged into the depths of a black hole. After four repetitions, the same exact riff is transposed down a 4th to E, where it sounds verbatim three times. To transition back to the home key of A, Blackmore and Lord walk chromatically up E–F–F♯–G in quarter notes as the spaceship is righted once again. Note that, if sped up and played all in fifth position with one-finger-per-fret, measure 1 makes quite a nice fingering exercise.

Space Truckin'

Words and Music by Ritchie Blackmore, Ian Gillan, Roger Glover, Jon Lord and Ian Paice

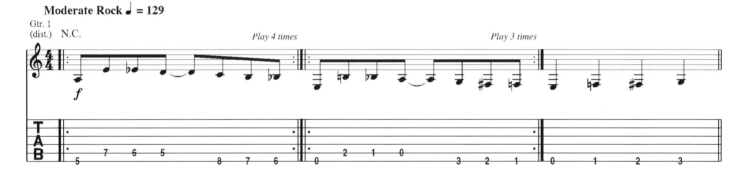

Spoonman

Performed by Soundgarden
From *Superunknown* (1994)

After being the first Seattle giant to sign with a major label in 1990, Soundgarden's powerful *Badmotorfinger* album (1991) got temporarily lost in the debris after the monumental explosion of Nirvana's *Nevermind* and Pearl Jam's *Ten*. Rather than get bitter, however, the band collected themselves, took their time, and delivered their tour de force, *Superunknown,* in 1994. By the time of its release, grunge had fully taken over the airwaves, and the novelty had worn off, meaning that just any lackluster album wasn't going to cut it. Luckily, their sound had expanded dramatically, with a newfound emphasis on harmonies and melody. A fair number of the band's trademark sludgy riffs were included, but they also branched out into Beatles-esque psychedelic pop with "Black Hole Sun" and understated dark pop rock in "Fell on Black Days," the latter of which can only be described as sounding like Soundgarden. The result was a #1 album and the band's crowning achievement.

One link to the Soundgarden of old was "Spoonman," which sounds a bit like a rewrite of *Badmotorfinger's* "Outshined." Although originally composed by Chris Cornell for the soundtrack to the 1992 film *Singles* (an acoustic version can be heard in the movie), the band thought the tune had more potential and began working on an electric version for their upcoming album. Inspired by a Seattle street musician known as Artis the Spoonman, the track features pots, pans, and spoons, the latter performed by Artis himself.

Working with his Guild S-100, drop D tuning, and a Mesa Boogie Dual Rectifier, Kim Thayil pounds out the song's signature riff in the odd (though not so much for Soundgarden) meter of 7/4. As is most often the case in drop D tuning, the riff is in D; what's less common is that very few open D5 power chords are used, relatively speaking. The one-fingered power chord afforded by drop D tuning is on full display here — hammered-on and slid around the entire range of the first 12 frets. The roots of all the chords here can be found within the D minor pentatonic scale (D–F–G–A–C), which is a little tame for the band's usual harmonic vocabulary, but the rhythms are syncopated in typical Soundgarden fashion, which lends a staggering, tripped-up feel to the proceedings as the chords wind their way down from fret 12 to open position. If the rhythms trip you up, slow the tempo down and set a metronome to eighth notes, working out the difficult bits until it feels natural. Playing in odd meters takes practice.

Spoonman
Words and Music by Chris Cornell

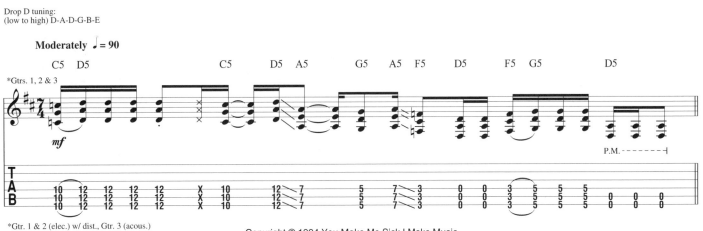

Start Me Up

Performed by the Rolling Stones
From *Tattoo You* (1981)

Although *Tattoo You* is often described as the Stones's last great album, it was hardly a collaborative effort on the band's part. Mick Jagger and Keith Richards were hardly speaking to each other at the time, so it wasn't a great time for the lads to hunker down in the studio for weeks on end. When the label began pressing for a new album, producer Chris Kimsey suggested assembling the album from the mass of unused tracks recorded over the years. For instance, "Start Me Up" had actually begun life as a reggae-tinged song recorded in 1975 for the *Black and Blue* album. It resurfaced for the *Some Girls* (1978) sessions (as well as the *Emotional Rescue* sessions in 1979), where it was given a more standard, rock 'n' roll treatment. It was the *Some Girls* version that was plucked for *Tattoo You,* to which Mick added his vocals. What did the band get for its trouble? Only a #1 album and three Top 40 hits in "Hang Fire" (#20), "Waiting on a Friend" (#13), and "Start Me Up" (#2).

Keith Richards "starts it up" with his timeless riff in F, making use of his tried-and-true five-string open G approach on his trusty Telecaster through a Mesa Boogie Mark I amp. The riff makes use of Richards' classic barre chord technique in which he alternates a one-fingered barre chord — C in this case — with another by adding the second and third fingers on strings 4 and 2, respectively, within a one-finger-per-fret position. The resulting second chord is Fadd9/C. Although many Stones riffs can be copied fairly well in standard tuning by way of some adjusted positioning, this particular voicing can not be (without a capo, at least). It's a subtle touch, but it's always a dead ringer for open G tuning.

After alternating between the C (V) and F (I) chords for two measures, Keith shifts down two frets to play off the B♭ barre chord at fret 3. Instead of strumming all five strings, however, he works only off of the bottom three (that's strings 5–3, remember?), alternating B♭5 with B♭6 in an open G variation on the standard Chuck Berry 5th-6th boogie pattern. Whereas measures 1 and 2 are filled with dramatic rests and full-sounding chords, measures 3 and 4 are by contrast softer, more compact, and rhythmically churning. It's this constant fluctuation between the two that gives this riff its perpetual momentum, once again affirming Keith's genius in the realm of rhythm guitar.

Start Me Up
Words and Music by Mick Jagger and Keith Richards

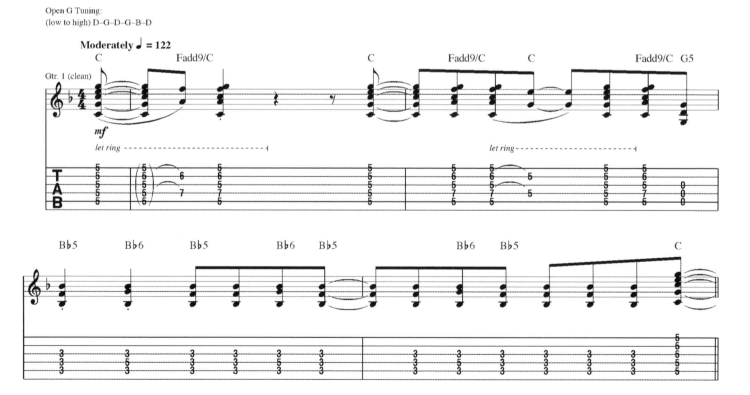

Stayin' Alive

Performed by the Bee Gees

From *Saturday Night Fever: The Original Movie Sound Track* (1977)

Although for many the Bee Gees will be forever thought of as the kings of disco, they actually got their start in the 1960s with a sound closer to Beatles-esque pop. A listen to their debut album, *Bee Gees' 1st* from 1967, would shock many in this regard. They found success right off the bat, with three Top 20 singles pushing the album to #7. A slew of moderately successful albums followed, but the turning point arrived with 1975's *Main Course* — the album on which Barry Gibb debuted his falsetto voice. Although the band felt their music to be part of a sub-genre at the time known as "blue-eyed soul," the disco fans took a liking and lifted the band up as champions of the craze. This popularity reached its apex with the monumentally successful soundtrack to *Saturday Night Fever*, which contained three #1 hits and remained at the top of the charts for 24 weeks, crowning the band as rulers of disco.

Interestingly, the rock solid groove of "Stayin' Alive" never really existed in the traditional sense. After the initial tracking was completed in a studio outside Paris, drummer Dennis Byron had to fly back to England because his father had just passed away. Upon relistening, no one was quite satisfied with the drum performance. After a failed attempt at trying to use the drum machine onboard a Hammond organ, they decided to find a two-bar section of the drums from "Night Fever" (recorded at near the same tempo) and create a tape loop for "Stayin' Alive." It was a bit tedious, but the result was an incredibly steady drum track that fit the bill perfectly. When Dennis returned from England, he only had to overdub some toms, the crash cymbal, and the hi-hat. That very same drum loop also wound up on "More Than a Woman" and Barbara Streisand's "Woman in Love."

The producer for the "Stayin' Alive" session, Ahlby Galuten, wanted a repetitive bass register line on guitar and suggested one to guitarist Alan Kendall. When Kendall wasn't able to cop him exactly, he settled on his own version, which Galuten liked just as much. Kendall most likely plugged his Fender Strat direct into the API console while recording this song. Working entirely from the F minor pentatonic scale, Alan crafts a memorable, syncopated line in first position for measures 1–2. Notice how beats 1–2 of measure 2 is a direct transposition down a 4th of beats 1–2 in measure 1. This lends a sense of cohesion to the lick and makes it more easily memorized and therefore singable. In other words, it makes a killer hook. In contrast to the busy riff of measures 1 and 2, Kendall sustains a B♭5 chord for a full two measures in 3 and 4.

Stayin' Alive

from the Motion Picture SATURDAY NIGHT FEVER

Words and Music by Barry Gibb, Robin Gibb and Maurice Gibb

Still of the Night

Performed by Whitesnake

From *Whitesnake* (1987)

Whitesnake roared onto the hard rock scene in the late 1980s, dominating the airwaves with their eponymous album in 1987. What few people knew then, however — especially in the U.S. — is that the band had already been at it for ten years with seven studio albums under their belt. As he was known to do, vocalist David Coverdale had put together an entirely new lineup before recording *Whitesnake*, with guitarist John Sykes taking on a prominent role, co-writing seven of the nine tracks and penning many of the album's memorable guitar riffs, including "Still of the Night."

On the strength of "Still of the Night" (#79), the recycled #1 hit power ballad "Here I Go Again" (which had appeared five years earlier on *Saints & Sinners*), and the runner-up ballad "Is This Love" (#2), the album reached #2 on the charts and plastered them all over MTV, along with Coverdale's sexy girlfriend-at-the-time, Tawny Kitaen. True to form, however, Coverdale again fired the entire line-up, enlisting Adrian Vanderburg and Vivian Campbell on guitars, Rudy Sarzo on bass, and Tommy Aldridge on drums for the supporting tours (not to mention videos!). Although he's largely unknown to most outside of the guitar world, Sykes was responsible for nearly all the guitar work on the album.

For "Still of the Night," Sykes bypassed his trusty Marshalls in favor of two Mesa Boogie Coliseum heads, presumably through 4x12 Marshall cabinets. In the effect department, he used the famed Lexicon PCM 41 for delay and a PCM 70 for chorus and other modulation effects. He made it all come alive with his 1978 Gibson Les Paul Custom, which then featured a Gibson "Dirty Fingers" humbucker in the bridge position.

The song seems to have its foot in two different key centers at times, including F♯ minor and E minor. The riff shown here is in F♯ minor and occurs during the verses. This is British blues metal at its finest, and as such makes use of the F♯ blues scale in its lowest register for maximum grind. After the "snakey" 16th-note sequence in measure 1, two beats of F♯ octaves ground things briefly before E5 and B chords give a boost of momentum for the riff's repeat in measure 3. Measure 4 again features the F♯ octave riff, but a recasting of the chords on beats 3 and 4 — this time as B and A, respectively — succinctly bring the riff home to the following tonic F♯5 (not shown).

Still of the Night

Words and Music by David Coverdale and John Sykes

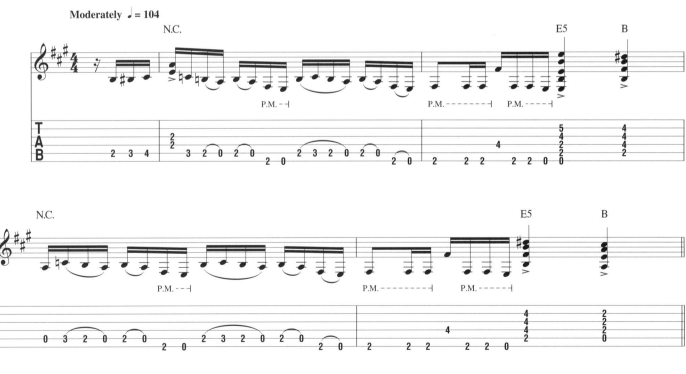

Stone Cold Crazy

Performed by Queen
From *Sheer Heart Attack* (1974)

With their eponymous debut in 1973, Queen hinted at nearly everything for which they would become legends. The dramatic vocals of Freddie Mercury, orchestral-like guitar overdubs of Brian May, and their sly sense of humor were all present, if a little unfocused. The story would remain somewhat the same for their follow-up, *Queen II*, in 1974. With 1974's *Sheer Heart Attack,* however, the band began to hit its stride. On the strength of the #12 single "Killer Queen," the album shot to #12 as well, heightening the band's profile on both sides of the pond and setting the stage for their first magnum opus: 1975's *A Night at the Opera.* Although the songwriting credit for "Stone Cold Crazy" is shared by all the band members, the song actually predates Queen. Freddie Mercury had played a different, slower version of the song with his previous band, Wreckage, during the late 1960s. Once introduced to Queen, however, the changes introduced by the band members essentially created a different song, prompting the shared credit.

"Stone Cold Crazy" has been called the first thrash or speed metal song, thanks to its brisk tempo and heavy sound. Metallica even recorded a cover of the song in 1990 for *Rubáiyát* — Elektra's 40th Anniversary — which was later used as a B-side for "Enter Sandman" and earned them a Grammy award. Brian May made use of his famous homemade Red Special guitar, Vox AC30 amp (cranked full), and Dallas Rangemaster for the track to achieve the thick, distorted tone. The main riff is in the key of G minor and mostly makes use of the G blues scale. After answering an eight-note assault on the tonic G note in measure 1 with a syncopated B♭5 chord in measure 2, the band joins in for a unison line in measures 3 and 4 that blends a G blues scale lick with a chromatically ascending line (B–C–C♯–D) to round out the phrase. This all goes by in a flash, so slow it down at first to make sure you've got the timing right.

Stone Cold Crazy
Words and Music by Freddie Mercury, Brian May, Roger Taylor and John Deacon

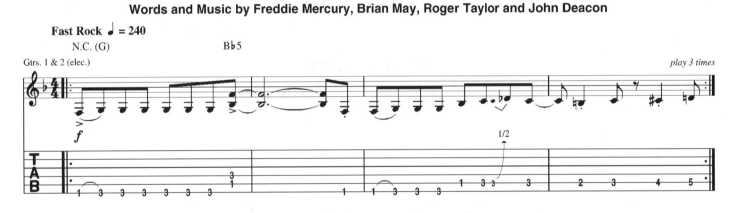

Stone in Love

Performed by Journey
From *Escape* (1981)

Two clearly delineated versions of Journey exist: B.S.P. and A.S.P. — before Steve Perry and after Steve Perry. The first incarnation of the band, featuring Neal Schon on guitar and Greg Rollie on keys and vocals, recorded their eponymous debut in 1975. Nearly unrecognizable to the casual fan of the Perry years, the album combined wayward pop songs with instrumental jazz-rock fusion. After only marginally gaining ground with the next two albums, the band decided to hire a dedicated lead vocalist before recording their fourth album. With Steve Perry on board, the resulting *Infinity* album (1978) permanently altered the band's direction and placed them on the path to eventual superstardom. The focus fell strictly on pop rock, and the songwriting improved drastically, sending the album to #21 on the strength of the hits "Lights," "Anytime," and "Wheel in the Sky."

The band continued to focus its efforts on *Evolution* (1979) and *Departure* (1980), the latter of which would be the last with Greg Rollie. With Perry and Schon now fully in control, everything coalesced perfectly for *Escape* (1981). Sporting three Top 10 hits in "Who's Crying Now," "Open Arms," and "Don't Stop Believing," the album easily topped the charts and sold millions. Journey had fully arrived.

"Stone in Love" is arena rock if anything is. Opening the song unaccompanied with the signature chordal riff, Neal Schon muscles his way through the progression with his Gibson Les Paul running through a cranked Marshall. The intro immediately casts images of a long guitar slinger on a darkened stage, illumined by a sole spotlight as he breaks the relative silence with 100 dB of power chord rock. Essentially a I–IV–V–I progression in G major, Neal does much to dress things up. The rhythm is especially dramatic, as single downbeat strums in measures 1–3 are followed by syncopated, staggering quarter-note triplets. Schon voices the chords so that a common tone of G is maintained on string 1 throughout, with the only exception being the D chord in measure 2 — although, he does move the F♯ up to G for the last chord to create a brief Dsus4. As if to goose things a little for the repeat, he finishes off in measure 4 with a rhythmically unambiguous 16th-note flourish consisting of a moving bass-register melody beneath a held G5 on top. The final G5/F♯ is an especially nice touch, as it flows effortlessly back into G5 for the repeat.

Stone in Love
Words and Music by Steve Perry, Neal Schon and Jonathan Cain

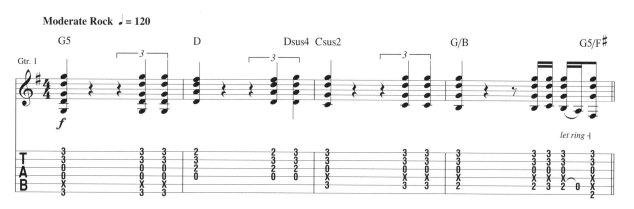

Sunday Bloody Sunday

Performed by U2
From *War* (1983)

With their constant touring, a unique sound that blended the energy of punk with a spacious, ethereal mood (mostly thanks to The Edge's unorthodox guitar playing), and their ambitious, often politically charged ideas and themes, U2 gained a steady following throughout the early 1980s. They gradually extending their reach out across the world from the home base of Dublin. After making a name for their brand of rock with 1980's *Boy* and 1981's *October,* they experienced their first breakout success with *War* in 1983. On the strength of "Sunday Bloody Sunday" and "New Years Day," the album peaked at #12 on the *Billboard* charts and made the band a huge concert draw in the States for the first time., World domination lay only four short years away with *The Joshua Tree*. "Sunday Bloody Sunday" is based on two separate instances nicknamed "Bloody Sunday" — one in 1972 and one in 1920 — in which numerous civilians were killed by soldiers. The band made it a point in the early years to state that the song is a pacifist anthem and "not a rebel song."

Although digital delay seems inextricably tied to most of The Edge's guitar parts, the band actually made a conscious decision on *War* to leave that out for the most part, giving the guitar a more direct and present sound. And although the Vox AC30 has undoubtedly fueled the tones of countless U2 tracks, The Edge revealed in the book *U2 on U2* that the tones on "Sunday Bloody Sunday" were coaxed from a Fender amp; it wasn't specified beyond that, but a good bet would be a Tweed Deluxe. In the guitar department, he made use of his trusty 1973 black Strat set to the bridge pickup — a DiMarzio FS-1. Atop Larry Mullen Jr.'s military beat, The Edge states this harmonic riff in unadorned fashion by arpeggiating the chords in straight eighth notes on the top three strings. The voicings used represent the epitome of efficiency and the entire riff can be comfortably played in second position, with the second finger remaining on the common D note on string 2 throughout. On the PopMart tour (1997–1998), The Edge performed an intimate, potent solo version of this song using a capo on fret 5 and singing the melody an octave lower than normal. This treatment can be seen on the accompanying video, *PopMart: Live from Mexico City* (1998), which is certainly worth checking out, because it gives the song (and its message) an entirely new slant.

Sunday Bloody Sunday
Words and Music by U2

* Gtr. 1 (clean elec.); Gtr. 2 (12-str. acous.)
   ** Chord symbols reflect implied tonality.

Sunshine of Your Love

Performed by Cream

From *Disraeli Gears* (1967)

Cream were doomed to have a short life from the beginning, but they certainly made the most of their time together, helping to send rock to unprecedented heights of instrumental prowess. After introducing the world to its first supergroup with *Fresh Cream* in 1966 (#39), containing a blend of mostly Jack Bruce originals and high-volume blues/traditional covers, the band teamed up with producer Felix Pappalardi for *Disraeli Gears* in 1967. This helped to focus the band's efforts, and, while less emphasis was placed on traditional blues (as traditional as Cream got, anyway), the songwriting grew more confident and cohesive. "Sunshine of Your Love" gave the band their first Top Ten hit at #5 and helped to send the album to #4. In a sly gesture, Eric Clapton quotes the melody of "Blue Moon" in the opening lines of his guitar solo as if to balance the references to celestial bodies.

The "Sunshine of Your Love" main riff came from bassist Jack Bruce, who wrote it one night after witnessing a Jimi Hendrix concert. Clapton contributed the chorus section and, consequently, the song's title. The epitome of Clapton's famous "woman tone," the song features his legendary Gibson SG guitar, known as "The Fool," plugged into his Marshall 100 watt with the volume, bass, mid, and treble all on 10. He used his neck pickup with the volume all the way up and the tone rolled all the way off. He also occasionally made use of a fixed wah pedal as a filter, but it's unclear whether it was used on this riff. Regarding the notes, this is pretty much blues scale 101. If you want to know how to make a D blues scale (D–F–G–A♭–A–C) talk, listen to this riff. Performed in the 10th-fret box position and lower extension box in eighth position, the riff also features Clapton's glorious vibrato on the F note in measure 2. This may reveal the thought process in moving down to the lower extension box for the riff's conclusion, as it allows him to apply the vibrato with his first finger — the strongest in this regard. Interestingly, Clapton's vibrato does not come from the wrist — the common method preferred by Jimi Hendrix, Stevie Ray Vaughan, and countless others. Instead, Clapton leaves his fret-hand finger perpendicular to the fretboard and shakes his entire forearm. It may be a bit unorthodox, but you can't argue with the results!

Sunshine of Your Love

Words and Music by Jack Bruce, Pete Brown and Eric Clapton

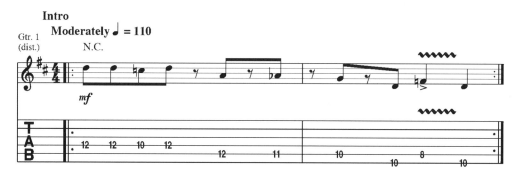

Super Freak

Performed by Rick James
From *Street Songs* (1981)

After a triumphant debut with *Come Get It* in 1978, which reached #13 on the pop charts with the help of singles "You and I" (#13) and "Mary Jane" (#41), Rick James treaded water for a bit with *Bustin' Out of L Seven* (1979) and *Fire It Up* (1979). He tried changing things up a bit for 1980's *Garden of Love,* mellowing out his sound a bit and working more ballads into the mix, but this wasn't as well-received as he (or the Motown label) had hoped. He decided to return to the raunchy funk that graced his debut for 1981's *Street Songs,* and the move paid off big time. With "Super Freak" reaching #16 and "Give It to Me Baby" hitting #40, the album shot to #3 and achieved platinum status — a first for the punk funker. "Super Freak" included backing vocals by the Temptations, one of which (the bass singer, Melvin Franklin) is Rick James's uncle.

Tom McDermott played guitar on almost all of Rick James's hits, including "Super Freak." Although his use of Charvel guitars is well documented, much less is out there with regards to his choice of amp. Nevertheless, he can be seen in several videos with a Marshall half stack (what looks like a 50 watt model), so that's a strong probability. The guitar is not prominently featured in this song, as it predominantly doubles the bass line, so the exact tone is not of paramount importance. The line here, which was famously sampled by M.C. Hammer for "U Can't Touch This," is derived from the A minor hexatonic scale — basically an A minor pentatonic with an added 2nd degree: A–B–C–D–E–G. There are six notes — hence the term "hexatonic." This is a great way to add a bit of flair and sophistication to the minor pentatonic scale, which contains all relatively safe notes. The 2nd (or 9th if you prefer) provides much more melodic possibility, and it's exploited nicely here, because it surrounds the tonic, A, along with the ♭7th, G. Remember to apply a slight palm mute for the appropriate sound and pay extra special care to the rests; they're what gives the riff its rhythmic punch.

Super Freak
Words and Music by Rick James and Alonzo Miller

Susie-Q

Performed by Creedence Clearwater Revival
From *Creedence Clearwater Revival* (1968)

With their eponymous debut in 1968, Creedence Clearwater Revival split their time between flirting with the psychedelic side of things ("I Put a Spell on You" and "Susie-Q") and the tuneful, swampy rock for which they would become known ("Porterville"). Fogerty's songwriting hadn't fully bloomed yet, which is one of the reasons why two of the chosen singles were covers, but he was certainly on his way. This was immediately confirmed with the #7 *Bayou Country* the following year, which contained two classics in "Born on the Bayou" and "Proud Mary" (#2). By 1969's *Green River*, the hit machine was in full swing, and Fogerty effortlessly churned out classics one after another over the course of the next three years and five albums, putting together one of the most prolific and successful runs in all of classic rock.

Interestingly, Creedence's first hit, "Susie-Q," was only recorded in the hopes of getting radio airplay on a local progressive rock station in San Francisco. It marks one of the few tunes on a CCR album in which John and brother Tom share lead vocals, with brother Tom taking the second verse. After Doug Clifford's drums settle into the right side of the stereo spectrum, John joins in on the left with the song's signature riff, which is articulated with hybrid picking (pick and fingers). With his Rickenbacker in hand — it had been modified with, among other things, a Gibson PAF pickup in the bridge position — he ran through his trusty Kustom K-200 amp to get the thick, throaty tone heard on the recording.

The riff is an excellent example of right-hand independence. The pick is used to peck out open E bass notes every quarter note (save for the final half-step bend on G), while the second and third fingers are used to play the syncopated melodies on top. If you're not used to this kind of playing, it'll take a while to develop. Take your time at first and learn each part separately before trying to combine them. Once you've got each one down, put them together at a slow tempo and increase it incrementally until you reach the target tempo. In the beginning your pick may try to jump ship and play the rhythms that your fingers are playing. With practice, though, the coordination will come, and your pick (or thumb if playing with a thumb pick or fingers only) will become a solid time keeper while your fingers are able to play any rhythms you can imagine on top.

Susie-Q
Words and Music by Dale Hawkins, Stan Lewis and Eleanor Broadwater

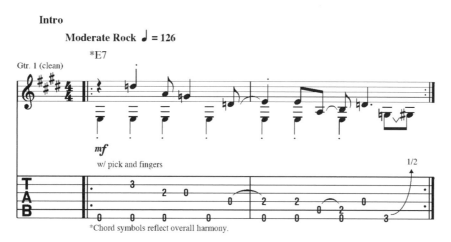

Sweet Child o' Mine

Performed by Guns N' Roses
From *Appetite for Destruction* (1987)

Appetite for Destruction (1987) holds the title of best-selling debut album of all time in the U.S. On the strength of three Top Ten singles — "Welcome to the Jungle" (#7), "Sweet Child o' Mine" (#1), and "Paradise City" (#5) — the album easily shot to #1 and has gone on to sell over 28 million copies worldwide. Borrowing heavily from the stripped down, sleazier stylings of Aerosmith and AC/DC, the band told a darker tale of excess than what was popular for the day. The notable exception to this formula is, of course, "Sweet Child o' Mine," the pop ballad-turned-hard rocker that's segmented into two distinct sections: a sweet tale of love and innocence, and a dark, dramatic breakdown and coda that asks, "Where do we go now?"

Although it contains one of the most widely known guitar riffs of the 1980s, the song actually started as a joke. Slash started playing what he called a "stupid string-skipping exercise" at a jam session with drummer Steven Adler. But Axl was in the next room, and, upon hearing the spontaneous jam, begin writing lyrics about his girlfriend at the time, Erin Everly. By the time he returned to practice, the song was nearly complete.

To create the iconic riff, Slash plugged one of his trusty Les Pauls (set to the neck pickup and tuned down a half step, of course) into a rented 1960s Marshall 1959 model head, which had been modded by Tim Caswell. The first thing you should notice about this riff is that only the first note changes; the rest of the riff is exactly the same. All the notes are derived from the D major scale, and every note of the scale is played except for the 7th, C#. Interestingly, the band chose to harmonize this riff with a progression based off D Mixolydian, which just so happens to be a D major scale with a ♭7th instead of a natural 7th. The picking and fingering in this riff can be tricky, so experiment with several different ways until you find something that feels good to you.

Sweet Child o' Mine
Words and Music by W. Axl Rose, Slash, Izzy Stradlin', Duff McKagan and Steven Adler

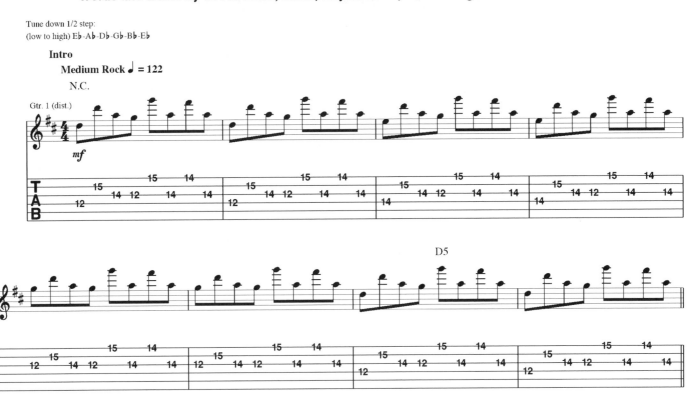

Sweet Emotion

Performed by Aerosmith
From *Toys in the Attic* (1975)

With their eponymous debut in 1973, Aerosmith established the basic format for their sound, which involved a combination of Rolling Stones swagger with the muscle of Led Zeppelin. They came off as a bit more risqué than either, however, thanks in no small part to the flamboyant nature of frontman Steven Tyler. They raced quickly out of the gate, with the classic power ballad "Dream On" reaching #6 and helping to propel the album to #21. And though their follow-up, *Get Your Wings* (1974), failed to produce a hit single and stalled at #74, it was a worthwhile experiment, because it helped the band solidify their trademark sound and shed the overly conspicuous influences that were present on their debut. Those two steps backward paid off as three steps forward with the release of *Toys in the Attic* in 1975. With all the critical elements fully in place, the band hit its stride and reached its potential with two Top 40 hits in "Sweet Emotion" and "Walk This Way." These two signature songs helped push the album to #11 and cement its status as the first true classic in their catalog.

"Sweet Emotion" was long rumored to have been written (by Tyler) about Joe Perry's wife, around whom much tension in the band centered at the time. Tyler later revealed that although some of the lyrics addressed this issue, the majority of the song did not. The song boasts one of the most famous uses of the talk box ever (obviously not surpassing that of Peter Frampton, of course), when Perry rides atop Hamilton's iconic bass line with his own electronic "Sweet Emotion" refrain prior to the true vocal entrance. At the end of the verses, in trademark Aerosmith fashion, the band erupts into a unison ensemble riff played entirely on strings 5 and 6. With both Perry and Brad Whitford running Strats through Marshalls for a cumulative, fat, muscular tone, the effect is quite massive. Although the riff starts with a pull-off from A minor pentatonic, the scale is quickly abandoned in favor of a staggering, ascending riff that climbs chromatically from F# back up to A. The effect is that of a stumble, a struggle to get back on your feet, and then another stumble. When the riff is repeated, Perry breaks off into harmony (not shown), thickening the texture considerably.

Sweet Emotion
Words and Music by Steven Tyler and Tom Hamilton

Sweet Home Alabama

Performed by Lynyrd Skynyrd
From *Second Helping* (1974)

Lynyrd Skynyrd is southern rock, plain and simple. When you look up the term in a dictionary, it should just show a picture of them. With a string of successful albums spanning the mid -1970s, the band defined everything about the genre. Each of their first two albums contained a song that would live in infamy among bars everywhere: "Freebird" on *Pronouned Leh-Nerd Skin-Nerd* (1973) and "Sweet Home Alabama" on *Second Helping* (1974). The band would, of course, suffer the first of several tragedies in 1977 when a plane crash took the life of several band members (and members of the plane crew), including singer/songwriter Ronnie Van Zant.

For all its universal appeal, "Sweet Home Alabama" is the subject of one of the longest-standing debates in music history: what key is the song in? Upon first listening, the song seems to tonicize the D chord, as the vocal melody regularly resolves on the note D. This would translate to a I–♭VII–IV progression — a staple of classic rock that's been heard in countless songs, including "Can't You See" by the Marshall Tucker Band and "Takin' Care of Business" by Bachman-Turner Overdrive. The other possible analysis is IV–V–I in the key of G. If you listen to the classic solo in this song, you'll discover that, in fact, Ed King soloed over the progression as if it were in the key of G.

The song also possesses one of the most easily recognizable intros in all of rock history. Arpeggiating through D5, Csus2, and G chords, Ed King played his 1960s Fender Strat through a Fender Twin to create the classic riff. He does much to dress things up, however, mixing palm muted bass notes with ringing treble notes, and adding bluegrass-style open-string runs over the G chords. In classic question-and-answer phrasing, notice how King plays near identical fills for the G chords in measures 2 and 6 but answers with different fills for the G chords in measures 4 and 8. In the former, he pulls off (literally) a syncopated pattern on the G string, pivoting notes from the G major scale against the open G string. The latter nicely wraps up the intro for the approaching verse (not shown) with the minor 3rd (B♭ or A♯) sliding into the major 3rd (B) on string 5, followed by the open D and G strings to form a first-inversion G chord (B–D–G, low to high).

Sweet Home Alabama
Words and Music by Ronnie Van Zant, Ed King and Gary Rossington

Sweet Leaf

Performed by Black Sabbath
From *Master of Reality* (1971)

Most agree that Black Sabbath invented the genre of heavy metal with their eponymous debut in 1970. Yes, Led Zeppelin played heavy, distorted blues riffs on *Led Zeppelin* and *II* in 1969, and yes, the Who had recorded head-banging, decibel-crushing music with "I Can See for Miles" in 1967. But not before 1970's *Black Sabbath* had all of the elements of heavy metal — the mammoth power chord riff, the crunchy tones, the dark subject matter, and the gothic imagery — so perfectly coalesced. In fact, Ozzy and the other members have recounted how some other bands and members of the press were actually afraid of Black Sabbath in the early days because they'd simply never seen or heard anything similar. The band had obviously tapped into something with widespread appeal and they enjoyed a string of six Top 40 albums right from the start. In addition to their debut, *Paranoid* (1970), *Master of Reality* (1971), and *Black Sabbath Vol. 4* (1972), are considered masterpieces and essential listening for any burgeoning metal head.

At the age of seventeen, while working his last day at a sheet metal factory, guitarist Tony Iommi accidentally chopped off the tips of his fret-hand middle and ring fingers. After attempting to learn right-handed (Iommi is a left-handed player), he instead attached thimbles to the ends of his fingers to serve as false fingertips. This got him through the first two Sabbath albums, but it wasn't a walk in the park. In an attempt to make guitar-playing easier on his fret hand, he switched to extremely light-gauged strings and began tuning his guitar down a minor 3rd (to C#) for the *Masters of Reality* album. This technique would have massive influence on generations of metal heads and grungers. When bassist Geezer Butler followed suit by tuning his bass down a minor 3rd, a new sound was born: detuned metal. This process is still in wide use today, with bands tuning down even further in search of ultimate heaviness.

As for the "Sweet Leaf" riff, it's basic power chords, all played on the 6–5 string set and slid around in typical Iommi fashion. He interjects some scratch rhythms to add some percussive heaviness, which is achieved by slightly releasing pressure with the fret hand and strumming the deadened strings. Iommi plugged his Gibson SG with custom made pickups into a Rangemaster treble booster, which had been modified by one of his roadies (although what the modification was is not clearly documented). From there, he ran into his Laney Supergroup head, which is somewhat similar in sound to a Marshall Plexi. Interestingly, the treble booster was not used so much to boost the treble as it was to overload the input stage of the Laney, which helped create the wooly, fuzzy distortion heard on the album.

Sweet Leaf
Words and Music by Frank Iommi, John Osbourne, William Ward and Terence Butler

Talk Dirty to Me

Performed by Poison
From *Look What the Cat Dragged In* (1986)

When someone mentions glam rock (or glam metal), you think of Poison; it's like a knee-jerk reaction. No band better epitomized the genre, whether you're talking music or off-stage antics. Most of their lyrics were about sex, drugs, and rock 'n' roll, and most of their time off stage was devoted to sex and drugs. Nevertheless, they managed to hold it together long enough to sell over 30 million albums and rack up three Top Ten albums before falling out of public favor with the great grunge overthrow of 1991.

Arriving on the scene in 1986 with *Look What the Cat Dragged In,* Poison couldn't have timed things better. Hair metal had infiltrated millions of teenager's bedrooms across the nation, and musical substance had all but been replaced with a rebellious party-'til-you-drop mentality. Poison's debut took the adolescent rock world by storm, reaching #3 on the charts and catapulting them to super stardom on the strength of two Top Ten singles: the punkish "Talk Dirty to Me" (#9) and the obligatory power ballad, "I Won't Forget You" (#13). Their follow-up in 1988, *Open Up and Say…Ahh!,* would prove their pinnacle of success, again reaching #3 on the charts and rewarding the band with their only #1 single: the acoustic-driven "Every Rose Has Its Thorn."

The opening riff to "Talk Dirty to Me" is just about as simple as three-chord punk rock gets. C.C. Deville sounds IV–V–I progression in the key of G with simple, three-string power chords: C5, D5, and G5. To help provide a bit of ear-tickling, he slides into the tonic G5 by a half step below (F#5), resulting in a chordal hook that drives the riff. Other subtleties include the slide from C5 to D5, the gliss up from D5 (to F#5), and the scratch rhythm strums on beat 2 of measure 2 of measures 1 and 2. All of these help lend a greasy, sleazy character to the proceedings that matches the lyrical content quite well. Remember to tune down a half step if you want to play along with the original. To achieve his dirty tone, C.C. plugged either his Jackson or Charvel into a tri-amp setup: a Crate G-60 (solid state), a Marshall JTM45, and a custom-made Soldano. He mixed the three together, mainly using the Crate for high end, to form the complete tone heard on record.

Talk Dirty to Me

Words and Music by Bobby Dall, C.C. Deville, Bret Michaels and Rikki Rockett

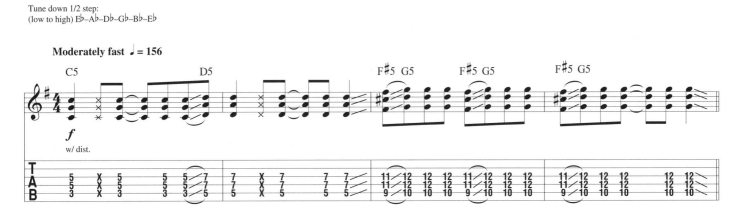

Tears in Heaven

Performed by Eric Clapton
From *Unplugged* (1992)

Originally appearing on the soundtrack to the 1991 drama *Rush*, "Tears in Heaven" more famously appeared on Clapton's massively successful *Unplugged* album in 1992, where it reached #2 on the *Billboard* charts. After the tragic, accidental death of his four-year-old son, Conor, Clapton wanted to write a song to help deal with the loss, seeking the partnership of co-writer Will Jennings. Though Jennings was reluctant at first (understandably so) to help with such an intimately personal subject matter, he came around eventually. The song won three Grammy awards and is one of Clapton's signature songs. He stopped performing it in 2004, stating that he finally didn't feel the loss anymore, and he didn't want those feelings to return.

The *Unplugged* album, which hit #1 and has been certified diamond platinum, helped to rejuvenate Clapton's career after his string of glossier pop-tinged albums had estranged him from some long-time fans during the 1980s. (He would continue this trend back toward his blues roots with 1994's *From the Cradle,* which also shot to #1 and fulfilled the long-time pining of many fans for an all-blues Clapton album.) Along with "Tears in Heaven," *Unplugged* also contained a slowed-down shuffle version of "Layla" (#12) and a rousing stomp through Bo Diddley's "Before You Accuse Me (Take a Look at Yourself)," among other celebrated performances.

Clapton performed "Tears in Heaven" on a 1992 Jose Ramirez III nylon string, playing fingerstyle throughout the song, which is not something he was known for before the album. The song is in the key of A major, and the intro riff, which also serves as interludes, makes use of a I–V–vi–I–IV–V–I progression, with all the chords lasting two beats except the final I chord. Clapton does much to dress this up, however. For example, he makes use of many inversions (chords with notes other than the root on bottom) throughout, resulting in a descending bass line of A–G♯–F♯–E in measures 1–2. He also adds ornamental hammer-ons and pull-offs, as seen in the pickup and measure 1, and decorates the E7 chord with a sus4 in measure 3. These devices create melodic hooks that help lift the part from a simple accompaniment to a memorable featured guitar part.

Tears in Heaven
Words and Music by Eric Clapton and Will Jennings

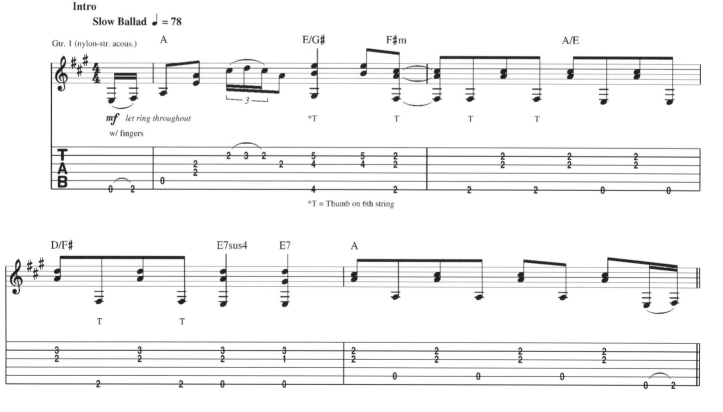

Too Rolling Stoned

Performed by Robin Trower

From *Bridge of Sighs* (1974)

British blues rock legend Robin Trower first made a name for himself in the late 1960s with Procol Harum, joining shortly after the band's classic rock staple "A Whiter Shade of Pale," was released. After remaining with them through five albums and steadily increasing his profile, Robin left the band in hopes of finding a project that allowed him more room to stretch out on the guitar. Eventually, Trower put together a power trio consisting of James Dewar on bass/vocals and Reg Isidore on drums. He issued his solo debut with the band, *Twice Removed from Yesterday,* in 1973, which failed to make much of an impact on the charts. The follow-up, however, would make Trower a household name. *Bridge of Sighs* (1974) sounded remarkably similar to Hendrix's brand of psychedelic blues rock, and its success helped to fill a void in the hearts of many Hendrix fans so soon after his untimely death.

On the strength of such concert favorites as "Day of the Eagle," "Too Rolling Stoned," and the title track, the album reached #7 on the U.S. charts and helped cement Trower's reputation as a guitar god in the making. Unfortunately, the similarities to Hendrix — the Strat guitar, the effects used, and the overall obvious influence — would eventually plague Trower. The comparisons to the late legend would make it difficult for Trower to truly surface with his own identity. Similar to an actor known for a specific role, Trower became typecast by many as a Hendrix clone, which eventually led to a decline in popularity.

"Too Rolling Stoned" is perhaps Trower's signature song and adds a bit of funk flair to his normal blues-tinged rock. The song is in the key of C minor, and the intro riff is derived mostly from the C minor pentatonic scale (C–E♭–F–G–B♭) with one very important addition: the natural 7th (B). Inserted between B♭ and the tonic C, the B note creates a chromatic three-note ascent that repeats in a "rolling" motion, gathering no moss in the process. The only other note present in the riff is the E♭, which is used to turn the riff around at the end of measure 1. Note that measure 2 ends differently with a syncopated B♭ on the "and" of beat 3, resulting in a question-and-answer format — a commonly used device among classic riffs. In keeping with the Hendrix M.O., Trower rolled through this riff with a Fender Strat plugged into a 100W Marshall.

Too Rolling Stoned

Words and Music by Robin Trower

*Chord symbols reflect overall harmony.

The Trooper

Performed by Iron Maiden

From *Piece of Mind* (1983)

With a career spanning over 35 years and over 85 million albums sold worldwide, Iron Maiden is one of the most successful British metal bands in history. And although the additions of Adrian Smith in 1981 *(Killers)* and Bruce Dickinson in 1982 *(Number of the Beast)* played huge roles in the band's emergence as metal gods, it wasn't until 1983 that the definitive line up (in most people's opinion) was cemented. Nicko McBrain joined for the band's fourth album, *Piece of Mind* (#14), providing the perfect complement to bassist Steve Harris's galloping bass lines and the dueling riffs of guitarists Dave Murray and Adrian Smith. Along with concert staples such as "Flight of Icarus" and the epic "Revelations," the album also contained "The Trooper," which soon became one of Maiden's signature songs.

Piece of Mind didn't contain any U.S. charting singles (although both "Flight of Icarus" and "The Trooper" were Top 40 hits in the UK), but the tour was successful in building Iron Maiden's fan base, and the band had finally settled into a lineup with which they could become comfortable. "The Trooper," written by Harris, is based off the Alfred Lord Tennyson poem "The Charge of the Light Brigade." Its dynamic riffs and stop-time ensemble hits paint a convincing picture of the tumultuous battlefield and the story of a fallen soldier.

In the favorite metal key of E minor, the classic "Trooper" riff is built on the tried-and-true minor chord progression of i–♭VII–♭VI, which has been used in literally thousands of metal and hard rock songs. In the key of E minor, this translates to Em, D, and C, though the implied harmony here is more of the power chord variety (E5, D5, and C5). Maintaining a common rhythm, Smith and Murray transpose a rapid pull-off figure down to each root note of the chord changes: E, D, and C. Notice that, while the figure is an exact transposition for the E5 and D5 chords, it's altered over the C5 chords — i.e., the pull-off is only a half step — in order to remain diatonic to the key of E minor. To wrap up the two-measure assault, a turnaround riff of D–G–D–E ends on the "and" of beat 4, providing an extra jolt of energy as the riff charges forward again for the repeat. To fuel their frontline march, Dave Murray plugged his trusty Fender Strat into a 100W Marshall, while Smith sent his Gold Top Les Paul through an Ibanez Tube Screamer into 50W Marshalls.

The Trooper

Words and Music by Steven Harris

*Chord symbols refelect overall harmony.

Trust

Performed by Megadeth
From *Cryptic Writings* (1997)

In one of the greatest rock rivalries, Megadeth founder Dave Mustaine set out to outdo Metallica after being booted from the band's original lineup in 1983 for drug and alcohol abuse and personality conflicts. His number one ambition at the time, he admitted, was to be faster and heavier than the commercial kings of thrash metal. Although he can't claim to have topped them in sales or widespread appeal, Mustaine certainly gave it the ol' college try. With over 30 million albums sold worldwide and ten Grammy nominations for Best Metal Performance, he can't be too disappointed with his efforts.

Megadeth has had more personnel changes throughout their thirty-year history (as of this writing) than ellipses in their album titles, with Mustaine the sole constant. Marty Friedman joined the band as lead guitarist in 1990, which revealed a newly sober Dave Mustaine and the release of *Rust in Peace* — the band's highest charting album to date at #23. Friedman remained through a string of the band's most successful albums — *Countdown to Extinction* (1992), *Youthanasia* (1994), and *Cryptic Writings* (1997) — all of which went platinum and hit the Top Ten. The opening track from the latter, "Trust," hit #5 on the Hot Mainstream Rock Tracks chart. More textured and less thrash than their earlier material, the song has much in common with Metallica's commercialized sound of the same period.

Dave plugged his Jackson V into his 100W Marshall amp to obtain the smooth distorted tone heard in the intro. This riff, which also serves as the backdrop for the chorus, is built primarily from the E natural minor scale (E–F♯–G–A–B–C–D), but, like so many classic metal riffs, also contains the ♭5th — B♭ in this case. Although the notes used in measures 1–2 (E, C, and B) are compelling, it's the rhythm that really makes this riff interesting. Notice that the same four-note pattern of (low) E–(high) E–C–B is repeated, but after the initial four-note statement in eighth notes, the notes are only stated three at a time. If you ignore the rhythm altogether and only focus on the note pattern in measures 1–2, you'll see (low) E–(high) E–C–B completed three times. The staggered rhythm, however, allows this to fill two full measures. This is answered in measures 3–4 with a wicked phrase that employs the B♭ for a sinister sound. Remember: this riff is performed without any palm muting, which means you need to be careful to not let the notes ring together.

Trust

Words and Music by Dave Mustaine and Marty Friedman

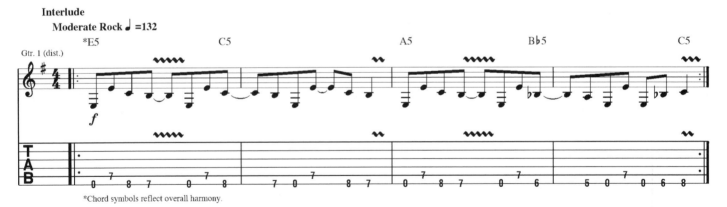

*Chord symbols reflect overall harmony.

25 or 6 to 4

Performed by Chicago
From *Chicago* (1970)

Chicago's original sound was tougher than the ballads of the mid-1980s and beyond. With muscular horn arrangements, stinging, angular guitar solos by Terry Kath, and an earthy production, it's hard to even believe that this band would eventually release songs like "You're the Inspiration." To be precise, they didn't. Lineup changes throughout the years played a crucial role in the evolution of the band's sound. No change, however, was more drastic than the tragic death of guitarist Terry Kath in 1978. (A gun enthusiast, Kath accidentally shot himself.) With killer guitar chops, a rough-n-gruff voice, and a rocker's spirit, Kath had provided much of the band's edginess. After his death, the sound steadily moved more toward the poppy and polished variety with an emphasis on ballads sung by Peter Cetera.

"25 or 6 to 4" appears on the band's second album, *Chicago* (1970). This album has retroactively come to be known as "Chicago II," as the third album, *Chicago III* (1971), began a series of Roman numeral-based album titles. *Chicago II* shot to #4 on the charts on the strength of singles "Make Me Smile" (#9), "Colour My World" (#7), and "25 or 6 to 4" (#4), easily achieving gold status in 1970 (eventually hitting platinum status in 1991).

The main riff serves as the backdrop for the intro (including the classic horn lines) and verses, as well as the guitar solo. Aside from the final E5, the rest of the A minor progression (A5–G5–D/F♯–F5–E5) is articulated as octaves on the guitar, with no 5th. To perform this part with the necessary aggression, you need to employ some careful fret-hand muting. Use your first finger on string 6 and either your third or fourth finger on string 4. Then make sure to deaden string 5 by lightly touching it with either fretting finger. You should also allow the curvature of your first finger to deaden all the treble strings as well. This way, you can strum through the octave shapes with full force and rest assured that only the notes you want will sound. To create his unusually thick tone, Kath plugged his 1980s model Strat into a Bogen P.A. head. He then ran the Bogen's speaker out into a Dual Showman, which overdrove its preamp, resulting in sizzling distortion.

25 or 6 to 4
Words and Music by Robert Lamm

Up Around the Bend

Performed by Creedence Clearwater Revival

From *Cosmo's Factory* (1970)

By the time they released *Cosmo's Factory* in 1970, CCR were on a serious roll. Having released four Top Ten albums in a row (all within the span of two years) and touring consistently, the Fogerty hit-making machine was well-oiled and in full flight. Including their eponymous debut album in 1968 (#58), that's six albums in two years, making them one of the most prolific bands in history. And five of those albums hit the Top Ten. In fact, Creedence wouldn't slip out of the Top Ten until 1972's *Mardi Gras,* which still reached #12. Only few others (including the Beatles) have topped such a successful streak. John may have had a reputation for being a bit of a control freak, but you can't say he didn't know what he was doing!

Although rightly celebrated as a treasure of classic rock, John Fogerty never seems to get enough credit for his guitar playing. Granted, he wasn't a virtuoso, but he *could* play, and he could write some seriously catchy guitar parts. Along with staples such as "Born on the Bayou," "Proud Mary," and "Bad Moon Rising," "Up Around the Bend" (#4) is a case in point. Fogerty wastes no time getting your attention in this song, kicking things off in style with a seriously stinging tone.

Fogerty plugs his Les Paul into his Fender Vibrolux and lets it rip on this one. Simplicity is the key here, but it's the deceptive kind. Moving between the I (D) and V (A) chords in the key of D major, John intelligently uses the open fourth and fifth strings as bass notes, respectively, and crafts a singable riff atop each with a first-inversion triad. The 3rd of each chord (F♯ and C♯, respectively) is enhanced by a grace-note slide on beat 2 of each measure, which kicks the riff in the pants and generates significant momentum. Take special care (as John does) to mute the D string when moving to the A chord in measure 3. Failing to do so will only muddy things up and diminish the riff's effectiveness.

Up Around the Bend

Words and Music by John Fogerty

Wake Up Little Susie

Performed by the Everly Brothers
From *The Everly Brothers* (1958)

Appearing on the Everly Brothers's eponymous debut album in 1958, "Wake Up Little Susie" hit #1 on the charts and helped propel the brothers to stardom. It certainly didn't hurt that the album also contained their other signature single, "Bye Bye Love." Both songs were penned by the husband/wife songwriting team of Felice and Boudleaux Bryant — the same writers responsible for countless other classics of the day, including "All I Have to Do Is Dream" and "Love Hurts." The Everly Brothers were particularly suited to the Bryant/Bryant style, and this is evidenced by the fact that most of their songs were performed by Don and Phil.

This song had to fight an uphill battle after a knee-jerk reaction to the lyrics. Because of its "suggestiveness," the song was banned from many Boston radio stations, among others, even though the lyrics clearly state that no indecency occurred; the couple simply fell asleep in their car while watching a boring movie. Leave it to the propaganda machine!

With their trusty Gibson J-200 jumbo acoustics, the brothers Everly get this rockin' romp going with a signature riff based off the open D chord. After strumming a measure of eighth-note D chords, they move the fretted portion of the chord up three and then five frets while allowing the open D string to sound. The result is F/D and G/D chords, respectively. Notice also, the syncopated (accenting the weak beat) rhythm in measure 2, which provides a welcome contrast from the driving, continuous eighth notes in measure 1. Interestingly, although this riff is played as straight eighth notes, when the band comes in, the song shifts to a swing feel.

The idea of moving the fretted portion of a chord against an open droning string (or strings) is a device used by many to create lush voicings that are often otherwise unplayable. For examples of how far you can take this concept, check out "Across the Universe" (The Beatles), "Hole Hearted" (Extreme), and "Wanted Dead or Alive" (Bon Jovi), to name but a few.

Wake Up Little Susie
Words and Music by Boudleaux Bryant and Felice Bryant

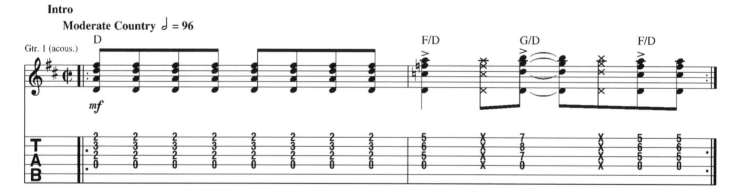

Walk This Way

Performed by Aerosmith

From *Toys in the Attic* (1975)

Aerosmith is one of the few bands to enjoy two hugely successful periods, which can broadly be divided into pre-1980 and post-1986 periods. Although they were big in the 1970s, they grew even bigger in the late 1980s and, after slightly angling their sound more toward the adult contemporary side of rock, continued soaring through the 1990s and 2000s. Along with "Dream On," "Walk This Way" is one of their signature songs from their first period. Originally released on 1975's *Toys in the Attic* and inspired by a phrase heard in the Mel Brooks film *Young Frankenstein,* the song hit #10 on the charts in 1977 and, along with the first single, "Sweet Emotion," helped to push the album to multi-platinum success.

Penned by vocalist Steven Tyler and guitarist Joe Perry, the songwriting team responsible for the large majority of the band's material, "Walk This Way" experienced a huge resurgence in popularity when Run DMC covered it for their 1986 album, *Raising Hell.* The version helped spawn a new breed of rap rock and also helped introduce Aerosmith to a younger generation. The band wasted no time capitalizing on this opportunity, employing the pop rock sensibilities of songwriter Desmond Child (who had worked with Bon Jovi) for their 1987 album, *Permanent Vacation.* The experiment proved a major success, the album hit #11 and went multi-platinum, and Aerosmith firmly established themselves in the new musical arena of the 1980s.

"Walk This Way" is one of the most immediately recognizable songs in the history of rock. If you're still not convinced after Joey Kramer's über famous drum intro, Joe Perry's even-more-famous guitar riff will seal the deal. Based off the E blues scale, Perry creates a tour-de-force of syncopation, chromaticism, and swagger on the lower strings. Running his Les Paul through his trusty Marshall, he achieves a mid-rangey raunchy tone that's as dry and in your face as it is rude. Notice that the same four-note run (A–A♯–B–E) is repeated after a sixteenth note rest, which places the riff at a different spot rhythmically on the repeat — an exceptionally cool riff-writing device.

Walk This Way

Words and Music by Steven Tyler and Joe Perry

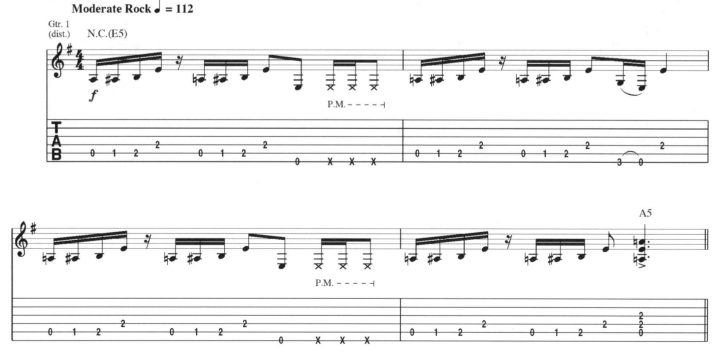

Wanted Dead or Alive

Performed by Bon Jovi
From *Slippery When Wet* (1986)

Ah, the 1980s. You had the new wave punk sound, and you had hair metal. And no band perhaps represents the latter like Bon Jovi — the undisputed kings of pop hair metal. After limited success with their eponymous debut in 1984 and 7800° Fahrenheit in 1985, the band simply *exploded* in 1986 with *Slippery When Wet.* An instant smash, it holds the distinction of the being the first hard rock album to ever contain three Top Ten singles ("You Give Love a Bad Name," "Living on a Prayer," and "Wanted Dead or Alive"). It's gone on to achieve diamond platinum status and is currently listed as the 21st top selling studio album of all time.

Jon Bon Jovi claims that the song is a tribute to life in the Old West, stating that the lifestyle of a rock band is similar to that of outlaws: riding into town and stealing money, girls, and booze before the sun came up. He's also credited the Bob Seger song "Turn the Page" as a huge inspiration for "Wanted Dead or Alive." After listening to "Turn the Page" on a tour bus in 1985, he told guitarist Ritchie Sambora, "We gotta write a song like this." A year later, the songwriting team penned "Wanted…" and took it into the studio for the *Slippery When Wet* sessions. With its epic sound, combining twelve-string acoustic guitars and power chord riffs with an irresistible chorus, the song hit #7 on the charts and remains a radio staple today.

To create the lush intro riff, Sambora played his Guild F-50 twelve string, arpeggiating through a descending series of 6th intervals against an open D-string drone. The notes are all derived from the D Dorian mode (D–E–F–G–A–B–C), which is the same thing as a D minor scale, but with a raised 6th tone. Following the arpeggio descent (which is played twice), he segues into the verse by way of a bluesy riff played in open position, which is largely derived from the D minor pentatonic scale (save for the open high E string, which is the 9th or 2nd).

Wanted Dead or Alive

You Really Got Me

Performed by the Kinks
From *Kinks* (1964)

After failing to chart with their first two singles, the Kinks were under heavy pressure from the Pye label to strike it big. Little did they know that their next single would still be showing up in nearly every "Top 100 Rock Songs of All Time" list in the new millenium. The song, reaching #1 on the U.K. charts and #7 in the U.S., launched the band's career and lifted them to the upper echelon of the British Invasion bands, including the Beatles, the Rolling Stones, and the Who (though they preceded the Who.)

In a 1998 interview, songwriter Ray Davies states that he wrote the song as a tribute to the blues greats of the past, such as Leadbelly and Big Bill Broonzy, although he's also stated that it came about while experimenting with the chords to "Louie Louie" (The Kingsmen). Regardless of the source, the result was undeniably one of the catchiest riffs in rock history, and the song has been famously covered by many artists since — the most famous being Van Halen on their 1978 eponymous debut.

"You Really Got Me" has also been the source of one of the most stubborn rock guitar solo myths in recent history. For years, rumors ran rampant that then-session player Jimmy Page played the solo (even though he would deny it repeatedly in interviews). But Dave Davies (Ray's brother), in fact, played the solo. Ray even claims that, upon close listening through headphones, you can hear Dave shouting an expletive at Ray right before the solo (actually in response to Ray's encouragement to play well — that's brotherly love for ya.)

With "You Really Got Me," the Kinks rewrote the book on guitar tone — so much so that some have proclaimed them the inventors of heavy metal. To achieve the famous distorted tone on the track, Dave Davies plugged his 1962 Harmony Meteor semi-hollowbody into his low wattage Elpico amp and ran the speaker leads into the input of his Vox AC30. He then sliced the Elpico's speaker cone with a razor blade to produce the raspy distortion that turned the world on its ear. As for the riff, it's power chords in the key of G. Play it with attitude!

You Really Got Me

Words and Music by Ray Davies

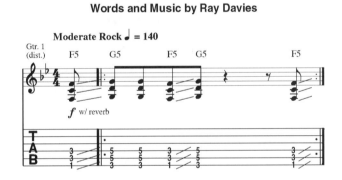

Welcome to the Jungle

Performed by Guns N' Roses

From *Appetite for Destruction* (1987)

In every decade, there are albums that simply take over. In the late 1980s, this was *Appetite for Destruction.* Seemingly out of nowhere, Guns N' Roses were suddenly *everywhere.* Suddenly, after seeing the top hat-donning Slash tear it up, guitarists started drooling over Les Pauls instead of the Kramers, Jacksons, Charvels, and other "superstrat" types that had pervaded the market since Eddie Van Halen's arrival nearly a decade earlier. With the most charismatic frontman since David Lee Roth in Axl Rose, and a brutally aggressive blues metal sound like Aerosmith on steroids, the band took over the charts and dethroned Bon Jovi as the world's biggest band.

Appetite for Destruction hit #1 on the charts, spawning five hit singles and going on to sell over 28 million copies worldwide (and counting). "Welcome to the Jungle" was the first song to be co-written by Axl and Slash, and in one interview Slash remembers the song taking about three hours to complete and credits other members of the band with adding certain sections. Axl wrote the lyrics to the song while visiting a friend in Kingston, Washington (outside of Seattle).

The main riff is split between the guitar duo of Slash and Izzy Stradlin' and consists mostly of power chords derived from the A Dorian mode (A–B–C–D–E–F♯–G). Whereas Slash states the riff more plainly by sliding power chords around on strings 6 and 5, Izzy articulates it with a mixture of single notes and power chords, employing bluesy half-step bends and a bit of palm muting to give it some life. In measure 4, Slash peels off a bluesy descending phrase from the A blues scale to lead into the verse. Taken together, the two parts combine into a wall of sound that runs over you like a jungle stampede. As for Slash, plug a Les Paul into a Marshall and fire away. Izzy used a then-unfashionable Gibson Hollow-body (most likely an ES-175) and ran through a Mesa Boogie Mark III into a 4x12 cabinet with EV and Celestion speakers.

Welcome to the Jungle

Words and Music by W. Axl Rose, Slash, Izzy Stradlin', Duff McKagan and Steven Adler

Tune down 1/2 step:
(low to high) Eb–Ab–Db–Gb–Bb–Eb

Intro

Moderate Rock ♩ = 124

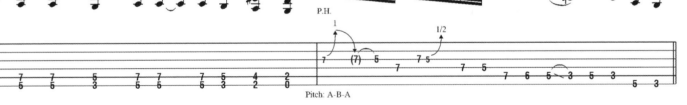

Pitch: A-B-A

You Were Meant for Me

Performed by Jewel
From *Pieces of You* (1995)

The debut album from Alaska-based singer/songwriter Jewel Kilcher made little impact upon its initial release in 1995. Eventually, "Who Will Save Your Soul" began to gain airplay, and the album entered the *Billboard* charts at #4 two full years after its release. Once it had some momentum, it eventually sold over 12 million copies in the U.S. alone on the strength of its three Top 10 hits: "Who Will Save Your Soul," "You Were Meant for Me," and "Foolish Games." It should be noted that each one of these sounds quite different on the originally released album than it did on the radio. The album was mostly recorded live at the Innerchange Coffeehouse in San Diego, and the three aforementioned hits were re-recorded in a studio and added to a later edition of the album.

A long-time user of Taylor guitars, Jewel bought her first, a 912ce, from the Taylor factory as a "second" (a guitar that features some slight imperfection) early in her career before her first album, and it's been her main guitar ever since. (The instrument, which features a striking floral inlay on the neck, can be seen in the video for "Who Will Save Your Soul.") She kicks off "You Were Meant for Me" with this gentle, shuffled fingerpicking riff, which forms the basis of the verses. Notice how she dresses up standard C and G chords by including a few open strings to add color. The open D string is allowed to ring over the C chord, creating a Csus2, and the open E string is allowed to ring through the G chord, creating a G6/B. Consequently, this also makes the high E string a common tone throughout all four measures. Jewel has a unique fingerpicking style and therefore doesn't normally play the riff exactly this way when playing live. She tends to flail downward on beat 3 with her index finger. An altered Travis-picking approach, with the thumb handling all the notes on the downbeats, will work perfectly for this riff. Give the D note on string 2 a slight wiggle in measure 1 to add a bit of ear candy.

You Were Meant for Me
Words and Music by Jewel Murray and Steve Poltz

The Zoo

Performed by the Scorpions
From *Animal Magnetism* (1980)

Most American fan of hard rock think the Scorpions first arrived on the scene around 1980. And that's correct — if you're talking about the *American* scene. The truth is, the Scorpions had been cranking out blues-tinged European metal since 1969 and released their debut album, *Lonesome Crow,* in 1972. By the time they finally disrupted the airwaves in America, they had enjoyed nearly a decade of steadily-building success in Europe and Asia — most notably in Japan.

With the release of *Animal Magnetism* in 1980, containing two minor hits in "The Zoo" (#75 in the UK) and "Make It Real," the "wind of change" began to blow, and they had their first gold album (in America) on their hands. Guitarist Matthias Jabs had been hired on to replace Michael Schenker, and the stage was set for world domination. They would soon realize that dream with the release of 1982's *Blackout* (#10 with "No One Like You"), 1984's *Love at First Sting* (#6 with "Rock You Like a Hurricane," "Big City Nights," and "Still Loving You"), and 1988's *Savage Amusement* (#5 with "Rhythm of Love").

To achieve the thick, distorted tone of the main riff, Rudolf Schenker used a bit of an unusual setup. With his trusty Gibson Flying V, he plugged into a Hiwatt 50W head and ran the speaker out to the input of a non-master volume Marshall 50W head, which drove the Marshall cabinet. He set the preamp volume of the Hiwatt on 10 and the master volume very low; the volume on the Marshall head was cranked.

The song is in the key of E minor, as are many heavy metal songs, and it makes use of a classic metal riff device: 3rd dyads alternated with a palm-muted open E string. This is something you hear in riffs by countless metal/hard rock bands, including Ratt, Mötley Crüe, Van Halen, White Lion, Yngwie Malmsteen, and Winger. The 3rds, played on strings 5 and 4, are all diatonic to E minor and walk up and down the scale to create a winding melody atop the chugging bass note. Be sure to slap the palm mute down on the low E string between the dyads so you get a clear separation of parts. This'll help the dyads speak clearly and prevent things from getting muddy.

The Zoo
Words and Music by Rudolf Schenker and Klaus Meine

GUITAR NOTATION LEGEND

Guitar music can be notated three different ways: on a *musical staff*, in *tablature*, and in *rhythm slashes*.

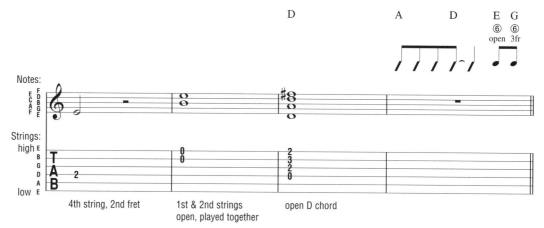

RHYTHM SLASHES are written above the staff. Strum chords in the rhythm indicated. Use the chord diagrams found at the top of the first page of the transcription for the appropriate chord voicings. Round noteheads indicate single notes.

THE MUSICAL STAFF shows pitches and rhythms and is divided by bar lines into measures. Pitches are named after the first seven letters of the alphabet.

TABLATURE graphically represents the guitar fingerboard. Each horizontal line represents a string, and each number represents a fret.

4th string, 2nd fret   1st & 2nd strings open, played together   open D chord

Definitions for Special Guitar Notation

HALF-STEP BEND: Strike the note and bend up 1/2 step.

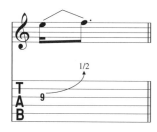

WHOLE-STEP BEND: Strike the note and bend up one step.

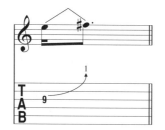

GRACE NOTE BEND: Strike the note and immediately bend up as indicated.

SLIGHT (MICROTONE) BEND: Strike the note and bend up 1/4 step.

BEND AND RELEASE: Strike the note and bend up as indicated, then release back to the original note. Only the first note is struck.

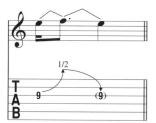

PRE-BEND: Bend the note as indicated, then strike it.

PRE-BEND AND RELEASE: Bend the note as indicated. Strike it and release the bend back to the original note.

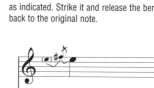

UNISON BEND: Strike the two notes simultaneously and bend the lower note up to the pitch of the higher.

VIBRATO: The string is vibrated by rapidly bending and releasing the note with the fretting hand.

WIDE VIBRATO: The pitch is varied to a greater degree by vibrating with the fretting hand.

HAMMER-ON: Strike the first (lower) note with one finger, then sound the higher note (on the same string) with another finger by fretting it without picking.

PULL-OFF: Place both fingers on the notes to be sounded. Strike the first note and without picking, pull the finger off to sound the second (lower) note.

LEGATO SLIDE: Strike the first note and then slide the same fret-hand finger up or down to the second note. The second note is not struck.

SHIFT SLIDE: Same as legato slide, except the second note is struck.

TRILL: Very rapidly alternate between the notes indicated by continuously hammering on and pulling off.

TAPPING: Hammer ("tap") the fret indicated with the pick-hand index or middle finger and pull off to the note fretted by the fret hand.

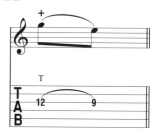

NATURAL HARMONIC: Strike the note while the fret-hand lightly touches the string directly over the fret indicated.

PINCH HARMONIC: The note is fretted normally and a harmonic is produced by adding the edge of the thumb or the tip of the index finger of the pick hand to the normal pick attack.

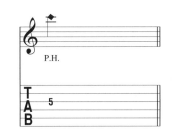

HARP HARMONIC: The note is fretted normally and a harmonic is produced by gently resting the pick hand's index finger directly above the indicated fret (in parentheses) while the pick hand's thumb or pick assists by plucking the appropriate string.

PICK SCRAPE: The edge of the pick is rubbed down (or up) the string, producing a scratchy sound.

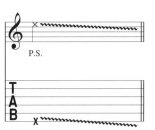

MUFFLED STRINGS: A percussive sound is produced by laying the fret hand across the string(s) without depressing, and striking them with the pick hand.

PALM MUTING: The note is partially muted by the pick hand lightly touching the string(s) just before the bridge.

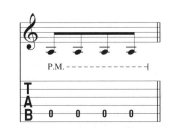

RAKE: Drag the pick across the strings indicated with a single motion.

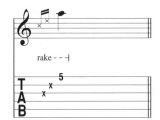

TREMOLO PICKING: The note is picked as rapidly and continuously as possible.

ARPEGGIATE: Play the notes of the chord indicated by quickly rolling them from bottom to top.

VIBRATO BAR DIVE AND RETURN: The pitch of the note or chord is dropped a specified number of steps (in rhythm), then returned to the original pitch.

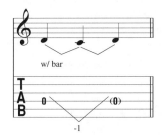

VIBRATO BAR SCOOP: Depress the bar just before striking the note, then quickly release the bar.

VIBRATO BAR DIP: Strike the note and then immediately drop a specified number of steps, then release back to the original pitch.

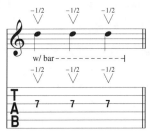

Additional Musical Definitions

(accent)	• Accentuate note (play it louder).	
(accent)	• Accentuate note with great intensity.	
(staccato)	• Play the note short.	
⊓	• Downstroke	
∨	• Upstroke	

D.S. al Coda • Go back to the sign (𝄋), then play until the measure marked "*To Coda*," then skip to the section labelled "**Coda.**"

D.C. al Fine • Go back to the beginning of the song and play until the measure marked "*Fine*" (end).

Rhy. Fig. • Label used to recall a recurring accompaniment pattern (usually chordal).

Riff • Label used to recall composed, melodic lines (usually single notes) which recur.

Fill • Label used to identify a brief melodic figure which is to be inserted into the arrangement.

Rhy. Fill • A chordal version of a Fill.

tacet • Instrument is silent (drops out).

• Repeat measures between signs.

• When a repeated section has different endings, play the first ending only the first time and the second ending only the second time.

NOTE: Tablature numbers in parentheses mean:
1. The note is being sustained over a system (note in standard notation is tied), or
2. The note is sustained, but a new articulation (such as a hammer-on, pull-off, slide or vibrato) begins, or
3. The note is a barely audible "ghost" note (note in standard notation is also in parentheses).

GUITAR *signature licks®*

Signature Licks book/CD packs provide a step-by-step breakdown of "right from the record" riffs, licks, and solos so you can jam along with your favorite bands. They contain performance notes and an overview of each artist's or group's style, with note-for-note transcriptions in notes and tab. The CDs feature full-band demos at both normal and slow speeds.

AC/DC
14041352 .... $22.99

ACOUSTIC CLASSICS
00695864 .... $19.95

AEROSMITH 1973-1979
00695106 .... $22.95

AEROSMITH 1979-1998
00695219 .... $22.95

DUANE ALLMAN
00696042 .... $22.99

BEST OF CHET ATKINS
00695752 .... $22.95

AVENGED SEVENFOLD
00696473 .... $22.99

BEST OF THE BEATLES FOR ACOUSTIC GUITAR
00695453 .... $22.95

THE BEATLES BASS
00695283 .... $22.95

THE BEATLES FAVORITES
00695096 .... $24.95

THE BEATLES HITS
00695049 .... $24.95

JEFF BECK
00696427 .... $22.99

BEST OF GEORGE BENSON
00695418 .... $22.95

BEST OF BLACK SABBATH
00695249 .... $22.95

BLUES BREAKERS WITH JOHN MAYALL & ERIC CLAPTON
00696374 .... $22.99

BLUES/ROCK GUITAR HEROES
00696381 .... $19.99

BON JOVI
00696380 .... $22.99

KENNY BURRELL
00695830 .... $22.99

BEST OF CHARLIE CHRISTIAN
00695584 .... $22.95

BEST OF ERIC CLAPTON
00695038 .... $24.95

ERIC CLAPTON – FROM THE ALBUM UNPLUGGED
00695250 .... $24.95

BEST OF CREAM
00695251 .... $22.95

CREEDANCE CLEARWATER REVIVAL
00695924 .... $22.95

DEEP PURPLE – GREATEST HITS
00695625 .... $22.95

THE BEST OF DEF LEPPARD
00696516 .... $22.95

THE DOORS
00695373 .... $22.95

TOMMY EMMANUEL
00696409 .... $22.99

ESSENTIAL JAZZ GUITAR
00695875 .... $19.99

FAMOUS ROCK GUITAR SOLOS
00695590 .... $19.95

FLEETWOOD MAC
00696416 .... $22.99

BEST OF FOO FIGHTERS
00695481 .... $24.95

ROBBEN FORD
00695903 .... $22.95

BEST OF GRANT GREEN
00695747 .... $22.95

BEST OF GUNS N' ROSES
00695183 .... $24.95

THE BEST OF BUDDY GUY
00695186 .... $22.99

JIM HALL
00695848 .... $22.99

JIMI HENDRIX
00696560 .... $24.95

JIMI HENDRIX – VOLUME 2
00695835 .... $24.95

JOHN LEE HOOKER
00695894 .... $19.99

HOT COUNTRY GUITAR
00695580 .... $19.95

BEST OF JAZZ GUITAR
00695586 .... $24.95

ERIC JOHNSON
00699317 .... $24.95

ROBERT JOHNSON
00695264 .... $22.95

BARNEY KESSEL
00696009 .... $22.99

THE ESSENTIAL ALBERT KING
00695713 .... $22.95

B.B. KING – BLUES LEGEND
00696039 .... $22.99

B.B. KING – THE DEFINITIVE COLLECTION
00695635 .... $22.95

B.B. KING – MASTER BLUESMAN
00699923 .... $24.99

THE KINKS
00695553 .... $22.95

BEST OF KISS
00699413 .... $22.95

MARK KNOPFLER
00695178 .... $22.95

LYNYRD SKYNYRD
00695872 .... $24.95

THE BEST OF YNGWIE MALMSTEEN
00695669 .... $22.95

BEST OF PAT MARTINO
00695632 .... $24.99

MEGADETH
00696421 .... $22.99

WES MONTGOMERY
00695387 .... $24.95

BEST OF NIRVANA
00695483 .... $24.95

THE OFFSPRING
00695852 .... $24.95

VERY BEST OF OZZY OSBOURNE
00695431 .... $22.95

BRAD PAISLEY
00696379 .... $22.99

BEST OF JOE PASS
00695730 .... $22.95

JACO PASTORIUS
00695544 .... $24.95

TOM PETTY
00696021 .... $22.99

PINK FLOYD – EARLY CLASSICS
00695566 .... $22.95

THE GUITARS OF ELVIS
00696507 .... $22.95

BEST OF QUEEN
00695097 .... $24.95

BEST OF RAGE AGAINST THE MACHINE
00695480 .... $24.95

RED HOT CHILI PEPPERS
00695173 .... $22.95

RED HOT CHILI PEPPERS – GREATEST HITS
00695828 .... $24.95

BEST OF DJANGO REINHARDT
00695660 .... $24.95

BEST OF ROCK 'N' ROLL GUITAR
00695559 .... $19.95

BEST OF ROCKABILLY GUITAR
00695785 .... $19.95

THE ROLLING STONES
00695079 .... $24.95

BEST OF JOE SATRIANI
00695216 .... $22.95

THE BEST OF SOUL GUITAR
00695703 .... $19.95

BEST OF SOUTHERN ROCK
00695560 .... $19.95

STEELY DAN
00696015 .... $22.99

MIKE STERN
00695800 .... $24.99

BEST OF SURF GUITAR
00695822 .... $19.95

BEST OF SYSTEM OF A DOWN
00695788 .... $22.95

ROBIN TROWER
00695950 .... $22.95

STEVE VAI
00673247 .... $22.95

STEVE VAI – ALIEN LOVE SECRETS: THE NAKED VAMPS
00695223 .... $22.95

STEVE VAI – FIRE GARDEN: THE NAKED VAMPS
00695166 .... $22.95

STEVE VAI – THE ULTRA ZONE: NAKED VAMPS
00695684 .... $22.95

STEVIE RAY VAUGHAN – 2ND ED.
00699316 .... $24.95

THE GUITAR STYLE OF STEVIE RAY VAUGHAN
00695155 .... $24.95

BEST OF THE VENTURES
00695772 .... $19.95

THE WHO – 2ND ED.
00695561 .... $22.95

JOHNNY WINTER
00695951 .... $22.99

NEIL YOUNG – GREATEST HITS
00695988 .... $22.99

BEST OF ZZ TOP
00695738 .... $24.95

HAL•LEONARD®
CORPORATION
7777 W. BLUEMOUND RD. P.O. BOX 13819
MILWAUKEE, WISCONSIN 53213

www.halleonard.com

COMPLETE DESCRIPTIONS AND SONGLISTS ONLINE!
Prices, contents and availability subject to change without notice.

1213

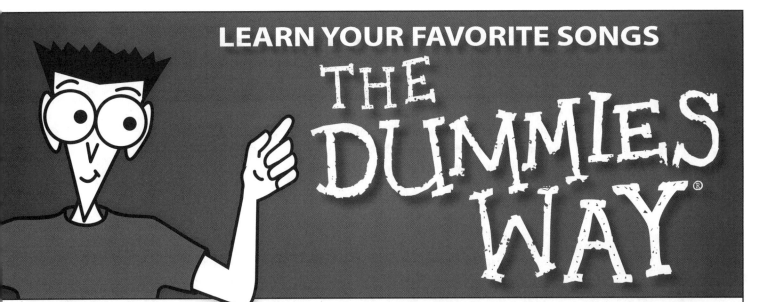

HAL•LEONARD GUITAR PLAY•ALONG®

This series will help you play your favorite songs quickly and easily. Just follow the tab and listen to the CD to the hear how the guitar should sound, and then play along using the separate backing tracks. Mac or PC users can also slow down the tempo without changing pitch by using the CD in their computer. The melody and lyrics are included in the book so that you can sing or simply follow along.

INCLUDES TAB

VOL. 1 – ROCK	00699570 / $16.99
VOL. 2 – ACOUSTIC	00699569 / $16.95
VOL. 3 – HARD ROCK	00699573 / $16.95
VOL. 4 – POP/ROCK	00699571 / $16.99
VOL. 5 – MODERN ROCK	00699574 / $16.99
VOL. 6 – '90S ROCK	00699572 / $16.99
VOL. 7 – BLUES	00699575 / $16.95
VOL. 8 – ROCK	00699585 / $14.99
VOL. 9 – PUNK ROCK	00699576 / $14.95
VOL. 10 – ACOUSTIC	00699586 / $16.95
VOL. 11 – EARLY ROCK	00699579 / $14.95
VOL. 12 – POP/ROCK	00699587 / $14.95
VOL. 13 – FOLK ROCK	00699581 / $15.99
VOL. 14 – BLUES ROCK	00699582 / $16.95
VOL. 15 – R&B	00699583 / $14.95
VOL. 16 – JAZZ	00699584 / $15.95
VOL. 17 – COUNTRY	00699588 / $15.95
VOL. 18 – ACOUSTIC ROCK	00699577 / $15.95
VOL. 19 – SOUL	00699578 / $14.99
VOL. 20 – ROCKABILLY	00699580 / $14.95
VOL. 21 – YULETIDE	00699602 / $14.95
VOL. 22 – CHRISTMAS	00699600 / $15.95
VOL. 23 – SURF	00699635 / $14.95
VOL. 24 – ERIC CLAPTON	00699649 / $17.99
VOL. 25 – LENNON & MCCARTNEY	00699642 / $16.99
VOL. 26 – ELVIS PRESLEY	00699643 / $14.95
VOL. 27 – DAVID LEE ROTH	00699645 / $16.95
VOL. 28 – GREG KOCH	00699646 / $14.95
VOL. 29 – BOB SEGER	00699647 / $15.99
VOL. 30 – KISS	00699644 / $16.99
VOL. 31 – CHRISTMAS HITS	00699652 / $14.95
VOL. 32 – THE OFFSPRING	00699653 / $14.95
VOL. 33 – ACOUSTIC CLASSICS	00699656 / $16.95
VOL. 34 – CLASSIC ROCK	00699658 / $16.95
VOL. 35 – HAIR METAL	00699660 / $16.95
VOL. 36 – SOUTHERN ROCK	00699661 / $16.95
VOL. 37 – ACOUSTIC METAL	00699662 / $16.95
VOL. 38 – BLUES	00699663 / $16.95
VOL. 39 – '80S METAL	00699664 / $16.99
VOL. 40 – INCUBUS	00699668 / $17.95
VOL. 41 – ERIC CLAPTON	00699669 / $16.95
VOL. 42 – 2000S ROCK	00699670 / $16.99
VOL. 43 – LYNYRD SKYNYRD	00699681 / $17.95
VOL. 44 – JAZZ	00699689 / $14.99
VOL. 45 – TV THEMES	00699718 / $14.95
VOL. 46 – MAINSTREAM ROCK	00699722 / $16.95
VOL. 47 – HENDRIX SMASH HITS	00699723 / $19.95
VOL. 48 – AEROSMITH CLASSICS	00699724 / $17.99
VOL. 49 – STEVIE RAY VAUGHAN	00699725 / $17.99
VOL. 51 – ALTERNATIVE '90S	00699727 / $14.99
VOL. 52 – FUNK	00699728 / $14.95
VOL. 53 – DISCO	00699729 / $14.99
VOL. 54 – HEAVY METAL	00699730 / $14.95
VOL. 55 – POP METAL	00699731 / $14.95

VOL. 56 – FOO FIGHTERS	00699749 / $15.99
VOL. 57 – SYSTEM OF A DOWN	00699751 / $14.95
VOL. 58 – BLINK-182	00699772 / $14.95
VOL. 59 – CHET ATKINS	00702347 / $16.99
VOL. 60 – 3 DOORS DOWN	00699774 / $14.95
VOL. 61 – SLIPKNOT	00699775 / $16.99
VOL. 62 – CHRISTMAS CAROLS	00699798 / $12.95
VOL. 63 – CREEDENCE CLEARWATER REVIVAL	00699802 / $16.99
VOL. 64 – THE ULTIMATE OZZY OSBOURNE	00699803 / $16.99
VOL. 65 – THE DOORS	00699806 / $16.99
VOL. 66 – THE ROLLING STONES	00699807 / $16.95
VOL. 67 – BLACK SABBATH	00699808 / $16.99
VOL. 68 – PINK FLOYD – DARK SIDE OF THE MOON	00699809 / $16.99
VOL. 69 – ACOUSTIC FAVORITES	00699810 / $14.95
VOL. 70 – OZZY OSBOURNE	00699805 / $16.99
VOL. 71 – CHRISTIAN ROCK	00699824 / $14.95
VOL. 72 – ACOUSTIC '90S	00699827 / $14.95
VOL. 73 – BLUESY ROCK	00699829 / $16.99
VOL. 74 – PAUL BALOCHE	00699831 / $14.95
VOL. 75 – TOM PETTY	00699882 / $16.99
VOL. 76 – COUNTRY HITS	00699884 / $14.95
VOL. 77 – BLUEGRASS	00699910 / $14.99
VOL. 78 – NIRVANA	00700132 / $16.99
VOL. 79 – NEIL YOUNG	00700133 / $24.99
VOL. 80 – ACOUSTIC ANTHOLOGY	00700175 / $19.95
VOL. 81 – ROCK ANTHOLOGY	00700176 / $22.99
VOL. 82 – EASY SONGS	00700177 / $12.99
VOL. 83 – THREE CHORD SONGS	00700178 / $16.99
VOL. 84 – STEELY DAN	00700200 / $16.99
VOL. 85 – THE POLICE	00700269 / $16.99
VOL. 86 – BOSTON	00700465 / $16.99
VOL. 87 – ACOUSTIC WOMEN	00700763 / $14.99
VOL. 88 – GRUNGE	00700467 / $16.99
VOL. 90 – CLASSICAL POP	00700469 / $14.99
VOL. 91 – BLUES INSTRUMENTALS	00700505 / $14.99
VOL. 92 – EARLY ROCK INSTRUMENTALS	00700506 / $14.99
VOL. 93 – ROCK INSTRUMENTALS	00700507 / $16.99
VOL. 95 – BLUES CLASSICS	00700509 / $14.99
VOL. 96 – THIRD DAY	00700560 / $14.95
VOL. 97 – ROCK BAND	00700703 / $14.99
VOL. 98 – ROCK BAND	00700704 / $14.95
VOL. 99 – ZZ TOP	00700762 / $16.99
VOL. 100 – B.B. KING	00700466 / $16.99
VOL. 101 – SONGS FOR BEGINNERS	00701917 / $14.99
VOL. 102 – CLASSIC PUNK	00700769 / $14.99
VOL. 103 – SWITCHFOOT	00700773 / $16.99
VOL. 104 – DUANE ALLMAN	00700846 / $16.99
VOL. 106 – WEEZER	00700958 / $14.99
VOL. 107 – CREAM	00701069 / $16.99
VOL. 108 – THE WHO	00701053 / $16.99

VOL. 109 – STEVE MILLER	00701054 / $14.99
VOL. 111 – JOHN MELLENCAMP	00701056 / $14.99
VOL. 112 – QUEEN	00701052 / $16.99
VOL. 113 – JIM CROCE	00701058 / $15.99
VOL. 114 – BON JOVI	00701060 / $14.99
VOL. 115 – JOHNNY CASH	00701070 / $16.99
VOL. 116 – THE VENTURES	00701124 / $14.99
VOL. 118 – ERIC JOHNSON	00701353 / $14.99
VOL. 119 – AC/DC CLASSICS	00701356 / $17.99
VOL. 120 – PROGRESSIVE ROCK	00701457 / $14.99
VOL. 121 – U2	00701508 / $16.99
VOL. 123 – LENNON & MCCARTNEY ACOUSTIC	00701614 / $16.99
VOL. 124 – MODERN WORSHIP	00701629 / $14.99
VOL. 125 – JEFF BECK	00701687 / $16.99
VOL. 126 – BOB MARLEY	00701701 / $16.99
VOL. 127 – 1970S ROCK	00701739 / $14.99
VOL. 128 – 1960S ROCK	00701740 / $14.99
VOL. 129 – MEGADETH	00701741 / $16.99
VOL. 131 – 1990S ROCK	00701743 / $14.99
VOL. 132 – COUNTRY ROCK	00701757 / $15.99
VOL. 133 – TAYLOR SWIFT	00701894 / $16.99
VOL. 134 – AVENGED SEVENFOLD	00701906 / $16.99
VOL. 136 – GUITAR THEMES	00701922 / $14.99
VOL. 138 – BLUEGRASS CLASSICS	00701967 / $14.99
VOL. 139 – GARY MOORE	00702370 / $16.99
VOL. 140 – MORE STEVIE RAY VAUGHAN	00702396 / $17.99
VOL. 141 – ACOUSTIC HITS	00702401 / $16.99
VOL. 142 – KINGS OF LEON	00702418 / $16.99
VOL. 144 – DJANGO REINHARDT	00702531 / $16.99
VOL. 145 – DEF LEPPARD	00702532 / $16.99
VOL. 147 – SIMON & GARFUNKEL	14041591 / $16.99
VOL. 149 – AC/DC HITS	14041593 / $17.99
VOL. 150 – ZAKK WYLDE	02501717 / $16.99
VOL. 153 – RED HOT CHILI PEPPERS	00702990 / $19.99
VOL. 157 – FLEETWOOD MAC	00101382 / $16.99
VOL. 158 – ULTIMATE CHRISTMAS	00101889 / $14.99
VOL. 161 – THE EAGLES – ACOUSTIC	00102659 / $17.99
VOL. 162 – THE EAGLES HITS	00102667 / $17.99
VOL. 163 – PANTERA	00103036 / $16.99
VOL. 166 – MODERN BLUES	00700764 / $16.99
VOL. 168 – KISS	00113421 / $16.99
VOL. 169 – TAYLOR SWIFT	00115982 / $16.99
VOL. 170 – THREE DAYS GRACE	00117337 / $16.99

Complete song lists available online.

Prices, contents, and availability subject to change without notice.

HAL•LEONARD® CORPORATION
7777 W. BLUEMOUND RD. P.O. BOX 13819 MILWAUKEE, WI 53213

www.halleonard.com

0713